Clarke H. Irwin

A History of Presbyterianism in Dublin and the South and West of Ireland

Clarke H. Irwin

A History of Presbyterianism in Dublin and the South and West of Ireland

ISBN/EAN: 9783337323196

Printed in Europe, USA, Canada, Australia, Japan

Cover: Foto ©ninafisch / pixelio.de

More available books at **www.hansebooks.com**

A HISTORY

OF

PRESBYTERIANISM IN DUBLIN

AND THE

SOUTH AND WEST OF IRELAND.

BY

CLARKE H. IRWIN, M.A.,

MINISTER AT BRAY.

London:

HODDER AND STOUGHTON,

27, PATERNOSTER ROW.

MDCCCXC.

TO MY FATHER,

REV. WILLIAM IRWIN, D.D.,

OF CASTLEROCK, CO. DERRY,

I DEDICATE THIS

BOOK.

PREFACE.

THE history of the Irish Presbyterian Church, in its successive stages, has been already well told by such historians as Adair, Reid, Killen, Witherow, and Hamilton. In the present work the writer has confined himself mainly to the history of Presbyterianism in Dublin and the South and West. He hopes that he has succeeded in putting in permanent form some facts regarding Presbyterianism outside Ulster which hitherto were not generally known.

The materials for the following pages were compiled in the spare hours of a busy pastorate. But they have not been hastily put together. No statement has been taken at second-hand where it was possible to consult original sources of information. Even so, it is possible that there are many mistakes. Should any such be discovered, the writer will be glad to be informed of them.

References have been made to the general history of the country, and to the general history of the Irish Presbyterian Church, where these seemed necessary to preserve the continuity of the narrative, and to throw light upon the circumstances of Presbyterianism in the South and West.

The writer desires gratefully to acknowledge the courtesy and kindness received by him from the Librarians of Trinity College, Dublin; the Royal Irish Academy; Assembly's College, Belfast; Magee College, Derry; and the Advocates' Library, Edinburgh; from the Deputy-Keeper of the Records, and other officials of the Record Office, Dublin; from the Registrar and Trustees of the General Fund; from the Clerks of Presbyteries; from the Rev. George MacFarland, M.A., Belfast; and from the Rev. D. D. Jeremy, M.A., minister of the Unitarian church, Stephen's Green, Dublin. Nor must he omit here to mention, in grateful remembrance, the valuable assistance received from the late lamented Professor Witherow, of Derry, who not only helped him in exploring the historical collections in the library of Magee College, but also placed at his disposal the rich treasures of his own private library.

This book is now given to the public as a small contribution to the ecclesiastical history of Ireland. It has been the writer's endeavour to record faithfully the story of the past. Of necessity, that story includes the recital of old conflicts. Not to perpetuate strife, but to end it, would be our earnest desire. But the interests of peace, as well as the interests of truth, are best promoted by a clear understanding of the causes which led to strife in the past. Let us hope that the day is speedily approaching when Irishmen of all creeds and parties will work together for the common good of our beloved land.

BRAY, IRELAND,
June, 1890.

AUTHORS AND WORKS CONSULTED.

Abernethy, "Reasons for Repeal of the Sacramental Test." Dublin, 1733. [Library, Magee College, Derry.]

Adair, "A True Narrative of the Rise and Progress of the Presbyterian Church in Ireland (1623-70). With Introduction and Notes by W. D. Killen, D.D." Belfast, 1866.

"Agreement and Resolution of Severall Associated Ministers in the County of Corke for the Ordaining of Ministers." Cork, 1657. [Library, Assembly's College, Belfast.]

"Agreement and Resolution of the Ministers of Christ Associated within the City of Dublin and Province of Leinster; for Furthering of a Real and Thorough Reformation according to the Written Word of God." Dublin, 1659. [Library, Assembly's College, Belfast.]

Armstrong, "A Short Account of the General Fund." Dublin, 1815.

Armstrong, "Ordination Service, at Ordination of Rev. James Martineau. With an Appendix, containing a Summary History of the Presbyterian Churches in the City of Dublin." Dublin, 1829. [Library, Magee College.]

Boyse, "Works." 2 vols. London, 1728. [Library, Trinity College, Dublin.]

Briggs, "American Presbyterianism." New York, 1885.

Campbell, "Vindication of the Principles and Character of the Presbyterians of Ireland." An Answer to the Bishop of Cloyne (Woodward) on "The Present State of the Church of Ireland." 1788. [Library, Magee College.]

Carlile, "A Series of Sermons on the Nature and Effects of Repentance and Faith." Dublin, 1821.

Clarendon, "The State Letters of Henry, Earl of Clarendon, Lord Lieutenant of Ireland, during the reign of James II., and his Lordship's Diary for the years 1687, 1688, 1689, 1690." Oxford and Dublin, 1765. [Library, Assembly's College.]

"Controversial Tracts and Sermons, chiefly by Ministers of the Presbytery of Antrim," 1725-78. [Library, Assembly's College.]

Croskery, "Irish Presbyterianism." Dublin, 1884.

Croskery and Witherow, "Life of Rev. A. P. Goudy, D.D." Dublin, 1887.

Dill, "Prelatico-Presbyterianism; or, Curious Chapters in the Recent History of the Irish Presbyterian Church." Dublin, 1856.

"Downpatrick Missionary Herald." Edited by Sidney Hamilton Rowan, Esq., 1837-40. [Library, Assembly's College.]

Emlyn, "A True Narrative of the Proceedings of the Dissenting Ministers of Dublin against Mr. Thomas Emlyn." London, 1719. [Library, Magee College.]

Frazer, "Manuscript History of the General (Presbyterian) Fund for the South and West of Ireland." Compiled by Dr. William Frazer, and presented to the Trustees by him, 1862. [Records of General Fund.]

Froude, "English in Ireland." 3 vols. London, 1886.

Gibson, "The Year of Grace: a History of the Ulster Revival of 1859."

Gilbert, "History of the City of Dublin." Dublin, 1859.

Hamilton, "History of the Irish Presbyterian Church." Edinburgh, 1886.

Huston, "Letters on the Present Position, Enemies, Prospects, and Duties of Presbyterians." Derry, 1843.

"Irish Ecclesiastical Journal." 1842-48. [Library, Magee College.]

"Irish Worthies." By Rev. Thomas Hamilton, M.A. Belfast, 1875.

"Journals of Irish House of Lords." [Record Office, Dublin.]
"Journals of Irish House of Commons." [Record Office, Dublin.]

Kelburn, "Sermons by Rev. Sinclaire Kelburn, A.B." [Library, Assembly's College.]

Killen, "Ecclesiastical History of Ireland."

Kirkpatrick, "An Historical Essay upon the Loyalty of Presbyterians in Great Britain and Ireland from the Reformation to this Present Year, 1713." Belfast, 1713.

Lecky, "England in the Eighteenth Century."

"Liber Munerum Publicorum Hiberniæ." [Record Office, Dublin.]

"Life and Times of Selina, Countess of Huntingdon. By a member of the Houses of Shirley and Hastings." 2 vols. London, 1841.

Mathews, "Account of the Trial of Rev. Thomas Emlyn." Dublin, 1839. [Library, Assembly's College.]

"Memorial Services in connection with the Removal of the Congregation of Mary's Abbey to Rutland Square, Dublin. Edited by Rev. W. B. Kirkpatrick, D.D." Dublin, 1865.

"Minutes of General Assembly," 1840-89.

"Minutes of Synod of Ulster," 1694—1831. [Library, Assembly's College.]

"Minutes of Synod of Ulster," 1830-40. [Library, Assembly's College.]

"Miscellaneous Sermons by Ministers of the Seceding Synod," 1799—1839. [Library, Assembly's College.]

"Missionary Sermons and Speeches delivered at a Special Meeting of the General Synod of Ulster, held in the Scots' Church, Mary's Abbey, Dublin, in September, 1833." Belfast, 1834.

"MS. Minutes of Synod of Ulster," 1770—1801. [Library, Assembly's College.]

"MS. Minutes of General Fund." [Records of General Fund, Dublin.]

"MS. Notes of Lectures on Theology, delivered in Manor Street College." By Rev. David Stuart. [Library, Magee College.]

Musgrave, "History of the Irish Rebellion."

Neal, "History of the Puritans."

O'Keeffe, "Life and Times of Daniel O'Connell." 2 vols. Dublin, 1864.

Orrery, "A Collection of the State Letters of the Earl of Orrery, Lord President of Munster. Correspondence between the Duke of Ormonde and his Lordship, from the Restoration to the Year 1668." [Library, Assembly's College.]

Pamphlets. Volumes of Pamphlets on Irish and Ecclesiastical Affairs in the Royal Irish Academy, and the Libraries of Trinity College, Dublin, Assembly's College, and Magee College.

"Pamphlets by George Mathews, Esq." Dublin, 1836. [Library, Assembly's College.]

Porter, "Life and Times of Dr. Cooke." London, 1871.

Reid, "History of the Presbyterian Church in Ireland." 3 vols. Belfast, 1867.

"Report of the Proceedings in Chancery, 1850, in the Case of the Attorney-General, at the Relation of George Mathews and John Black, against Rev. James Carlile, D.D., relative to the General Fund." Dublin, 1851.

"Reports of the Home Mission and Schools of the Synod of Ulster," 1832-40. [Library, Assembly's College.]

"Reports of the Irish Evangelical Society," 1815-31. [Library, Assembly's College.]

Sullivan, "New Ireland." Seventh Edition. Glasgow and London, 1882.

Swift, "A Letter from a Member of the House of Commons in Ireland to a Member of the House of Commons in England, concerning the Sacramental Test." London, 1709. [By Jonathan Swift, afterwards Dean of St. Patrick's.] [Library, Assembly's College.]

"Synod's Reports," 1820-29. Extracts from Minutes of Synod of Ulster. [Library, Assembly's College.]

"*Ware's* Works." Edited by Harris. 2 vols. Dublin, 1745.

Webster, "History of the Presbyterian Church in America." Philadelphia, 1857.

Witherow, "The Boyne and Aghrim." Belfast.

Witherow, "Derry and Enniskillen." Belfast, 1885.

Witherow, "Historical and Literary Memorials of Presbyterianism in Ireland." 2 vols. London and Belfast, 1879 and 1880.

Wodrow MSS. Collection in Advocates' Library, Edinburgh. Correspondence of Rev. Robert Wodrow, Minister at Eastwood, near Glasgow, and many other important Papers, bearing dates from 1636 to 1729.

CONTENTS.

PART I.

GENERAL HISTORY.

CHAP.	PAGE
I. BEGINNINGS	3
II. PATRONAGE AND PERSECUTION	14
III. THOMAS EMLYN	18
IV. THE TEST ACT	24
V. THE GENERAL (OR EUSTACE STREET) FUND	32
VI. THE PRESBYTERY OF DUBLIN IN RELATION TO ULSTER AND AMERICA	37
VII. BISHOPS AND BIGOTRY	42
VIII. BETTER DAYS	50
IX. THE SUBSCRIPTION CONTROVERSY	54
X. DUBLIN PRESBYTERIANS AND IRISH GRIEVANCES	62
XI. THE SECEDERS	66
XII. GENEROUS LAYMEN AND REPRIMANDED MINISTERS	68
XIII. PRESBYTERIANS AND THE VOLUNTEERS	71
XIV. CONCILIATION AND CONCESSION	75
XV. PRESBYTERIANS AND THE REBELLION OF 1798	79
XVI. THE LEGISLATIVE UNION	84

CHAP.		PAGE
XVII.	Lord Castlereagh and the Rev. James Carlile	91
XVIII.	Mission Work in the South and West	95
XIX.	Activity and Growth	103
XX.	Intolerance again	119
XXI.	The General Fund Law-suit	123
XXII.	The Marriage Question	128
XXIII.	Church Extension	131
XXIV.	The General Assembly of 1850 and the Land Question	134
XXV.	The Magee College Controversy	139
XXVI.	The Ulster Revival	149
XXVII.	Disestablishment	151
XXVIII.	The Present Outlook	158

PART II.

HISTORY OF CONGREGATIONS OUTSIDE ULSTER.

I. Presbytery of Athlone.

Congregation of	Athenry		165
„	„ Athlone		165
„	„ Ballinasloe		166
„	„ Creggs and Roscommon		168
„	„ Corboy		169
„	„ Ennis		169
„	„ Galway		171
„	„ Longford		172
„	„ Moyvore		173
„	„ Mullingar		173
„	„ Tully		174

CONTENTS.

	PAGE
II. PRESBYTERY OF BAILIEBOROUGH.	
Congregation of Kells, Co. Meath	177
III. PRESBYTERY OF CONNAUGHT.	
Congregation of Ballina	179
,, ,, Ballinglen	182
,, ,, Ballymote	183
,, ,, Boyle	184
,, ,, Clogher	185
,, ,, Creevelea	186
,, ,, Dromore West	186
,, ,, Hollymount	187
,, ,, Killala	188
,, ,, Newport	191
,, ,, Sligo	192
,, ,, Turlough and Castlebar	193
,, ,, Westport	196
IV. PRESBYTERY OF CORK.	
Congregation of Bandon	199
,, ,, Castlemartyr and Aghada	204
,, ,, Clonakilty	205
,, ,, Fermoy	206
,, ,, Lismore	208
,, ,, Mallow	209
,, ,, Queen Street, Cork	210
,, ,, Queenstown	211
,, ,, Tralee	211
,, ,, Trinity Church, Cork	212
V. PRESBYTERY OF DUBLIN.	
Congregation of Abbey Street, Dublin	215
,, ,, Adelaide Road, Dublin	219

		PAGE
Congregation of Athy	.	221
,, ,, Ballacolla	.	223
,, ,, Birr, or Parsonstown	.	223
,, ,, Bray	.	225
,, ,, Brunswick Street, Dublin	.	229
,, ,, Carlow	.	230
,, ,, Clontarf	.	232
,, ,, Donore, Dublin	.	234
,, ,, Drogheda	.	235
,, ,, Duncannon	.	239
,, ,, Enniscorthy	.	239
,, ,, Greystones and Kilpedder	.	241
,, ,, Kilkenny	.	243
,, ,, Killucan	.	244
,, ,, Kingstown	.	245
,, ,, Lucan	.	247
,, ,, Mountmellick	.	248
,, ,, Naas	.	249
,, ,, Nenagh and Cloughjordan	.	250
,, ,, Ormond Quay, Dublin	.	251
,, ,, Rathgar, Dublin	.	261
,, ,, Rutland Square, Dublin	.	263
,, ,, Sandymount	.	278
,, ,, Tullamore	.	279
,, ,, Wexford	.	281
,, ,, Wicklow	.	282

VI. PRESBYTERY OF MUNSTER.

Congregation of Clonmel	.	286
,, ,, Fethard	.	288
,, ,, Kilrush	.	290
,, ,, Limerick	.	290

	PAGE
Congregation of Portlaw	. 293
,, ,, Summerhill	. 293
,, ,, Tipperary	. 299
,, ,, Waterford	. 302

VII. PRESBYTERY OF NEWRY.

Congregation of Carlingford 305
,, ,, Castlebellingham 307
,, ,, Dundalk 307

The United Presbyterian Church, Lower Abbey Street, Dublin 311

SOME CONGREGATIONS NOW UNITARIAN.

Strand Street, Dublin 313
Eustace Street, Dublin 325

CONGREGATIONS NOW EXTINCT.

Aughmacart 328
Ballybrittas 330
Edenderry 331
Leap 332
Rahue 333
Stratford 334

PART I.

GENERAL HISTORY.

CHAPTER I.

BEGINNINGS.

PRESBYTERIANS, as a separate religious body, can hardly be said to have existed in Dublin before the passing of the Act of Uniformity. But Presbyterianism, in all its distinctive features of doctrine, government, and worship, was a powerful factor in the reformed Church of Ireland long before that time. Until the Established Churches of England and Ireland became narrower than they were immediately after the Reformation, Presbyterians remained within their pale.

In Dublin, indeed, the Presbyterian influence was felt at an earlier date than in any other part of Ireland. The first elected Fellows of Trinity College were two Presbyterians from Scotland—Fullerton and Hamilton, the latter of whom afterwards became Lord Claneboy. The first regular Provost of Trinity College was also a Presbyterian—Walter Travers. It is worth while to note some facts in the history of Travers, as showing how little his Presbyterianism prevented him from occupying a high position of honour and of usefulness in the Protestantism of Ireland at that time.

Travers was one of the leaders of English Puritanism. He was the friend and associate of Thomas Cartwright, Professor of Divinity at Cambridge, who for his Presbyterianism was deprived of his professorship by the

Prelatical party, and was more than once arrested, imprisoned, and brought before the Star Chamber and the High Commission Court. In 1572 was held the memorable Conference at Wandsworth, near London, by which Presbyterianism was first established in England. As a result of this Conference a Synod was held in London in 1584, to which a Book of Discipline was submitted, which had been prepared by Travers and Cartwright. Travers was silenced by Whitgift, Archbishop of Canterbury, but in 1594 he was invited over to Ireland by Loftus, Archbishop of Dublin, who had been honorary Provost of Trinity College, and whom he succeeded in that important office. Here Travers became the teacher of Ussher, and exercised upon him and many others of the rising generation an influence which bore fruit in the subsequent history of Irish Presbyterianism.[1]

The Plantation of Ulster, by which is meant the colonization of that province chiefly with Scotch settlers by James I., was the great event which led to the firm establishment of Presbyterianism in Ireland. Though, as we shall see, Presbyterian Churches were formed in Dublin and the South, irrespective of Scotch or North-Irish influence, still it was the influence of Ulster Presbyterianism which mainly preserved from decay the Presbyterianism of Dublin and the South.

From about the year 1605 there continued a steady flow of Scotch Presbyterians into Ulster, and in 1642 the first Irish Presbytery met at Carrickfergus. The earliest Presbyterian ministers in Ulster came over not as Dissenters at all. All of them who were ordained between 1622 and 1642 were ordained in the Presby-

---

[1] Reid: *History of the Presbyterian Church in Ireland.* Briggs: *American Presbyterianism.* Neal: *History of the Puritans.*

terian fashion, the Bishop joining with other ministers in the act of ordination. They were ministers of parish churches, and received the tithes and endowments ; they frequently met and consulted with the Bishops about matters concerning religion, and some of them were members of the Convocation in 1634.[1] Yet all the while they remained Presbyterian, and did not use the liturgy, whilst they strictly maintained the forms and discipline of the Church of Scotland. This pleasant state of matters, however, did not last. They were silenced at various times by Echlin and Leslie, successively Bishops of Down, and by Bramhall, Bishop of Derry. Their people suffered also, many of them being imprisoned under the authority of a commission of Wentworth, then Lord Deputy of Ireland. For about four years the prospects of Presbyterianism seemed very dark in Ulster, all the ministers, and many of their people, having been compelled to take refuge in Scotland. But in 1642 several ministers came over with the Scotch troops, and Presbyterianism once more took root in the northern province.

The Puritan spirit, so strong in Irish Protestantism from its earliest days, had not died out in Dublin and the South. In 1657 was published at Cork a most interesting little volume, entitled " The Agreement and Resolution of severall Associated Ministers in the County of Corke for the Ordaining of Ministers." In this "Agreement" the subscribing ministers advocate Presbyterian ordination, and resolve to practise it. In February, 1658, a number of ministers in Dublin and the province of Leinster formed a similar Association. The views which they held, and the objects which they

---

[1] Kirkpatrick's *Presbyterian Loyalty* (1713), Chap. iii.

set before them, are stated in a volume entitled "The Agreement and Resolution of the Ministers of Christ Associated within the City of Dublin and Province of Leinster; for furthering of a real and thorough Reformation according to the Written Word of God" (Dublin, 1659). This Agreement is of a most practical religious character. The ministers subscribing it resolve to cultivate personal holiness, to give themselves zealously to the work of the ministry, to practise brotherly love, and to avoid giving offence to one another. They also resolve to promote a revival of religion in the families committed to their care, by means of family worship and observance of the Lord's Day. In order to promote a reformation in their congregations generally, they propose and agree to the following means :—

1. Public Catechising of the younger and weaker sort on the Lord's Days. Their text-book for this catechising was to be the Shorter or Larger Catechism of the Westminster Assembly.

2. A public Profession of Faith by the older members. This was to include a statement that they received the Holy Scriptures as the inspired Word of God, and that they resolved to be guided by them as their rule of faith and life; that they still retained the Apostles' Creed; and that they received and held fast the Westminster Confession of Faith. The Irish Presbyterian Church of modern times expects parents to make a somewhat similar profession when presenting children for baptism; but the language used in this *Agreement* implies that the profession of faith was to be of a general or congregational character, the minister and people joining in the act.

3. Conducting all the ordinances of public worship

as near as possible to the teachings of the Word of God. They resolved to lay aside "the antiquated Service Book, and to be guided in their public services by the Westminster Assembly's *Directory for God's Public Worship.*"

4. Exhorting Christians to more frequent religious conferences, that thus they may enjoy the communion of saints.

5. A restoration in all their congregations of "that Church government and discipline which Jesus Christ hath appointed in His Holy Scripture." Here may be seen the thoroughly Presbyterian character of this Dublin Association of 1658. In one paragraph under this last head it is stated "that the ordinary and standing officers which Christ hath appointed in His Church for the edifying and perfecting of His body are *Pastors and Teachers, Ruling Elders,* and *Deacons.*" Another paragraph states that it is the duty of all the churches and ministers of Christ "to meet together in Synods and Assemblies of the officers and delegates of the churches, if need require; where they have power to determine difficulties and controversies according to the Word of God."

Three prominent features of this Dublin Association may be noticed, as we find them expressed in this memorable *Agreement and Resolution*: 1. Its decidedly Presbyterian character, in doctrine, worship, and government. 2. Its spirit of brotherly love. 3. Its belief in the advantage and power of Creeds and Confessions of Faith. The attitude which the Presbyterianism of Dublin afterwards assumed in the non-subscription controversy was certainly not the attitude of its early founders.

After the death of Oliver Cromwell, which occurred

the same year as this Association was formed, events seemed for a time to favour the Presbyterians. They were still members of the Established Church, and their ministers received the tithes and other emoluments of parish ministers. When the Restoration came, and Charles II. became king, it seemed for a time as if Presbyterianism was likely to be the State religion of Ireland. This, at any rate, was the opinion of the Convention which met in Dublin in lieu of a Parliament in the year 1660. The religious opinions of the new king had not then been declared, and even the supporters of prelacy feared that he was likely to take the side of the presbytery. The Convention accordingly chose for their chaplain the Rev. Samuel Cox, minister of St. Catherine's Church, who was reputed the soundest Presbyterian in Dublin. In the Irish Parliament of 1660 its devotions were conducted every morning by this Presbyterian minister. Moreover, the Convention summoned eight ministers, most of whom were Presbyterians, two from each province, to give advice to the Convention as to the settlement of the Church in Ireland, both as to the appointment of ministers and arranging for colleges and schools.[1]

But once again Presbyterian prospects were doomed to be blighted. In 1662 the English Act of Uniformity was passed, by which more than 2,000 ministers were compelled to give up their parishes and leave their homes. In 1665 a similar Act was passed in the Irish Parliament, which enjoined the use of the Book of Common Prayer in all places of public worship, and required not only ministers, but also *schoolmasters and private tutors*, to take the oath of abjuration (declaring

---

[1] Adair's *Narrative*, pp. 231-233.

it unlawful to take arms against the king, conforming to the liturgy of the Established Church, and abjuring the Solemn League and Covenant). No person who was not episcopally ordained could hold an ecclesiastical living, and any minister not episcopally ordained who dared to administer the sacrament was liable to a penalty of one hundred pounds.[1]

This Act, which was intended to be fatal to Presbyterianism, in reality established it on a firmer basis than ever. Its immediate result in Dublin was the formation of four new Presbyterian congregations. These were the congregations of Wood Street, New Row, Cook Street, and Capel Street. There had already been a Presbyterian Church at Bull-Alley, formed in 1660 or 1661 by North of Ireland Presbyterians. A large number of the most eminent and godly ministers of the city seceded from the Established Church and joined the Presbyterian Church. Amongst the number were the Rev. Samuel Winter, D.D., Provost of Trinity College ; Rev. Samuel Mather, Senior Fellow of Trinity College ; Rev. Edward Veal, S.F.T.C.D. ; Rev. Josiah Marsden, F.T.C.D. ; Rev. Stephen Charnock, F.T.C.D. ; Rev. Nathaniel Hoyle, F.T.C.D. ; Rev. Robert Norbury, F.T.C.D. ; Rev. Gamaliel Marsden, F.T.C.D. ; Rev. Thomas Harrison, D.D., Minister of Christ Church ; Rev. Edward Baynes, Minister of St. John's ; Rev. Robert Chambers, Minister of St. Patrick's ; Rev. Samuel Cox, Minister of St. Catherine's ; and Rev. William Leclew, Minister of Dunboyne.[2]

The strength of Presbyterianism throughout Ireland

---

[1] *Liber Munerum*, Part VI., p. 20 (Irish Record Office). Mr. Froude says of this Act that it "was like the offspring of lunacy."— *English in Ireland*, I., 172.

[2] Armstrong : *History of Dublin Churches*.

at this time may be seen from a letter written by the Earl of Orrery, Lord President of Munster, to the Duke of Ormonde. In this letter, dated Charleville, December 14th, 1666, Lord Orrery says, "I consider Ireland as consisting of three sorts of people: the protestants, the Scotch presbyters and other sectaries, and the papists. By the best calculation I could make, I cannot find the protestants, including the army, to amount to above forty thousand men, fit to bear arms. I believe the Scotch presbyters and other sectaries are double that number, and the papists quadruple the number of both. But then the protestants, to counterbalance the greatness of the other two, have the king's authority in their hands, together with the arms and garrisons."[1]

The growing power of Presbyterianism in Dublin seems to have been a source of great annoyance to the dignitaries of the Established Church. In 1669 Boyle, who was then Archbishop of Dublin and Lord Chancellor of Ireland, and afterwards Lord Primate, tried to induce the Lord Lieutenant to suppress Presbyterian "meetings" in Dublin. His efforts, however, were not successful. To the credit of the Lord Lieutenant (Lord Robarts) be it said that at a time when Bishops were sending Presbyterian ministers to prison for daring to preach, he had the courage to resist a man so powerful and so intolerant as the Archbishop-Chancellor. He answered him that if the Nonconformists were not Papists, and were peaceable and civil, he had no commission to meddle with them.[2]

In the following year an attempt of a different kind to stir up odium against the Presbyterians met with a

---

[1] *State Letters of Lord Orrery.*
[2] Adair's *Narrative*, p. 291.

peculiar fate. To quote from Adair's *Narrative:* "There had been, a while before, builded at Dublin, a large stately house with three storeys of galleries, for acting the stage-plays. . . . . To this house came a great number of noblemen and ladies, besides other persons, and clergymen, the first day of Christmas, being Monday (26th December). The play acted was one called by them 'The Nonconformist.' And there, among other parts of the play, the poor shadow of a Nonconformist minister is mocked and upbraided, and at last is brought to the stocks, prepared for this purpose, that his legs may be fastened. Those of the greatest quality sat lowest; those next in quality sat next above, and the common people in the upmost gallery. But, behold, when this shadow is brought to the stocks, as an affront upon Presbyterian ministers, and to teach great persons to deal with like severity toward them, down came the upper gallery on the middle one, where gentlemen and others sat, and that gallery broke too, and much of it fell down on the lords and ladies. Divers were killed, and many hurt. Among those that were hurt was one of the Lord Lieutenant's sons, and the Lady Clanbrassil, who, the year before, had caused to be pulled down the preaching-house at Bangor."

Yet amid all the persecution and ridicule thus heaped upon the Irish Presbyterians by their Episcopalian neighbours of that time, there were some gleams of favour from those in high place, and occasional indications that their loyalty and peaceable spirit were not absolutely forgotten. In 1672 Sir Arthur Forbes afterwards Earl of Granard, who was then one of the Lords Justices of Ireland, sent for four leading Presbyterian ministers to come to him to Dublin. He told them that he had had an interview with Charles II. in

London a short time before. The king told him how good an account he had received of the Irish Presbyterians, of their loyalty and their sufferings in the cause of loyalty, notwithstanding the many hardships they had endured. Sir Arthur confirmed this account, and mentioned that the ministers "lived in no great plenty, although they had the affection of the people where they did reside, but that they were not in a capacity to afford them a comfortable subsistence, being under many heavy burdens." The king, "of his own meer motion," told Sir Arthur that there was a sum of £1,200 in the revenue of Ireland which he had not yet disposed of, and that he thought the best use he could make of it was to give it to these ministers.[1] It was found, however, that there was only a sum of £600 available. This sum was paid as a pension out of the Irish Civil List. Coming to the Presbyterians at the time it did, when so little toleration was extended to them, it showed a considerable appreciation of their character and conduct.

Between the time of the Restoration and the Revolution of 1688 the Established Church seems to have been in a miserable condition. In a letter from the Earl of Clarendon, Lord Lieutenant of Ireland, to the Archbishop of Canterbury, dated Dublin Castle, May 25th, 1686, Clarendon says, "The ruinous state of the fabrick of most of the churches is very melancholy: very few of the clergy reside on their cures, but employ pitiful curates; which necessitates the people to look after a romish priest or nonconformist preacher; and there are plenty of both. I find it is an ordinary thing here for a minister to have five or six, or more, cures of

---

[1] This is the account given by Reid (II., pp. 333, 334) in the words of Rev. A. Hutchinson, of Saintfield, who had it from Sir A. Forbes.

souls, and to get them supplied by those who will do it cheapest ; and by this means some hold five, six, nay nine hundred pounds per annum in ecclesiastical preferments, get them all served for 150*l.* per annum, and not preach once a year themselves." Even the Bishops, he says, were largely absentees.[1] No wonder that the Bishops and parish clergy of that time disliked the presence of those early Presbyterian ministers, who, by their earnest and evangelical preaching, by their consistent and self-sacrificing lives, put to shame the indolence and the neglectfulness of their more favoured neighbours.

In 1687 the Irish Presbyterians obtained relief from the persecutions to which they had been subjected under the Act of Uniformity, by the "Declaration for Liberty of Conscience" issued by James II. The chief object of this Declaration on the king's part was unquestionably to prepare the way for the restoration of the Roman Catholic religion throughout the three kingdoms. But at that time, as at many other times in Irish history, the Presbyterians and Roman Catholics suffered the same oppression at the hands of Protestant Episcopacy. They endured the same wrongs. Civil and religious liberty was denied to both. Hence when the wrongs of one creed were redressed, as a rule, both received the benefit of the Act. Addresses of gratitude to King James for this Declaration were presented to him by Presbyterians in several parts of Ireland, and among the rest by the Presbyterian ministers and congregations in and near the city of Dublin.[2]

---

[1] *State Letters of Henry, Earl of Clarendon.*
[2] Reid, *History*, II. 351.

CHAPTER II.

PATRONAGE AND PERSECUTION.

THE accession and reign of William III. brought comparative peace and quietness to the Presbyterians. In this reign they received the first recognition of their services to religion and to the State in the form of a regular permanent endowment. The pension which was so generously granted by Charles II. has already been referred to. But this pension does not seem to have been regularly paid, and it ceased altogether during the closing years of Charles II. and all the brief reign of James II. It was William III. who first granted the *Regium Donum*, or Royal Bounty, which continued from his day until the passing of the Irish Church Act in 1869—a period of nearly two centuries. In 1689, before William came to Ireland, a deputation from the Irish Presbyterians waited on him in London. He then promised to grant their ministers a pension of £800 a year. But in the turmoil of the time the matter was overlooked until the following year. It was better that it was. The king had in the meantime come over to Ireland, and in his progress through Ulster had been impressed with the numbers and usefulness of the Presbyterians. The result was that he issued from Hillsborough, co. Down, a royal order to the collector of customs at Belfast, directing a sum of £1,200 to be paid annually to the

Presbyterian ministers of the North. In the following year, 1691, this Royal Bounty was placed upon the Irish establishment by letters patent.

During the closing years of King William's reign, the Episcopal clergy, alarmed at the growing power of the Presbyterians, made several attempts to restrict their liberty.[1] In particular, Dr. Walkington, Bishop of Down and Connor, forwarded a petition to the Government, in which he made several complaints against the Presbyterians of his diocese. The grave offences with which he charges them are such as these: That they "exercise jurisdiction openly, and with a high hand, over those of their own persuasion;" that "they generally everywhere celebrate the office of matrimony;" that "they celebrate the sacrament of the Lord's Supper in congregations so formidably numerous, by gathering the inhabitants of ten or twelve or more parishes together to one place, when they preach in the fields, and continue there a great part of the day together;" and that "they openly hold their sessions and provincial synods for regulating of all matters of ecclesiastical concern, and have set up at Killileagh a philosophical school, in open violation and contempt of the laws." A court, consisting of the lords justices and some of the judges and bishops, was held in Dublin to

---

[1] In a letter from Rev. George Lang, of Newry, dated October 23rd, 1699, to Rev. Robert Wodrow, he says, "The Bishops here have used endeavours to hinder our ministers to marry, but without success as yet. That they might the more safely compass their design they applied themselves to the Government, who proposed the Bishops' desire to the ministers, that they would leave that part of their office (marriage, viz.) to the Established Church. The ministers considered the matter at their General Synod in July, and returned a negative answer, since which time we have heard no more noise about it."—Wodrow MSS., Letters, Vol. I., No. 61.

consider these complaints. The only action which it took in the matter was to give a good advice to all parties. The Presbyterian ministers it advised "to carry rectably towards the Established Church," and the Bishops it advised "to carry moderately." Thus the Bishop's narrow-minded intolerance was defeated in its object.[1]

A worse case of persecution occurred at Galway. In this case it must be recorded to the credit of the local Episcopal clergy that they took the side of toleration. But notwithstanding this, the power of bigotry succeeded. The Rev. William Biggar, who was then minister of the Presbyterian Church in Limerick, came to Galway at the invitation of some Presbyterian families to conduct services for them. He was brought before the mayor, and committed to prison, on the charge of dividing the Protestant interest by preaching in Galway, where no Dissenting worship had been celebrated for twenty years, and "at a time when the Papists were rapidly conforming."[2] The Archbishop of Tuam procured his release, but he was subsequently brought before the Lords Justices in Dublin. They ordered that Mr. Biggar should return to Limerick, and that no Presbyterian minister should for the present preach in the capital of the West. This was in 1698, but in 1700 the Rev. Mr. Hooks was ordained as the minister of the Presbyterian congregation of Galway. Mr. Biggar seems to have been a special object of Episcopalian animosity, for he was subsequently imprisoned for the terrible offence of preaching at Drogheda.[3]

---

[1] Reid : *History*, II., pp. 472-478.
[2] *Account of Emlyn's Trial*, by George Mathews, 1839 (Appendix). Reid, II., pp. 478, 479. Lecky : *England in the Eighteenth Century*.
[3] See below, Chap. VII.

These individual cases of sectarian bitterness were but the single heavy drops which came before the shower of persecution and penalties which was yet to fall upon the Irish Presbyterians in the reign of Queen Anne.

CHAPTER III.

THOMAS EMLYN.

PROFESSOR WITHEROW[1] has well said that "the history of the Presbyterian Church in Ireland, from the accession of the House of Stuart down till the period of Disestablishment, may be divided into three periods, of nearly a century each. The first of these, covering the seventeenth century, is the period in which Presbyterianism first appears, and, in spite of persecution and opposition, secures for itself a footing in the country; the second, coinciding with the eighteenth century, is a time of religious declension—declension in doctrinal purity, in zeal, and in usefulness; the third, or nineteenth century, is a period of revival and recovery, characterized by growth in orthodoxy, in activity, and in every symptom of spiritual life."

The first instance of that Arian teaching which so seriously endangered the Presbyterianism of Ireland during the close of the eighteenth and the beginning of the nineteenth century unhappily occurred in Dublin. In 1698 the Synod of Ulster had enacted that no young man should be licensed to preach the Gospel unless he subscribed the Westminster Confession as the confession of his faith. This, of course, had no reference to

---

[1] *Historical and Literary Memorials of Presbyterianism in Ireland,* Second Series, p. 341.

ministers who had already been licensed, but was merely prospective in its intention. However, the Synod was soon obliged to take steps to secure the orthodoxy of all its ministers.

Thomas Emlyn, the first minister who introduced Unitarian principles into Ireland, was a native of England, and the son of Episcopalian parents. He was educated for the Nonconformist ministry. In 1691 he was invited by the Rev. Joseph Boyse, minister of Wood Street, Dublin, to become his colleague in the pastorate of that congregation, then vacant by the resignation of the celebrated Dr. Williams. Emlyn's faith in the doctrine of the Trinity was first shaken, strange to say, by reading a *Vindication* of the doctrine published by Dr. William Sherlock, Dean of St. Paul's. For a long time Emlyn successfully concealed his change of opinion on this subject, so much so that neither Mr. Boyse, his colleague, nor any member of the congregation, had any suspicion of his Arian views. But at last his opinions were called in question by Dr. Duncan Cumyng, a member of his congregation. Dr. Cumyng had been educated for the ministry, but afterwards entered the medical profession. He noticed that Mr. Emlyn never in his preaching referred to the Deity of Christ, and this led him to suspect that Emlyn did not hold that important doctrine. Dr. Cumyng accordingly communicated his suspicions to Mr. Boyse. Together they waited on Mr. Emlyn, who confirmed their fears by acknowledging himself to be an Arian. Emlyn offered to leave the congregation peaceably, that they might choose another, if they pleased, in his place. But Mr. Boyse thought it necessary to bring the matter before the meeting of the Dublin ministers. Their action on that occasion leaves us in no doubt about their orthodoxy, but we may well question the wisdom and Christian charity of the course they adopted. "After about two hours' discourse," to quote the words of Emlyn's *Narrative*, upon this first and only conference with him, the ministers immediately, the same day, agreed to cast him off, and that he should not preach any more. They may have thought that Arianism had taken such a hold of him that he could not shake it off, and possibly this was a correct view of the case. But at any rate they might have given him the opportunity to reconsider his position, especially when, on Dr. Cumyng's own acknowledgment, no other member of the congregation but himself suspected Emlyn's orthodoxy.

As far as Emlyn was personally concerned the matter might have ended there, but that he published some books vindicating his position, and declaring his views on the Deity of Christ. It was this that led to his prosecution in June, 1703, a year after he had been deposed by the Dublin Presbytery. Caleb Thomas, an officebearer in a Baptist church in Dublin, obtained a warrant from the Lord Chief Justice to seize Emlyn and his books. Emlyn was put on his trial on the charge of writing and publishing a book "wherein it was blasphemously and maliciously asserted that Jesus Christ was not equal to God the Father," etc. The trial, verdict, and sentence were a strange perversion of justice. There was absolutely no proof to substantiate the charge of blasphemy. But the Chief Justice told the jury that "presumption was as good as evidence," and that "if they acquitted the prisoner my lords the bishops were there" (six or seven Bishops were on the bench). Emlyn was found guilty. He was sentenced "to suffer a year's imprisonment, to pay a thousand pounds to the Queen, or to lie in jail till it was paid, and to find security for good behaviour during life." A paper was then attached to his breast, indicating his crime and the sentence pronounced on him, and he was led round the Four Courts (says Professor Witherow) like a captured wild beast, to be exposed to the rude gaze and insults of the populace. Emlyn was kept in prison for two years, but through the kindly interposition of Mr. Boyse with the Duke of Ormond, his fine was reduced to seventy pounds, which he paid into the Queen's exchequer.

"But it seems I had not yet done," says Emlyn, in his *Narrative*, "for the Primate, Dr. Narcissus Marsh (who with the Archbishop of Dublin had sat on the bench at my trial), demanded a shilling in the pound of the whole fine, as the Queen's almoner. I thought his fees must have been reduced proportionably to her Majesty's reducement, and that the Church was to be as merciful as the State; but I was mistaken herein. In short, after several applications and letters to him, he would have twenty pounds off me, and so it was paid him, who thought it no blemish to his charity or generosity to make this advantage of the misery of one who for conscience toward God had endured grief."

The Dublin Presbyterian ministers, though they had deposed Emlyn, had nothing whatever to do with this prosecution. Indeed, judging by the rancour and bitterness displayed against Emlyn by the Episcopalian dignitaries, his chief crime would appear to have been that he was a Nonconformist. Emlyn himself acknowledges the friendly feeling of his brethren towards him, and that it was only a sense of duty which led them to depose him. Of Dr. Duncan Cumyng he says, "He had done me formerly so many kind offices that I cannot impute what he now did to any ill-will to me, other than what a mistaken zeal is apt to inspire." To his other chief opponent in doctrine, Mr. Boyse, he thus refers: "Mr. Boyse made several attempts for my liberty; whose kindness I thankfully acknowledge, in that with great concern and much labour he pursued it from time to time; which has abundantly confirmed my affection and respects to him, and extinguished all uneasy resentments. I am sensible that what he did against me was with regret and grief, what he did for me was with choice and pleasure. So that I hope nothing in this history shall be any diminution to the character of his great worth and good temper; who endeavoured to allay the common odium against me as far as he could without the loss of his own reputation." Emlyn afterwards became minister of a congregation in London, where he died in 1743.[1]

Emlyn's case has been here narrated in detail for two reasons: first, it shows us that the Dublin ministers of that time were orthodox in their opinions on the Deity of Christ; secondly, it was the beginning of that famous controversy on Subscription which was destined to affect so seriously the Presbyterianism of Dublin and the South, and in which the Dublin ministers took so prominent a part. The immediate result of Emlyn's deposition in 1702 and his subsequent publications was that in 1705 the Synod of Ulster adopted the following resolution:—

"That such as are to be licensed to preach the Gospel subscribe the Westminster Confession of Faith to be the confession of their faith, and promise to

---

[1] Emlyn's *Narrative*. Mathews: *Account of Emlyn's Trial*. Witherow: *Presbyterian Memorials*, I., pp. 130-146.

adhere to the Doctrine, Worship, and Government of this Church, as also those who are licensed and have not subscribed be obliged to subscribe before being ordained among us," which was voted and unanimously approved.

CHAPTER IV.

THE TEST ACT.

WHILE the Irish Presbyterian Church was thus troubled by the danger of erroneous teaching within, its enemies were assailing its rights and liberties without. The Irish Parliament, in its first session after the accession of Queen Anne, showed that the spirit of animosity to the Presbyterians which had given such unpleasant proofs of its existence in Bishop Walkington's petition and in the imprisonment of Mr. Biggar at Galway was now determined to assert itself in the government of the country. The House of Commons, in October, 1703, resolved "That the pension of twelve hundred pounds per annum granted to the Presbyterian ministers in Ulster is an unnecessary branch of the establishment."[1] No action, however, was taken by the Government upon this resolution, and the Regium Donum still continued to be paid.

In the following month a Bill which had already been framed by the Irish House of Commons was sent to England for the consideration of the Queen and her ministers. It was entitled "A Bill to Prevent the Further Growth of Popery." Yet, strange to say, it became one of the most powerful methods which had yet been devised for oppressing the Presbyterians of Ireland.

---

[1] *Journals of Irish House of Commons*, October, 1703.

The Presbyterians had themselves to blame. So long as the Bill contained clauses referring only to the Roman Catholics, the Presbyterians joined with their own tyrannical persecutors, the Episcopalians, in supporting it. The very essence of Presbyterianism is the principle of civil and religious liberty. The way to overcome what we believe to be a religion of error is not by imposing disabilities and penalties upon the observance of it, but by fair argument and in a Christian spirit to endeavour to convince those who differ from us. Yet on this occasion the Irish Presbyterians were so far led astray by that very spirit of intolerance from which they themselves had suffered that they supported this iniquitous law. "And it was a singular occurrence," says Dr. Reid, a Presbyterian historian, "an instance, perhaps, of righteous requital, that they themselves, after having given their aid in Parliament to carry one of the most cruel of these statutes against the Romanists, should, by a clause added to that very statute, be deprived of their own civil rights, and subjected in their turn to serious grievances on account of their religion."[1]

It was when the Bill was under consideration by the English Government that the clause affecting the Presbyterians was added to it. This clause required that all persons holding any office, civil or military, or receiving any pay or salary from the Crown, or having command or place of trust from the sovereign, should take the sacrament in the Established Church within three months after every such appointment. Hence the Act is usually called the Sacramental Test Act, or more briefly the Test Act. We now know, on the

---

[1] Reid: *History*, II., p. 502.

authority of Sir Gilbert Dolben, one of the Judges of the Court of Common Pleas in Ireland, who was then in London, that the Queen and the leading dignitaries of the Church of England did their utmost to secure that this amendment should become law. In a letter written by Dolben to Sir Richard Cox, the Irish Lord Chancellor, he says that "this amendment was made by her Majesty's particular direction in Council, upon a due sense of the laws being defective in that great point."[1]

On the 14th of February, 1704, this infamous Bill, with this infamous addition, was read the first time in the Irish House of Commons. On the 4th March it received the royal assent.

Reid's summary of the effects of the Sacramental Test Act upon the Presbyterians is so excellent that it may be quoted here. "The Irish Presbyterians," he says, "were now, therefore, in a much worse position than their brethren in England. Like them, indeed, they were excluded from the public service, but their Church was still unrecognized in law, while the English Dissenters enjoyed full security for their worship and government. The disabilities created by this Act extended to all civil and military appointments under the Crown. No Presbyterian could henceforth hold any office in any department of the army or navy, nor in the customs, excise, or post-office, nor in or about any of the courts of law, whether in Dublin or in the provinces, nor in the magistracy of the kingdom, without conforming to the Established Church. They were also excluded by this Bill from all municipal offices in the corporate towns of Ireland. A remarkable instance

---

[1] Reid: *History*, II., p. 506.

of its operation in this respect occurred in the city of Derry. No fewer than ten out of twelve aldermen, and fourteen out of twenty-four burgesses, being Presbyterians, were turned out of their respective offices; and that, too, in a city which most of these very men had contributed to preserve, by their services and sufferings during the siege, but in which they were now ignominiously branded by the Government as unworthy to hold the humblest offices! Most of the magistrates throughout Ulster were in like manner deprived of their commissions, not more than two or three having qualified according to the Act, and great difficulty was experienced in filling their places." So general was the feeling of indignation throughout the kingdom at the way in which the Irish Presbyterians had been treated, that De Foe, the celebrated author of *Robinson Crusoe*, wrote a most sarcastic and powerful pamphlet on the subject, entitled "The Parallel; or, Persecution of Protestants the Shortest Way to Prevent the growth of Popery in Ireland."

But persecution, as is commonly the case, seemed only to have the effect of making the Presbyterians more earnest in extending that religion for which they had suffered so much. The Synod of Ulster began to feel the necessity of assisting the scattered Presbyterians throughout the South and West. In 1706 it inaugurated a missionary fund for this purpose, and by means of this fund not only were existing congregations aided in obtaining regular ministers, but ministers were also sent to visit and preach to isolated Presbyterians in places where no Presbyterian congregation already existed.

The Regium Donum granted by William III. was given to ministers of the Synod of Ulster. But there were several ministers and congregations in the South of Ireland not connected with that Synod. These congregations had been mainly formed by English Presbyterians, and in 1708, through the interest of Dr. Calamy and other Presbyterians in England, Queen Anne was induced to allow for the support of these Southern ministers £800 a year out of her Privy Purse. The ministers receiving the £800 a year (which was known as the English Bounty) were called "The Southern Association," afterwards the Synod of Munster.[1]

Once again the increasing activity of the Presbyterians excited the indignation of their Episcopalian neighbours. The case of Drogheda may be taken as a single instance. In that town there had been a regular Presbyterian congregation from the time of Cromwell to 1688. Dr. Daniel Williams, afterwards successively minister in Wood Street, Dublin, and in London, had been minister there. The occupation of the town, however, by King James's troops, from 1688 to 1690, was the means of dispersing the congregation, most of the members having taken refuge elsewhere. Kirkpatrick, in his *Presbyterian Loyalty*, which was written in 1713, tells us what happened in the intervening years. "The remains of that Congregation," he says, "have several times, at their own desire, enjoyed the occasional labours of divers Ministers of our Persuasion while they wanted a fixed Pastor of their own. And *upon their invitation and earnest request*, in the year 1708, several of our brethren preached among them, of whom Mr. Flemyng . . . was one, who, *for no other cause pretended or objected against him but that of preaching,*

---

[1] Mathews: *Account of the Regium Donum*. Report of Chancery Proceedings, Attorney-General *v.* Dr. Carlile (1850), pp. 12, 19.

was bound over to the next assizes at Drogheda ; though there is a vast number of Papists there, much superior to the whole Protestant inhabitants, openly going to mass undisturbed, while some of our Persuasion were obliged to pay *twelve-pence* a piece to prevent them from being *set in the stocks*, as they were peaceably going home from their Meeting, upon pretence of travelling upon the Lord's Day ; and yet others at the same time were really guilty of profaning it by carrying loads openly, with impunity." Dean Cox, the rector of the parish, was the originator of all these troubles. During the time that Mr. Flemyng was bound over to stand his trial, the Rev. William Biggar came to preach to the Presbyterians of Drogheda. We have already seen how he was imprisoned at Galway for preaching there in 1698. Immediately after he preached for the first time in Drogheda, Dean Cox had him brought before the mayor, and he was sent to prison for three months under the Irish Act of Uniformity. On representations made to the Lords Justices, however, he was released at the end of six weeks. But Mr. Flemyng was brought up for trial at the spring assizes in 1709. At the same time three other persons were prosecuted for travelling on a Sunday to hear him preach. The case was taken to the Court of Queen's Bench, but before the time for hearing it, the Earl of Wharton, then Lord Lieutenant, directed a *nolle prosequi* to be entered. This put an end to the trial, and for many years afterwards the Presbyterian congregation of Drogheda continued to enjoy the privilege of a regular ministry.

It was in this same year, or about the close of 1708, that Dean Swift appeared upon the scene of conflict, and threw all the weight of his genius into the scale against the persecuted Presbyterians. Petitions had already been forwarded to the Queen against the Sacramental Test, and when the Earl of Wharton, who had long been considered the leader of the Presbyterian interest in England, came to Ireland as Lord Lieutenant in 1709, the Episcopalians began to fear that the test would be abolished. In his speech at the opening of the Parliamentary session in May, Lord Wharton referred to "the necessity there is of cultivating and preserving a good understanding amongst all the Protestants of this kingdom." At the close of the session in August he said, "I am directed to declare it to you as her Majesty's fixed resolution, that as her Majesty will always maintain and support the Church as by law established, so it is her royal will and intention that the Dissenters shall not be persecuted or molested in the exercise of their religion."[1] Perhaps the Queen had begun to see that the Presbyterians were too important a part of the community to be recklessly alienated and embittered.

Dean Swift also saw the power of the Presbyterians, but instead of seeking to gain their sympathy for Episcopal Protestantism and for British rule, he did his best to make them the enemies of both. Froude says that the one great mistake of Swift's life was his misunderstanding the Presbyterians. Swift was determined to put down Presbyterianism in Ireland, and he therefore vehemently opposed every attempt to repeal the Sacramental Test. His first attack was made in a pamphlet entitled "A Letter from a Member of the House of Commons in Ireland to a Member of the House of Commons in England, concerning the Sacramental Test." In this pamphlet, amidst all the abuse

---

[1] *Irish House of Lords' Journals*, 1709.

and ridicule which he pours upon the Presbyterians, he cannot help bearing testimony to their industry and loyalty to their religion. He says, "We observe the Scots in our Northern parts to be a brave, industrious people, extreamly devoted to their religion, and full of an undisturbed affection towards each other. Numbers of that noble nation, invited by the fertilities of the soil, are glad to exchange their barren hills of Louquabar, by a voyage of three hours, for our fruitful vales of Doun and Antrim, so productive of that grain which at little trouble and less expence finds diet and lodging for themselves and their cattle. These people, by their extream parsimony, wonderful Dexterity in Dealing, and firm adherence to one another, soon grow into wealth from the smallest beginnings, never are rooted out where they once fix, and increase daily by new supplies. Besides, when they are the superior number in any tract of ground they are not over-patient of mixture; but such, whom they cannot assimilate, soon find it their interest to remove. I have done all in my power on some land of my own to preserve two or three English fellows in their neighbourhood, but found it impossible, though one of them thought he had sufficiently made his Court by turning Presbyterian. Add to all this, that they bring with them from Scotland a most formidable notion of our Church, which they look upon at least three degrees worse than popery, and it is natural it should be so, since they come over full fraught with that spirit which taught them to abolish Episcopacy at home."

CHAPTER V.

THE GENERAL (OR EUSTACE STREET) FUND.

THE persecutions to which the Presbyterians had been subjected, especially in the South and West, directed the attention of some of their leaders to the necessity for strengthening their position at the outposts of the Church. Cases like those of Galway and Drogheda showed them that in any effort to minister to the spiritual wants of their own isolated members, or in any effort to engage in missionary work, they must expect to be rewarded with imprisonment by the enlightened Episcopacy of the time. The Presbyterianism of Dublin was rich in laymen of influential position, high spirit, Christian thoughtfulness, and loyalty to their Church. By their services at this time of danger and distress they have laid the Presbyterianism of the South, and indeed the whole Presbyterian Church of Ireland, under a lasting debt of gratitude. Some of these gentlemen formed the idea of establishing a fund for the permanent endowment of the Presbyterianism of Dublin and the South. This idea soon ripened into the establishment of the "General Fund," which has supported many a struggling congregation, and aided many a missionary effort, for the greater part of two centuries.[1]

---

[1] Armstrong's *Short Account of General Fund* (1815). Frazer's MS. *History of the General Fund* (1862). *Report of Chancery Proceedings* (1850).

The first public mention of such a project was made in 1696. The Rev. Alexander Synclare, minister of Plunket Street congregation, Dublin, stated, at a meeting of the Southern ministers held that year in Clonmel, "That some gentlemen in London, and others in Dublin and elsewhere in this kingdom, had lodged some money in the hands of the Dublin ministers, to be by them distributed as they saw necessary, for the support and encouragement of the ministry in the southern parts of this kingdom."

In 1710 the General Fund was actually formed. The chief promoters of it first of all issued a "Proposal to establish a General Fund." The reasons which they give to induce persons to contribute to the fund are worth quoting. In an abridged form, they are these:—

1. The ends to be promoted.
   (a) Liberty of conscience, and the desire to secure this for others.
   (b) The paucity and poverty of country congregations make it desirable to encourage ministers to settle over them.
   (c) There are many places where congregations might be erected, and ministers sent to preach to scattered people.
   (d) To encourage students for the ministry.
2. The inconvenience and difficulty of private applications to particular persons on particular occasions and emergencies of this kind.
3. Persons who have wealth have both a peculiar capacity and a special obligation to promote these excellent ends.

There is the obligation of gratitude to God.

Wealth is a stewardship.

It is best to give in your lifetime. Then you can

see fruit of the seed which you have sown. "It is a just observation of a learned judge, that those who put off their charity to their last will show they have but little will to it, since they only give what they can no longer enjoy themselves."

4. All possible precautions will be taken to apply this fund to the uses for which it is designed.

The first contributors were Joseph Damer, Esq., £500; Richard Cooke, Esq., £100; James Martin, Esq., £100; John Curtis, Esq., £200; Hugh Henry, Esq., £100; Sir Arthur Langford, Bart., £500. Thus a total of £1,500 was subscribed, which, on the 1st of May, 1710, was settled by a deed of trust.

The trust deed thus states the purpose of the fund: "From a pious disposition and concern for the interest of our Lord Jesus Christ, and the welfare of precious souls, Sir Arthur Langford and Joseph Damer, Esq., with divers other well-disposed Christians, have designed and intended to set on foot a stock or fund for the support of religion in and about Dublin and the South of Ireland, by assisting and supporting the Protestant Dissenting interest against unreasonable prosecutions, and for the education of youth designed for the ministry among Protestant Dissenters; and for assisting Protestant Dissenting congregations that are poor and unable to provide for their ministers; and for such other pious and religious ends, and by such means, as shall by the subscribers hereunto be thought proper and reasonable for promoting the design and intention herein expressed."

The trustees were to be the ministers of the several Presbyterian congregations in Dublin, with two members of each congregation and all donors of a hundred pounds or more. As each of the five congregations in Dublin at that time had two ministers, there were ten ministers among the first trustees. These were the Revs. Joseph Boyse and Richard Choppin (Wood Street); Francis Iredale and Robert Craighead (Capel Street); Nathaniel Weld and John Hemingway (New Row, afterwards Eustace Street); Ralph Norris and Thomas Steward (Cook Street); and Alexander Sinclair and James Arbuckle (Plunket Street). The ten gentlemen chosen as members of the five congregations were Doctor Duncan Cumyng, Mr. James Kennedy, Mr. Thomas Kirkpatrick, Mr. Richard Bamber, Mr. Joseph Marriott, Mr. Christopher Litton, Joseph Kane, Esq., Mr. John Cuthbert, Mr. Ralph Norris, and Walter Stephens, Esq. The remaining trustees were the original contributors whose names are given above, with the addition of Mr. John Damer. There were in all twenty-seven trustees.

The fund must have been soon considerably augmented. Armstrong, in his History of the Dublin Churches, states that the capital of this fund was £7,670, of which the members of Wood Street congregation contributed £6,750. Professor Witherow, in his account of Rev. Richard Choppin (*Presbyterian Memorials*, First Series), repeats this statement, and adds, "The gentlemen who took the most active part in its collection were Mr. Choppin, Sir Arthur Langford, and Dr. Duncan Cumyng. . . . Of the money thus intrusted to them, the trustees invested the largest portion in the purchase of Mr. Choppin's estate at Rathfarnham."

This fund, thus formed by the energy and generosity of a few Dublin gentlemen, has proved of inestimable value to the Presbyterianism of the South and West.

It has aided in the education of students for the ministry, in the support of ministers where the congregations were weak and struggling, and in the erection of churches, manses, and schools. Presbyterians of the present day, whether in the North or in the South, who are devoted to the Church of their fathers, who believe in her power for doing good, and who would like to assist those who are doing her work, amid many difficulties, at the outposts, could not do better than contribute to the General Fund.

CHAPTER VI.

THE PRESBYTERY OF DUBLIN IN RELATION TO ULSTER AND AMERICA.

AT the time when the General Fund was established the Presbyterianism of Dublin was most vigorous and prosperous. There were five Presbyterian congregations in the city, some of them, as Wood Street, says a reliable narrator,[1] "having a thousand hearers on the Lord's Day, and all attended by wealthy and respectable members, holding, so far as we can ascertain, a truly orthodox creed, although from their origin, having been in great part English Puritan rather than Scottish Presbyterian, the Dublin Churches did not always attend to subscription of the Westminster Confession as they ought to have done. At the same time we have obtained clear proof that some at least were most particular, and would not accept of non-subscribing ministers as their pastors."

The founders of the General Fund had certainly little sympathy with that Arianism into whose hands the administration and the benefits of the Fund subsequently passed for a considerable time. One of the chief promoters of the Fund was Dr. Duncan Cumyng, the very man who first called attention to Emlyn's Arian views. Choppin, another of its promoters, was

---

[1] Dr. William Frazer : MS. *History of the General Fund.*

the man who succeeded Emlyn in the ministry of Wood Street, and he was not likely either to be chosen or to be continued as minister there if he had held views for which his predecessor had been deposed. Among the ministerial trustees of the Fund were several of the very men who had deposed Emlyn for denying the Deity of Christ. But though the Dublin ministers of that time were themselves orthodox, they unconsciously prepared the way for the Arianism which afterwards took possession of many of the pulpits in Dublin and the South. By the attitude which they took up in the Subscription controversy, objecting to the signing of any creed or confession as a test of orthodoxy, they opened the door for the entrance of various errors.

The attitude of Dublin Presbyterianism to the Synod of Ulster at this time was somewhat peculiar. The ministers of Dublin and surrounding districts were bound together in a Presbytery or associated body, which seems to have been a revival of the Brotherly Association of 1658. This Presbytery acted in some respects quite independently of the Synod of Ulster, and partly in conjunction with it. It sent corresponding members to the meetings of the Synod. But at the same time some of the Dublin congregations were under the control of a Presbytery in the North. The Dublin ministers were most anxious to avoid the danger of collision which might arise from this division of interests, and in 1709 they drew up some resolutions on this subject to be submitted to the Synod of Ulster. As the result of this, the Synod in 1710 and 1711 drew up a kind of agreement with the Presbytery of Dublin. The chief points of this agreement were—

1. " That in the ordination of any person in Dublin

to any congregation subject to a Northern Presbytery the said Presbytery do ordinarily appoint one of the brethren residing in Dublin that belongs to them to preside in the ordination," except in some case of emergency.

2. "That after the Presbytery in the North have taken what trials they think fit of any candidate of theirs to be ordained in Dublin, the Presbytery of Dublin may also take what trials they think needful; and in case the Presbytery of Dublin should not be satisfied with the said candidate's trial, then the final determination shall be by the Presbytery in the North and that in Dublin, or as many of their members as they think fit in conjunction."

3. The Presbytery of Dublin was to act in conjunction with a Northern Presbytery in any case of discipline affecting a member of a Northern Presbytery residing in Dublin.

4. Six weeks' notice was to be given to the Dublin Presbytery when an ordination by a Northern Presbytery was to take place in Dublin. The Dublin ministers were to take part in all such ordinations. In 1710 the Presbytery of Belfast had been directed to apologize to the Presbytery of Dublin for not having given notice of the intended ordination of Mr. Craghead in Capel Street congregation.[1]

Such an agreement as this shows that the Synod of Ulster recognized the Presbyterianism of Dublin and the South to be somewhat different from the Presbyterianism of the North, and that, notwithstanding, it was willing to modify its own arrangements to suit the different circumstances of the South.

---

[1] Statement of Lord Chancellor in giving judgment in the case of the General Fund, *Report of Chancery Proceedings* (1850), pp. 101, 102.

About this time the Presbytery of Dublin was brought into relationship with the young and growing Presbyterian Church of the United States. Already one of its former members, the Rev. Alexander Coldin, of Enniscorthy, had been invited to cross the Atlantic. He was one of the many ministers who were obliged to leave Ireland and take refuge in Scotland in the troublous times of 1689. In 1708 Francis Makemie wrote a letter to him by order of the Presbytery of Philadelphia, to signify the desire of the people of Lewistown that he should become their minister. Francis Makemie, the founder of American Presbyterianism, was himself an Irish Presbyterian from Co. Donegal, and had doubtless many opportunities of knowing the reputation of ministers in Ireland. Mr. Coldin was then minister of the parish of Oxam, in the Presbytery of Jedburgh, Scotland. As he had been at this time about thirty years a minister, he doubtless thought it was too late to make so great a change, for he remained at Oxam till his death in 1738.

Dr. Briggs, who mentions these particulars in his *American Presbyterianism*,[1] tells us that the Presbytery of Philadelphia was essentially a missionary Presbytery. "It was strengthened," he says, "in 1710, by the arrival of two able men, John Henry from the Presbytery of Dublin, and James Anderson from the Presbytery of Glasgow.... Mr. Henry became the successor of Makemie at Rehoboth, and the heir of his influence in Ireland."

"Mr. Henry received a letter soon after his arrival, dated November, 1709, from the Rev. Alexander Sinclair, minister of the Plunket Street Church, Dublin, desiring

---

[1] Chapter IV.

correspondence and an account of ecclesiastical affairs, and giving assurances of financial help." Mr. Henry was directed by the Presbytery of Philadelphia to write a letter from that Presbytery to the Presbytery of Dublin. This letter is quoted by Briggs from the records of the Philadelphia Presbytery. It requests the Presbytery of Dublin to give such aid to their brethren in Philadelphia as will support an itinerant minister. I do not know whether the request was granted, and Mr. Sinclair's assurance carried out, but it is most likely that among the wealthy and generous Presbyterians who resided in Dublin at that period the required sum would be easily raised. Irish Presbyterianism has had an important part in the formation of the Presbyterian Church in the United States, for during almost the whole of the eighteenth century there was a constant exodus of Irish Presbyterians to America, to escape the persecutions of Prelacy, and to obtain in that land of freedom the civil and religious liberty which was denied them at home.

CHAPTER VII.

BISHOPS AND BIGOTRY.

THE Presbyterians had little time to breathe between the attacks of intolerance in the reign of Queen Anne. Dean Swift's efforts against them had not been in vain. On the 6th November, 1711, the Irish House of Lords appointed a Committee to draw up a representation and address to the Queen, relating to the Dissenting ministers. What the representation was likely to be might be imagined from the composition of the Committee. The members of the Committee were:—

The Lord Archbishop of Dublin	The Lord Bishop of Kildare
The Lord Archbishop of Cashel	The Lord Bishop of Elphin
The Lord Archbishop of Tuam	The Lord Bishop of Clonfert
The Earl of Inchiquin	The Lord Bishop of Killala
The Earl of Mountrath	The Lord Bishop of Ossory
Lord Viscount Valentia	The Lord Bishop of Clogher
Lord Viscount Fitzwilliam	The Lord Bishop of Limerick
Lord Viscount Charlemont	The Lord Bishop of Killaloe
Lord Viscount Blessington	The Lord Bishop of Raphoe
Lord Viscount Mountjoy	The Lord Bishop of Cloyne
Lord Viscount Strabane	The Lord Bishop of Kerry
Lord Viscount Mount-Cashel	The Lord Bishop of Dunkellin.

No time was lost. Next day the Earl of Inchiquin reported to the House that the Committee had met and agreed to the following address. The address shows so plainly the spirit of intolerance with which the

Presbyterians had to contend that no apology is needed for giving it in full.

"To the Queen's most Excellent Majesty, the humble Representation and Address of the Lords Spiritual and Temporal in Parliament assembled.

"May it please your Majesty, we your Majesty's most dutiful and loyal subjects, the Lords Spiritual and Temporal in Parliament assembled, being touched at Heart to find the Members of our Church charged with Oppression and Persecution by the Dissenters; and that your Majesty's Name has been made use of in a Letter, dated the 8*th* of *April*, 1710, from the Earl of *Wharton*, then Lord Lieutenant of this Kingdom, to the Lords Justices; directing them to order *Noli prosequis* (thereby putting a stop to the Proceedings at Law against one Flemyng and others, who were sent by the Presbyterys of the North to set up a Meeting in the Town of *Drogheda*, where there had been none for 28 years past, to the great Disturbance of the Peace and Quiet of that Town), do, upon this present Occasion, think ourselves obliged, with all Duty and Submission, to represent unto your Majesty, that no Dissenters throughout this Kingdom have been disturbed in the exercise of their religious Worship where they had settled Congregations, either by your Majesty's Civil or Ecclesiastical Governors or by any of our Church: And yet, those unjust Complainers of Persecution, whilst they themselves enjoyed Ease and Security, have exercised great Severities towards their conforming Neighbours, by denying them common Offices of Humanity; and by threatening and actually ruining several, who, in Compliance with their Conscience, have left their sect.

"In many Towns they have refused to take Apprentices that will not covenant to go to their Meetings, and wherever they obtain the Majority in Corporations, they excluded all such as were not of their own Persuasion; they have also obliged those of their own Communion, who were married according to the Office of our Liturgy, to do publick Penance.

"And we farther beg Leave to observe to your Majesty, that a Right Rev. Bishop, a member of this House, lost his Bishoprick for not taking the Oath of Abjuration in due time, to which he was restored by your Majesty's Clemency and Goodness; and yet some Dissenting Ministers, who are under the same Obligation, whilst they openly refuse to take the Oath, preach on with Impunity and in Defiance of the Law.

"The Episcopal Order hath been stiled *Anti-Scriptural;* our holy and religious Worship called *superstitious* and *idolatrous;* and our Ministers have been openly and violently assaulted and hindered in the Discharge of their sacred Offices; and even the Legislature itself hath not escaped the Censure of a bold Author of their's, who hath published in Print that 'the Sacramental Test is only an Engine to advance a State Faction and to debase Religion, to serve mean and unworthy Purposes.'

"Amidst these many and repeated Provocations, we have been still easy, and have endeavoured, by gentle Usage, to melt them down into a more soft and complying Temper: But all our attempts of this kind have proved unsuccessful. They have returned us Evil for Good; our Forbearance hath only increased their Rage and Obstinacy, and by our Lenity, the Northern Presbyterys have been encouraged to seek out to enlarge their Borders: And, not content with the Enjoyment of the free Exercise of their religious Worship in places where they had settled Meetings, have assumed a Power to send out Missionaries into several Places of their Kingdom, where they have had no Call, nor any congregations to support them.

"And this, we beg Leave to acquaint your Majesty, they have been enabled to do, by misapplying that Bounty of £1,200 a Year (which your Majesty hath been pleased to extend to them for charitable Purposes) to the Propagation of Schism, the undermining of the Church, and to the Disturbance of the Peace and Unanimity of the Conformists of this Kingdom.

"From this Fund also we doubt not they have Supplies to employ and maintain Agents, support Law-Suits against the Church, to form Seminaries to the Poisoning of the Principles of our Youth; and, in Opposition to the Law, to set up Synods and Judicatories, destructive of your Majesty's Prerogative.

"And one *John Macbride*, a Non-juror, stiling himself *Minister of Belfast*, at a Provincial Synod held there, preached and printed a Sermon wherein he justifies these Meetings, and makes them independent on the Civil Power.

"By these means, Schism, which formerly, in a Manner, was confined unto the *North*, hath now spread itself into many other Parts of this Kingdom:

"So that we should not be just in our Duty to your Majesty

or our Country, if we did not acquaint your Majesty with the Dangers we apprehend from these great Advances which Presbytery and Fanaticism have made: which, if not checked, we doubt not, will in Time end in the Destruction of the Constitution both in Church and State.

"We therefore humbly submit it to your Majesty, Whether your Majesty will not think it, in your great Wisdom, proper to put a stop to these growing Evils, by withdrawing from them your Bounty of £1,200 a Year?

"And we earnestly intreat your Majesty that, whilst we do not disturb the Dissenters in their Way of Worship in their usual Places of Meeting, your Majesty will not think it unreasonable that we should by all lawful Means hinder the spreading of Schism, in order to preserve our own Peace and Unanimity and the Safety and Welfare of this Realm."[1]

The unchristian bigotry of this document is only equalled by its unblushing effrontery. Upon a series of accusations, of which not a shadow of proof is offered, followed by absolutely unfounded suspicions, these noblemen, in their high position of responsibility, do not scruple to base a request for the withdrawal of the scanty pittance by which three sovereigns had rewarded the loyalty of their Presbyterian subjects.

Two days later, the same House afforded another instance of the bigotry and tyranny which the Presbyterians had to expect. In the Lords' Journals of the 9th November occurs the following minute:—

"Resolved, on the Question that a book intitled 'Sermons preached on various Subjects, Vol. I., by J. B., Dublin, printed by S. Powell for the Use of the Author, 1708,' is false and scandalous, and contains matters highly reflecting on the Legislature, and on the Episcopal Order.

"Ordered, on Motion, that the Sheriffs of the City of Dublin do cause the said Book to be burnt by the hands of the common Hangman To-morrow, at Twelve of the Clock, before the Tholsel."

---

[1] *Journals of Irish House of Lords*, November, 1711.

The book which was thus honoured by what Dr. Witherow calls "the bonfire argument of the Bishops" was a volume of Sermons by the Rev. Joseph Boyse, minister of the Presbyterian congregation of Wood Street, Dublin. The sermon which was particularly obnoxious was one on "The Office of a Scriptural Bishop," which may be found in the first volume of Boyse's Works, and which is one of the fairest and most moderate of all treatises on the subject. So much for the religious freedom accorded to their fellow-Protestants by the Episcopal Protestantism of the eighteenth century!

The Synod of Ulster did not allow the calumnies of the House of Lords to remain unanswered. Their Committee prepared a statement vindicating themselves, and refuting the charges made in the "Representation and Address," and Mr. Iredell, minister of Capel Street, Dublin, was commissioned to proceed to London and lay it before the Queen. They also forwarded to Government an affidavit from Mr. Bryce Blair, of Belfast, who was agent for the distribution of the Royal Bounty. The unfounded charge of the House of Lords about the use made of this Bounty was completely disproved by Mr. Blair's statement that since his appointment to the office he had paid the Royal Bounty quarterly, in equal shares, among the ministers, and that he had never expended any portion of it "in setting up or maintaining seminaries, missionaries, law-suits, or agents, or in any other ways than to the said ministers."[1]

In 1712 a whole Presbytery was taken into custody at the instigation of the High Church party. The

---

[1] Reid: *History*, III., pp. 20, 21.

Presbytery of Monaghan resolved to meet at Belturbet, for the purpose of erecting into a congregation the Presbyterians residing in that town and its neighbourhood, who had already been supplied with preaching for about three years. On the day on which the Presbytery met its members were arrested and brought before the magistrates; they were charged with holding an unlawful and riotous assembly, and were bound over to appear for trial at the next assizes for the county of Cavan. In this case Mr. Iredell, of Dublin, again received from the Synod of Ulster's Committee the honourable commission of bearing to London addresses to the Queen and heads of Government on the subject. The case was ended by a statement on the part of the ministers, that "since the complaint was made, they have, to avoid giving offence, prevailed with their people to remove their meeting-house a mile farther from the town than it was before, and resolve never to give any uneasiness to the said town on that account." The proceedings were then stayed on the part of the Government. This gross attempt to interfere with the rights and liberties of ministers of the Gospel arose entirely from the alarm of the Episcopal clergy at the prospect of a place for Presbyterian worship being erected in the town of Belturbet. How relieved they must have been when the Presbyterians, to avoid imprisonment, agreed to remove their meeting-house a mile farther away! Modern Presbyterians who are acquainted with the North of Ireland must have often wondered why Presbyterian churches are so commonly found a considerable distance away from the village or town for whose inhabitants they have been mainly erected. They have in this case at Belturbet an illustration of the cause.

Several other instances of similar intolerance occurred about the same time. It was reported to the Synod of Ulster, at its meeting in 1713, that several ministers and laymen had been prosecuted—the ministers for the crime of celebrating marriages,[1] and the laymen for the grievous offences of refusing the office of churchwarden and teaching school.

The persistent attacks of the Episcopal clergy and of the House of Lords were at length successful in the matter of the Royal Bounty. In 1714 this grant was altogether withdrawn.[2] The same year witnessed another act of persecution in the passing of the Schism Act. By this oppressive Act any Presbyterian in Ireland who ventured to teach a school, except of the very humblest description, was liable to be imprisoned for three months. The passing of the Act led to various acts of violence against the Presbyterians. Dean Swift was then Rector of Laracor. He had been very much annoyed at the erection of the Presbyterian church of Summerhill by Sir Arthur Langford, within his parish. Accordingly he wrote the following letter to Sir Arthur Langford :—

"TRIM, *October* 30*th*, 1714.

"SIR,—I was to wait upon you the other day, and was told by your servant that you were not to be seen till towards evening, which, at the distance I am, at this time of the year, cannot easily be compassed. My principal business was to let you know that, since my last return from England, many persons have complained to me that I suffered a conventicle to be kept in my parish, and in a place where there never was any before. I mentioned this to your nephew, Rowley, in Dublin, when he came to me with this message from you; but I could not prevail with him to write to you about it. I have always looked upon

---

[1] See above, p. 15.
[2] Reid: *History*, III., p. 53.

you as an honest gentleman, of great charity and piety in your way; and I hope you will remember, at the same time, that it becomes you to be a legal man, and that you will not promote or encourage, much less give a beginning to, a thing directly contrary to law. You know the Dissenters in Ireland are supposed to have their conventicles only by connivance, and that only in places where they formerly used to meet. Whereas this conventicle of yours is a new thing, in a new place, entirely of your own erection, and perverted to this ill use from the design you outwardly seemed to have intended it for.

"It has been the weakness of the Dissenters to be too sanguine, and assuming upon events in the State which appeared to give them the least encouragement; and this, in other turns of affairs, hath proved very much to their disadvantage. The most moderate Churchmen may be apt to resent, when they see a sect, without toleration by law, insulting the established religion. Whenever the legislature shall think fit to give them leave to build new conventicles, all good Churchmen will submit; but till then we can hardly see it without betraying our Church. I hope, therefore, you will not think it hard if I take those methods which my duty obliges me to prevent this growing evil, as far as it lies in my power, unless you shall think fit, from your own prudence, or the advice of some understanding friends, to shut up the doors of that conventicle for the future.

"I am, with true friendship and esteem, Sir,
"Your most humble, obedient Servant,
"B."

Sir Arthur Langford not having "the prudence" to shut up the doors of the church which he had erected, Dean Swift caused them to be nailed up. Sir Arthur thereupon erected a parsonage-house for the Presbyterian minister of Summerhill, with a convenient place for worship in one of its largest apartments.[1] By a similar arbitrary exercise of authority, the Presbyterian churches at Antrim, Downpatrick, and Rathfriland were also nailed up.

---

[1] Report of Chancery Proceedings, 1850. Armstrong's *History of Dublin Churches*. *Swift's Works*.

CHAPTER VIII.

BETTER DAYS.

THE death of Queen Anne, and the accession of George I., raised once more the hopes of the Presbyterians. Mr. Iredell, of Dublin, was again commissioned by the Synod's Committee to proceed to London, in company with Colonel Clotworthy Upton, M.P. for co. Antrim, with an address to the new sovereign. The address was agreed to at a meeting which all the leading ministers and members of the Church were invited to attend, and embodied three principal requests: (1) for capacity to serve their country, by the repeal of the Sacramental Test; (2) for full legal protection for their worship and government; (3) for the restoration and increase of the grant of the Royal Bounty. The Commissioners afterwards reported to the Synod that the king received them graciously, and "appeared sensibly concerned" when he read the representation of their grievances. The only immediate result was that the Royal Bounty, payment of which had been suspended for more than a year, was at once renewed, and hopes were held out that it would be speedily increased.[1]

About this time an invasion by the Pretender was expected, and in order to strengthen the defences of the country the Irish Lords Justices resolved to call out

---
[1] Reid, *History*, III., pp. 60-63.

the militia. "This proposed measure," says Dr. Reid, "placed the members of the Presbyterian Church in a very embarrassing position. If they entered the militia, whether as officers, or even as privates, and received pay from the Crown, they exposed themselves to the penalties of Nonconformity under the Sacramental Test Act. On the other hand, if they refused to enter the service, they exposed themselves to what they no doubt dreaded more than civil penalties—the charge of basely deserting their sovereign and their country in the time of danger."[1] At a meeting of the leading Presbyterians held in Belfast, they resolved to take the first alternative, in the hope that the Government would protect them from the penalties under which religious intolerance had laid them. An Act of Parliament was subsequently passed, indemnifying such Presbyterians as had entered the militia from the penalties they had incurred. The incident illustrates the method in which, down to very recent years, successive English Governments have dealt with the Presbyterians of Ireland. They have been glad to avail themselves of their loyalty, their influence, and their courage in any time of danger, but when the danger was past the privileges which these qualities might be supposed to deserve have almost invariably been withheld, or given with grudging hand.

In 1716 the Presbytery of Dublin addressed a letter to the Synod of Ulster, urging their brethren in the North to join with them in preaching the Gospel in Irish in those parts of the country where the native language was spoken. The Synod heartily fell in with the proposal. They appointed such ministers and probationers as were capable of preaching in Irish to labour in succession in various districts. These Irish-speaking

---

[1] *History*, III., p. 67.

preachers were fourteen in number. The Synod also agreed to erect a school for teaching to read Irish in the town of Dundalk, and to print a catechism and a short grammar in the Irish tongue.[1] It is a pity that this patriotic movement has not always been maintained. It was vigorously prosecuted for five or six years, when the discussions which arose in the Church diverted attention from it, and the interest of Irish Presbyterianism was once more confined to Ulster.

The following years were marked by further attempts on the part of the Government to do justice to their Irish Presbyterian subjects. In 1718 an addition of £800 a year was made to the Royal Bounty, and half of this sum was to be paid to the ministers of Dublin and the South.[2] In 1719 the Duke of Bolton became Lord Lieutenant. In his address to the Houses of Parliament on the 1st July he said, "His Majesty leaves to your consideration, and has commanded me to acquaint you, that as he hath the welfare of the Church by law established under his peculiar care, and resolves always to support and maintain it, so it would be very pleasing to him if any method could be found (not inconsistent with the security of it) to render the Protestant Dissenters more useful and capable of serving his Majesty, and supporting the Protestant interest, than they now are; they having, upon all occasions, given sufficient proofs of their being well affected to his Majesty's person and government, and to the succession of the Crown in his royal house. And

---

[1] Reid: *History*, III., pp. 84-5.
[2] Reid (*History*, III., p. 89) says the Southern ministers' were not previously endowed. But see *Report of Chancery Proceedings* (1850), pp. 12, 19. See also Mathews's *Account of Regium Donum*, and above, p. 28.

this I am ordered to lay before you as a thing greatly importing his Majesty's service and your own security."[1]

In the following November a Toleration Act for the Presbyterians received the royal assent. It was entitled "An Act for Exempting the Protestant Dissenters of this Kingdom from certain Penalties to which they are now subject." The Bill was nothing more than a bare toleration for Dissenting worship. It really conferred no new privilege, for as a matter of fact Presbyterians were already enjoying that toleration. It simply legalized that which was already being permitted. Yet this Bill, so scanty in its measure of justice, excited the most violent and determined opposition from Archbishop King and the High Church party. When it was read the third time in the House of Lords it was passed by only thirty-nine to twenty-six. The minority entered on the journals of the House a protest against the Bill.[2] Of this minority three were Archbishops, and six were Bishops. Six Bishops supported the Bill, five of these six being Englishmen. As has often happened since, the defeated Churchmen raised that cry of alarm which has usually followed the giving of civil and religious liberty to any one else than themselves. Archbishop King, of Dublin, writing to Wake, Archbishop of Canterbury, said, "In truth, I can't see how our Church can stand here, if God do not by a peculiar and unforeseen providence support it." The truth is, if only the Archbishop had understood it, that it is not the toleration, but the persecution of its fellow-Christians which will bring about the overthrow of any Church.

---

[1] *Journals of Irish House of Lords*, 1st July, 1719.
[2] *Journals of Irish House of Lords*, September, October, and November, 1719.

CHAPTER IX.

THE SUBSCRIPTION CONTROVERSY.

IN the year 1720 began in the Synod of Ulster one of the most memorable internal conflicts in the history of Irish Presbyterianism. This was the famous Subscription Controversy.[1] Several years before this a number of ministers and laymen in Belfast and its neighbourhood had formed themselves into an association called the *Belfast Society*. They met together for mutual edification and improvement. But their chief bond of union was the opinion which they held in common, "that the Church had no right to require candidates for the ministry to subscribe to a confession of faith prepared by any man or body of men, and that such a required subscription was a violation of the right of private judgment, and inconsistent with Christian liberty and true Protestantism."

The Belfast Society and its opinions were first brought before the notice of the Synod by the publication of a sermon which had been preached by Mr. Abernethy, one of its members. Abernethy, who afterwards succeeded Boyse in the ministry of Wood Street, Dublin, was then minister of Antrim. "There can be no doubt," says Dr. Witherow, "that John Abernethy,

---

[1] Reid: *History*, III., pp. 110-211; Witherow. *Presbyterian Memorials*, I., p. 142; II., pp. 8, 9, 341-349. *Report of Chancery Proceedings* (1850), p. 36.

of Antrim, is the true father of the Freethinking School of Irish Presbyterians." In this sermon, entitled " Religious Obedience founded on Personal Persuasion," Abernethy taught, among other things, that every man's persuasion of what was true and right was the sole rule of his faith and conduct, and that it was unjust and unscriptural to exclude from Christian fellowship any who walk according to their own persuasion on non-essential points—non-essential points being those on which "human reason and Christian sincerity permitted men to differ."

When the Synod met in Belfast in June, 1720, the outgoing Moderator was Mr. Craghead, of Dublin, who was then colleague to Mr. Iredell in the ministry of Capel Street. In view of the subject which was expected to occupy the attention of the Synod, Mr. Craghead advocated toleration for those who held the disputed doctrines, on the ground that the latter were of secondary importance. Mr. Craghead showed, in his sermon, that he himself was a sound believer in the Divinity of Christ and the other fundamental doctrines of the Christian faith, but the temporising policy which he supported was full of danger to the Church. This policy, however, the Synod of 1720 very unwisely adopted. By the *Pacific Act* which the Synod adopted the door was left open for the introduction of erroneous doctrine. This Act, while declaring the Synod's adherence to the Westminster Confession of Faith, provided also a way of escape for any person called upon to subscribe it who should scruple any phrase or phrases in it, by permitting him to use his own expressions, subject to the Presbytery's approval. The results showed how short-sighted this policy was, for the controversy, instead of being ended, continued to disturb the peace of the Church for six years more, and to scatter more widely the seeds of those errors which afterwards wrought such havoc upon the Presbyterianism of Ireland.

Each of these six years which followed the Pacific Act witnessed fresh attempts on the part of those who were opposed to subscription to promulgate their views, and fresh advances in the path of erroneous doctrine. Each year also the Synod took a more decided stand against error, but it was a very hesitating position at the best.

The Synod of 1721, after Mr. Haliday had meantime been installed as minister of the Belfast congregation, though he refused to sign the Confession of Faith, passed a resolution simply permitting all the members of Synod who were willing to do so to subscribe the Westminster Confession. In accordance with this resolution, the vast majority of the ministers present signed the Confession. At this stage originated the two names *Subscribers* and *Non-subscribers*.

At this time also three of the Dublin ministers took a prominent part in supporting the Non-subscribers. Mr. Boyse, of Wood Street, had already proposed a resolution which was adopted by the Synod, declaring that the Synod did not intend any reflection on the non-subscribing brethren as if they were unsound in the faith, and also recommending ministers and people to exercise mutual tolerance in this matter. In the beginning of 1722 a pamphlet, written by Mr. Abernethy, was published, with this title: "Seasonable Advice to the Protestant Dissenters in the North of Ireland; being a Defence of the late General Synod's Charitable Declarations. With a recommendatory Preface by the Rev. Nath. Weld, J. Boyse, and R. Choppin."

THE SUBSCRIPTION CONTROVERSY. 57

Mr. Weld was minister of New Row, Dublin, and Messrs. 'Boyse and Choppin were both ministers of Wood Street. The pamphlet defended the attitude of the Non-Subscribers and the Synod's action in tolerating their continuance within the Church.

This pamphlet and other publications showed the prevalence of non-subscribing principles. The Synod was consequently obliged to take the matter up again this year, when five resolutions were adopted. The first three declared that it was not sufficient evidence of a person's soundness in the faith if he confessed his belief in Scripture words only; that the Synod was resolved to adhere to the Westminster Confession, and that it would maintain the Presbyterian government and discipline as hitherto exercised. But the two remaining resolutions left the door still open for the promulgation of error. In these the Synod declared its desire to exercise Christian forbearance towards the Non-Subscribers so long as they governed themselves according to the laws of the Synod, and did not disturb the peace of the Church, and it exhorted the people who were under the ministry of the Non-Subscribers to continue, as far as their consciences allowed them, to adhere to their pastors.

Further charges against non-subscribing ministers, of teaching erroneous doctrine, led to further action in the Synod of 1723. This year the resolutions which were passed in the Synod declared, among other things, "that the condemning all creeds and confessions, and declarations of faith in human words, as tests of orthodoxy, opens a door to let in errors and heresies into the Church," and also that though it was possible for candidates to declare their faith in words of their own, to the satisfaction of their ordainers, yet it was far too great a trust, and extremely dangerous to the Church, to commit to a few ordaining ministers the sole power of judging what must be satisfactory to the entire body. The Synod had already begun to see how wide a door had been left open by the Pacific Act of 1720, and how great was the danger to which it led.

The main business of the Synod of 1724 was the trial of Mr. Nevin, of Downpatrick, a leading non-subscribing minister, on the charge, amongst others, of denying the Divinity of Christ. After a protracted hearing of the case, and debate upon it, the Synod decided to require of Mr. Nevin an immediate declaration of his belief in the supreme Deity of Christ. Mr. Nevin refused to comply, on the ground that he objected to subscription, but added that his refusal did not proceed from any disbelief of the doctrine in question. Upon this the Synod resolved that, as Mr. Nevin had refused to make the declaration required of him, it would hold no further ministerial communion with him. Here again the Synod was at once hasty and halting. It excluded Mr. Nevin from its fellowship, although the sole offence proved against him was that he was a Non-Subscriber, whilst at the same time it retained the other Non-Subscribers in its communion. It was halting and inconsistent in that it cut off Mr. Nevin from communion with the Synod, but continued him in his congregation and in the ministerial office.

The Synod of 1725 took a further step in opposition to the Non-Subscribers. By one resolution it granted liberty to all persons who were under non-subscribing ministers to withdraw from their ministry if they chose. By another it declared that the Pacific Act did not warrant the questioning of any *doctrines* contained in the Westminster Confession, but only of the *phrases* in which they were expressed. And by a third it constituted a new Presbytery of Templepatrick, and placed in the Presbytery of Antrim all the non-subscribing ministers of the North. This last resolution was wise and effective. By concentrating the Non-Subscribers into one Presbytery it greatly narrowed the sphere of their influence, and diminished the influence itself.

Before and after this Synod of 1725 the non-subscribing ministers of Dublin took part in two proceedings, neither of which was much to their credit. Before the Synod met, a deputation of them, headed by Mr. Boyse, waited on the Lord Lieutenant, and gave him such a representation of the conduct of the Synod that they obtained from him a declaration that the divisions among the Northern Presbyterians were very displeasing to his Majesty, and a recommendation that such courses should be dropped. It was the last method to which friends of liberty of thought should have resorted, in order to gain their ends.

At the meeting of Synod a Mr. Colville had been suspended from preaching for three months. His offence was that when he was under call to the congregation of Dromore, co. Down, and when both the Presbytery and Sub-Synod of Armagh had declined to ordain him till he should subscribe the Confession of Faith, he had sought and obtained ordination from some English Dissenting ministers in London. Very properly the Synod suspended him, though only for a brief period, for this breach of ecclesiastical order. But he continued to preach despite the sentence of the Synod, and applied to the non-subscribing Presbytery of Dublin, complaining of the injustice which had been done him, and praying them to instal him as minister of the congregation of Dromore. After some communications between the Dublin Presbytery and the Presbytery and Sub-Synod of Armagh, in which the latter courts declined to act except in accordance with the law of the Synod, a deputation from the Dublin Presbytery installed Mr. Colville at Dromore. The deputation consisted of Messrs. Choppin, of Dublin, McJachy, of Athy, and Wood, of Summerhill. The ministers of Dublin should have disdained to act in such a way. Such conduct was not only opposed to all true Presbyterianism, but would overthrow the order and discipline of any Church. Mr. Iredell, of Capel Street, testifies that some of the best of the non-subscribing ministers of the city were opposed to the Presbytery's action in this case, but were outvoted by some brethren from the country. Mr. Iredell himself withdrew from the meetings of the Dublin Presbytery in consequence.

In 1726 the controversy in the Synod on the question of Subscription at last came to an end. The Synod at last saw the necessity of excluding the Non-Subscribers from ecclesiastical fellowship. The resolution which was adopted declared that by the principles which the Non-Subscribers persisted in maintaining "they put it out of our power to maintain ministerial communion with them in Church judicatories as formerly, consistently with the faithful discharge of our ministerial office and the peace of our own consciences." Here, again, the Synod did not act with the decision and thoroughness which the nature of the case demanded. If these ministers, by reason of the opinions which they held, were unfitted to continue members of the Ecclesiastical Courts, they should also have been regarded as unfitted to minister to the congregations of the Synod. This, however, was not done. They still continued to hold the office of Presbyterian ministers, and to minister to Presbyterian congregations. Nevertheless it was an advantage to the Church that their opinions were no longer permitted to guide the counsels, and to influence the decisions, of the Church courts. Though the Non-Subscribers were mostly men of great ability, the Synod did not lose much in numbers by their exclusion. Only twelve ministers were actually excluded from the communion of the Synod by the decision of 1726. These were all Northern ministers. The non-subscribing ministers of Dublin had hitherto been connected with the Synod of Ulster only as corresponding members. The subscribing ministers of Dublin had up to this time been connected with Northern Presbyteries of the Synod, while also acting as members of the Dublin Presbytery or Association. Now, however, the Synod formed a Presbytery of Dublin directly under its own control, and the non-subscribing ministers of Dublin and the South formed themselves into the Southern Presbytery of Dublin.

CHAPTER X.

DUBLIN PRESBYTERIANS AND IRISH GRIEVANCES.

THE continuance of the disabilities under which the Presbyterians laboured on account of their religion had already led to extensive emigration from Ulster. It was no wonder that men of independent spirit should seek in that land of freedom across the Atlantic those civil and religious liberties which were denied to them at home. At home Episcopalian landlords were very glad to receive Presbyterian rents, but they did all in their power to discourage the Presbyterian religion. They inserted clauses in their leases forbidding the erection of Presbyterian churches upon their property.[1] "The Sacramental Test," says Reid, "still excluded Presbyterians from all places of trust under the Crown. Though constituting, in several counties of Ulster, more than two-thirds of the Protestant population, they could not have a single gentleman of their Church in the office of magistrate or sheriff; and, in some cases, Presbyterian teachers could with difficulty keep open their schools. And, lastly, they were still subject to frequent prosecutions and expensive litigation in the Ecclesiastical Courts for marriages celebrated by their own clergy."[2] As their

---

[1] Commission and Private Instructions given to Rev. Francis Iredell, quoted by Witherow, *Presbyterian Memorials*, I., pp. 151-53.

[2] Reid: *History*, III., p. 221.

leases expired, their rents were enormously increased, and in addition to this they had to bear the burden of constantly increasing tithes. The result was twofold. They emigrated in large numbers to America, and they bore with them memories by no means pleasant of English rule, and a spirit far from friendly to it. Dr. Hodge, in his History of the Presbyterian Church in the United States, tells us that nearly 6,000 Irish are reported as having come to America in 1729, and before the middle of the century nearly 12,000 arrived annually for several years.[1] He adds that the Irish emigrants of that time were *almost all Presbyterians*, and that the flow of the Catholic Irish did not take place until a much later period. "It was the sons and the grandsons of these Presbyterian emigrants who gathered to the standard of General Washington in 1775, and struck the hardest blows for American Independence" (Croskery: *Irish Presbyterianism*). On the one hand, Irish Presbyterians may be said to have suffered more injustice than any others at the hands of the British Government, considering how loyal they had been and how faithfully they had often fought for their English sovereign. If they ever became rebels, it was in defence of their religion and their liberties. On the other hand, Irish Roman Catholics may be said to have drunk deepest of the cup of injustice and oppression, when we consider that they have formed for centuries the vast majority of the inhabitants of their native land.

The Lords Justices, who were then at the head of the executive Government in Ireland, consulted Mr. Iredell and Mr. Craghead, two of the Dublin ministers,

---

[1] See also Webster's *History of the Presbyterian Church in America.*

with a view to ascertaining the cause of this continued emigration. The Dublin ministers, having communicated with all the Northern Presbyteries, drew up a memorial to the Lords Justices, in which they enumerated, as causes of the emigration, the various grievances under which the Presbyterians laboured. The principal of these grievances which they mentioned were the extraordinary increase in their tithes, and the oppressions of the Ecclesiastical Courts in their recovery. The Archbishop of Dublin, writing in opposition to the memorial, laid all the blame of the Presbyterian discontent at the door of the landlords, whom he charged with imposing excessive rents.[1] An Archbishop might attack the landlords with impunity, but Presbyterian ministers, even in the nineteenth century, have been accused of disloyalty and lawlessness for seeking to obtain common justice for their people! The memorial of the Presbyterian ministers, however, received a striking confirmation from a report of a Committee of the Irish House of Commons in 1736. This report stated, "That a strong inclination has prevailed for some time among the Protestants of this kingdom to withdraw themselves and their effects to America. And that this temper of mind is greatly increased by the new and burdensome demand made by the clergy."

It is but justice to say that all the Episcopal dignitaries were not so hostile to the Presbyterians as the Archbishop of Dublin. When Mr. Craghead, of Dublin, was commissioned by his brother ministers to proceed to London in support of their memorial, and at the same time to request payment of some arrears of Royal Bounty, he bore with him a letter of introduction to

---

[1] Reid: *History*, III., p. 227.

the Prime Minister, Sir Robert Walpole, from the Primate, Archbishop Boulter. In this letter the Primate strongly supported the application of the ministers for the arrears of Bounty, and, among other things, said of the Presbyterian ministers, "It is but doing them justice to affirm that they are very well affected to his Majesty and the royal family."

Mr. Craghead succeeded in his mission so far as the payment of the Royal Bounty was concerned. But neither at that time nor subsequently, when he went over again on a similar mission, did he succeed in obtaining the redress of the grievances which pressed upon the Presbyterian people, or the repeal of the Sacramental Test. Mr. Abernethy, of Wood Street (afterwards Strand Street), another of the Dublin ministers, endeavoured by his pen to do what Mr. Craghead had already attempted to do by personal appeals. He published a pamphlet entitled "The Nature and Consequences of the Sacramental Test Considered, with Reasons humbly offered for the Repeal of it." But the efforts of the Presbyterians of Ireland, so ably headed by the ministers of Dublin, to obtain toleration and redress of their grievances, were once more doomed to failure. The only mitigation of the oppression under which they suffered was a sort of indemnity Bill passed in the year 1638, entitled "An Act for giving further Ease to Protestant Dissenters with respect to Matrimonial Contracts." This Act did not directly legalize Presbyterian marriages, but it exempted from all prosecutions the ministers who celebrated them, if they had qualified under the Toleration Act. Those who celebrated such marriages might thus escape punishment, but Presbyterian marriages were still illegal and their offspring illegitimate.

CHAPTER XI.

THE SECEDERS.

IN 1736 commenced a movement which was destined to change the current of Irish Presbyterianism and largely to counteract and check the spread of Moderatism. Three years previously State interference with the Church of Scotland had produced a secession similar to that which, more than a hundred years later, took place at the Disruption, and led to the formation of the Free Church. The secession of 1733, like that of 1843, was led by men of eminent piety and earnestness, chief among whom were the two Erskines, Ralph and Ebenezer. The United Presbyterian Church of Scotland at the present day is the modern representative of the secession.

A division in the Presbyterian Church of Lisburn led a section of the congregation to appeal to the Scotch Seceders to send them a minister. This request was not then complied with, but five years afterwards, in 1741, the first Seceding preacher visited Ireland in response to repeated invitations from the people of Lylehill, county Antrim. A Secession minister was formally ordained there in 1746. From this time forward the Seceders made rapid progress in Ireland. We need not delay here to narrate the divisions which arose amongst their number on the question of the oath for burgesses, and which divided them into the almost forgotten parties of Burghers and Antiburghers. The time came when Burghers and Antiburghers united and formed the Secession Synod of Ireland. And finally in 1840, after being separated for a whole century, the Synod of Ulster and the Seceders once more united, blending into one harmonious and energetic Church. It has been alleged that Presbyterian principles are disintegrating. The history of Irish Presbyterianism shows that if Presbyterians know how to divide they know also how to unite.

To the influence of the Seceders Irish Presbyterianism owes much. When "New Light" doctrines were sapping its vitality the Secession preachers infused into it a new life, a spiritual fervour, and a missionary spirit, the power of which remains to this day.

Let it not be imagined, however, that "New Light" doctrines were confined to the Presbyterians of Ireland. Bad as the state of the Synod of Ulster was at this time, the state of the Established Church was worse. One of the most eminent Arians of the eighteenth century was Dr. Clayton, Bishop successively of Killala, Cork and Ross, and Clogher.[1] Paradoxical though it may seem, it was the subsequent expulsion of the Arians from the Synod of Ulster which led many people to identify Arianism exclusively with Presbyterianism. The Arians retained the name of Presbyterians after they had given up everything of Presbyterianism except the form. But the Arians who remained in the Episcopal Church were allowed to disseminate their views unmolested.

---

[1] Reid: *History*, III., pp. 303-4.

CHAPTER XII.

GENEROUS LAYMEN AND REPRIMANDED MINISTERS.

THE Presbyterians of Dublin took the lead in an important philanthropic movement which began in 1750. This was the fund for the widows and families of ministers generally known as the Widows' Fund. To Mr. William Bruce, a Dublin bookseller, and an elder in Wood Street congregation, belongs the credit of originating this important fund. He proposed its adoption to the Synod of Ulster, at its annual meeting in Dungannon, and received the thanks of the Synod for his care and zeal in projecting and carrying on the scheme. Mr. Bruce had no family. His brother, Rev. Patrick Bruce, minister of Killyleagh, Co. Down, was great-grandfather of Sir Hervey Bruce, the present owner of Downhill, Co. Derry. Like many another Irish family whose ancestors were Presbyterians, Sir Hervey Bruce and his family are members of the Episcopal Church.

The first trustees of the Widows' Fund were all Dublin Presbyterians. One of them was Mr. Alexander Stewart, originally of Ballylawn, Co. Donegal, and afterwards proprietor of the estates of Comber and Newtownards, Co. Down. Mr. Stewart's son Robert became Marquis of Londonderry, and his grandson was the celebrated Lord Castlereagh. The other trustees were Mr. William Lennox, an elder of Wood Street congregation; Alderman James Dunn, an elder of Cook Street congregation; Dr. Martin, an elder of Capel Street congregation; Dr. George Machonchy, and the Rev. Robert McMaster, one of the ministers of Usher's Quay congregation. Not only were Dublin Presbyterians the first promoters of the Widows' Fund, but by contributions and legacies they continued to be among its most generous supporters. About this same time the Presbyterians of Ireland contributed upwards of £400 for the relief of poor and distressed Presbyterian ministers in America, and their widows and children. Colonel Dunne, of Dublin, was the agent through whom this generous contribution was transmitted.[1]

The attendance of the Dublin ministers at the meetings of the Synod of Ulster seems to have been somewhat irregular at this time. In 1758, when the Synod met at Lurgan, the only member of the Dublin Presbytery present was the Rev. Thomas Vance, of Usher's Quay. The next year only one, the Rev. William Wight, was present. In 1760 the Rev. Charles McCollum, of Capel Street, was the only Dublin minister present, but as he was Moderator of Synod that year, he could hardly have been absent. Passing on to 1782, we find that in that year the Rev. Benjamin McDowell, of Capel Street, was the sole representative of Dublin. In 1783 and 1784 no Dublin minister was present. Once more, in 1787, Mr. McDowell was the only Dublin minister at the Synod. In 1789 Dr. McDowell was accompanied by the Rev. Wm. Wilson, of Usher's Quay. In 1790 there was no representative and no report from the Dublin Presbytery. In 1792 Dr.

---

[1] Reid: *History*, III., pp. 324-25.

McDowell was not only accompanied by the Rev. James Horner, his newly ordained colleague in Capel Street, but actually by a representative elder also, Mr. William Gilbert, from the same congregation. In 1794 Mr. Horner was present, accompanied by an elder, Mr. John Stitt. In the successive years 1796, 1797, and 1798 no member of the Dublin Presbytery was present. This brought matters to a crisis. In 1798 the following resolution was adopted by the Synod :—

"This Synod, observing that the Presbyteries of Belfast, Ballymena, and Dublin have made no returns, and that no member from any of these Presbyteries appears at this time, express their pointed disapprobation of these Presbyteries, and enjoin that they shall account for their shameful neglect at next meeting of Synod."

After this sharp reprimand the Dublin ministers seem to have attended more regularly. In 1802, when the Synod met in Cookstown, there were four Dublin ministers present, Rev. Dr. McDowell and Rev. James Horner, of Capel Street, and Revs. Hugh Moore and Wm. Wilson, of Usher's Quay.[1]

---

[1] MS. *Minutes of Synod of Ulster*.

CHAPTER XIII.

PRESBYTERIANS AND THE VOLUNTEERS.

MATTERS much more serious than the attendance or non-attendance of one or two ministers at meetings of Synod occupied the attention of Irish Presbyterians during the closing years of the eighteenth century. The Presbyterians of Ireland are a loyal people. They have proved their loyalty in many times of disaffection. They have borne with patience social, civil, and religious disabilities of the most oppressive kind. But there is a time when even the most patient become weary of enduring wrongs. Such a time in Irish Presbyterian history was the last quarter of the eighteenth century. The attitude of the Presbyterians of Ulster during that period was unquestionably one of fearless, manly, determined revolt. I do not refer to the Rebellion of 1798, in which, after all, comparatively few Presbyterians were implicated. I refer to the Volunteer movement, in which the Presbyterians of Ulster mustered in their thousands, and, with arms in their hands, demanded and obtained the redress of grievances which had well-nigh crushed their spirit and driven thousands of emigrants to seek a home beyond the seas.

These grievances were mainly an oppressive landlordism and the tyranny of the dominant Church. In the year 1775 numerous petitions were presented to the Irish House of Commons, praying for the redress of grievances. The Commons' Journals of that year report that on October 25th petitions from Protestant Dissenters, inhabitants of the parish and congregation of Downpatrick, of the borough of Antrim, and of the town and neighbourhood of Dungannon, were severally presented to the House and read, setting forth—

"That the Petitioners are greatly alarmed by a Clause of an Act of last Session of Parliament, intitled 'An Act to Explain and Amend former Acts for better Keeping of Churches in Repair,' by which Clause the Petitioners are deprived of their legal constitutional right of voting in Church Vestries, and praying that the said Clause may be repealed or amended."

The petitions were ordered to lie on the table for the perusal of members. Whether the said members perused them or not, it is not recorded. But at any rate they did not profit by them. On subsequent days similar petitions were presented from Coleraine and Killowen; from the town and parish of Belfast; from inhabitants of the city of Londonderry, *members of the Established Church;* from Ardstraw and Newtownstewart; from Coagh; from Protestant Dissenters of the city of Londonderry, of the Barony of Dungannon and county of Tyrone, of the town and county of Carrickfergus, of the congregation of Cookstown, of the town and neighbourhood of Ballymure, of the united parishes of Larne and Raloo, Carn-Castle and Killwaughter, Glenarm and Ballyeaston, of the town and parish of Comber, Co. Down, of the parish of Carnmoney; from Protestant inhabitants of the parishes of Donagore, Killbride, and Nelteen; from inhabitants of the parish of Carnmoney, *members of the Church of Ireland as by law established;* from Protestant Dissenters of Ballyclare, Belfast, neighbourhood of Strabane, Antrim, Lisburn, Dundonald, Ballymena and neighbourhood, Newry, Armagh, Rathfriland, Benburb, Dromore, Bangor, Killyleagh, Seapatrick, Tullylish, Donochcloney, Clare, Dromballyroney, Drumgoolan, Dunmurray, Omagh, and Drumaragh. Thus from all parts of Ulster, from city and from hamlet, the petitions of the oppressed people kept flowing in. Even the members of the Established Church in some places joined their Presbyterian neighbours in protesting against this fresh disability that had been imposed upon them. But the petitions seem to have been as useless as the paper they were written on. Other methods must be tried.

In 1778 the first Volunteer company was formed at Belfast, and in a few months every district of Ulster witnessed the spectacle of armed men assembling for drill, and declaring their determination to redress the wrongs of their country. The failure of an attempt to repeal the Test Act in the House of Commons in the autumn of the same year intensified the discontent. Presbyterian Ulster was at last becoming thoroughly aroused. Its people were no longer in a temper to be trifled with. When Parliament reassembled in October, 1779, the armed Volunteers had increased to the number of 42,000 men. Parliament was at last brought to its senses. A Bill for the Relief of Dissenters was brought in by Sir Edward Newenham, member for County Dublin, and became law in a few months.[1]

Dr. Killen's words on this subject[2] are so emphatic and so memorable that I cannot forbear quoting them. He says, " Government, however, received little credit for a measure which had been so long denied, and

---

[1] *Liber Munerum*, 19 & 20 Geo. III. (1779-80), Chap. VI.
[2] Reid: *History*, III., p. 345.

which was now so ungraciously conceded; *and the Presbyterians felt that they were indebted for this piece of tardy justice, not so much to the enlightened wisdom of fraternal rulers as to the brilliant display of their own armed advocates.*" It was indeed a memorable day when the Volunteers assembled at Dungannon in 1782, and when, to quote again from Dr. Killen, "the Presbyterians of the North boldly asserted the independence of the Irish legislature, and proclaimed their joy at the relaxation of the penal laws affecting their Roman Catholic fellow-subjects." A hundred thousand Volunteers, well armed and well trained, were ready if necessary to give effect to the demand for constitutional freedom. The Volunteers succeeded where petitions had failed, and in 1782 the legislative independence of Ireland was formally proclaimed by the British Government. How quietly, yet how determinedly, this great revolution had been accomplished! There were no outrages, no assassinations. But there was an organization of all classes of Irishmen, rich and poor, Presbyterian and Episcopalian, which it was vain for any Government to attempt to crush, and whose just demands it was wise policy to concede.

CHAPTER XIV.

CONCILIATION AND CONCESSION.

THE Presbyterians had now shown that they were no longer to be trampled on. It is wonderful how soon a little determination on the part of the oppressed changes the tone and bearing of the oppressor. Conciliation now for a while took the place of coercion.

In 1782 a Marriage Act was passed, declaring the validity of all marriages celebrated among Protestant Dissenters by ministers of their own denomination:[1] It had a narrow escape in the Irish House of Lords, being carried by merely twenty-five against twenty-three. As usual, the prelates of the Episcopal Church were foremost in opposing any measures of toleration for their Presbyterian neighbours. A protest against the measure was entered on the Journals of the House of Lords, signed by three archbishops, ten bishops, and nine temporal peers.

In 1784 the Regium Donum, or Royal Bounty to ministers of the Synod of Ulster, was increased by £1,000. The Rev. Dr Campbell, of Armagh, and the Rev. Dr. McDowell, of Dublin, represented the Synod in making application to the Government for an increase of this grant. At the same time a grant was made to the Secession Synod of £500 per annum.

---

[1] *Liber Munerum*, 21 & 22 Geo. III. (1781-82), Chap. XXV.

In 1792 a further grant, of £5,000 per annum, was granted for the use of the Presbyterian ministers of Ireland. This was divided among the Synod of Ulster, the Seceders, and the Southern Association. For almost a century no increase had been made in the amount of State aid granted to the Irish Presbyterian Church. The amount of Regium Donum which its ministers received was mainly due to the personal gratitude of William III. for the help he had received from the Presbyterians. Though it was a generous gift and gratefully received, the increase in the number of ministers had of course diminished the amount available for each. In 1793 each minister was only receiving £9. Now, by the action of the Irish Parliament and the cordial sympathy of the Earl of Charlemont and Henry Grattan,[1] the State aid was more than tripled. The amount added to the income of each Presbyterian minister was £20 3s. 2d. Presbyterian ministers and people of to-day who make light of Grattan's Parliament should remember that it was the first to adequately recognize their services to the State. In spite of prelatic opposition, the Irish Parliament legalized Presbyterian marriages. In spite of similar opposition, the Irish Parliament added a very substantial endowment to the income of Presbyterian ministers.

In 1787 Dr. Campbell, above referred to, published a book entitled "A Vindication of the Principles and Character of the Presbyterians of Ireland." This book was a reply to Dr. Woodward, Bishop of Cloyne, who had made a fierce and unwarranted attack on the

---

[1] Reid: *History* III., p. 353. It was asserted by Grattan, in the Irish Parliament, that "the Presbyterian religion is the father of the free constitution of England."—Armstrong's *History of Dublin Churches*.

Presbyterians. In the edition of 1788 is added as an Appendix, that

"At a full meeting of the Southern Presbytery of Dublin, held on the 17th March, 1787, it was unanimously resolved to transmit a letter to Dr. Campbell approving of his book."

The letter, which is also given, thanks him for his learned, judicious, and able vindication of the Presbyterians, and is signed by the Moderator, William Dunn, D.D., minister of Cook Street, the clerk, William Bruce, and his colleague, John Moody, ministers of Strand Street,[1] Philip Taylor, of Eustace Street, and Patrick Vance, of Summerhill. These were the non-subscribing ministers of Dublin and its neighbourhood at that time.

The clouds were now rapidly gathering which ultimately broke in the Rebellion of 1798. The Earl of Fitzwilliam had been appointed Viceroy of Ireland in January, 1795, and during his brief Viceroyalty showed himself well disposed to redress wrongs, and to concede their just rights to the two oppressed classes of the community, the Presbyterians and the Roman Catholics. Fitzwilliam's kindly attitude led the people to expect that a new era of Irish government was about to dawn. A college for the education of the Roman Catholic priesthood was erected and endowed at Maynooth, and the Presbyterians were encouraged to expect that a Presbyterian college would be endowed in Ulster.

But the sudden recall of Lord Fitzwilliam, after a three months' Viceroyalty, dashed the bright hopes both of Roman Catholics and Presbyterians to the ground. It was the beginning of that exasperated

---

[1] The congregation of Cook Street joined Strand Street about this time.

feeling which ultimately caused the Rebellion. Not only in Dublin and the South, but in the Presbyterian North, the departure of the Viceroy called forth universal regret. A town meeting of the inhabitants of Belfast was held on the 4th March, when it was unanimously resolved to give an address to Lord Fitzwilliam on his departure. The 28th of March—the day of Fitzwilliam's departure from Ireland—was observed as a day of *national mourning* by the inhabitants of Belfast. "There was not," says the local historian,[1] "a shop or counting-house open during the whole day—all was one scene of sullen indignation."

---

[1] *Historical Collections relative to the Town of Belfast*, Belfast, 1815.

CHAPTER XV.

PRESBYTERIANS AND THE REBELLION OF '98.

THE sad story of 1798 has been so often recited that it is not necessary to repeat it here in detail. The mutual recrimination in which the different political and religious parties indulge regarding it is hardly warranted by facts. There were outrages, horrible and inhuman, committed by the rebels. There were outrages committed by the loyalist troops. So far as the rebellion itself was concerned, Episcopalians, Presbyterians, and Roman Catholics were all implicated in it. The ministers of the Synod of Ulster, as a rule, were on the loyalist side, though one of their number was executed, some were imprisoned, some banished, and others had to leave the country. The Synod passed resolutions condemning seditious practices, and voted £500 for the defence of the kingdom against the threatened French invasion. But in large Presbyterian districts in Ulster the sympathies of the people were entirely with the rebels. When, in the two years preceding the Rebellion, the leaders of the United Irishmen were arrested in various parts of counties Antrim and Down, in all parts of the country the people assembled to cut down the harvest for the imprisoned patriots.[1] The bitter memories of "the burning of Ballymoney,"

---

[1] *Historical Collections relative to the Town of Belfast.*

and other wanton acts of the loyalist troops, are not yet extinct in the farmhouses of county Antrim and county Derry.

The Rev. Sinclair Kelburn, of Rosemary Street Church, Belfast, one of the Presbyterian ministers imprisoned, was a man equally distinguished for his piety and scholarship. He was the author of at least seven published sermons which are still extant. One of these is entitled "The Morality of the Sabbath Defended;" another is an ordination sermon preached at Newtownards on *The Duty of Preaching the Gospel;* and there are *Five Sermons on the Divinity of the Lord Jesus Christ*, which show that he was a thoroughly orthodox and evangelical minister. He was son of the Rev. Ebenezer Kelburn, who was for about thirty years minister of Plunket Street congregation, Dublin. From long confinement in Kilmainham Gaol, Mr. Kelburn lost the use of his limbs, and died soon after his liberation.[1]

Another distinguished Presbyterian minister who took a leading part in the organization of the United Irishmen was the Rev. William Steele Dickson, D.D., of Portaferry. Dr. Dickson was arrested immediately before the rebellion broke out, and was kept for three years a State prisoner at Fort George, in Scotland. Professor Witherow says, "Certainly nothing was ever established against Dr. Dickson which would convict him now in any court of justice, and therefore we must think that, like so many others at that time, his own folly left him at the mercy of unscrupulous and unprincipled men, who, for their advantage, seized the

---

[1] Quotation from *Gentleman's Magazine*, written on back page of *Sermons* by Sinclaire Kelburn, A.B. Witherow: *Presbyterian Memorials*, II., p. 243-46.

opportunity to ruin a clever man whom they hated and feared, and whose guilt was strongly suspected without their being able to establish it by legal proof." Dr. Dickson, ex-prisoner though he was, was, after his release, invited by the congregation of the 2nd Keady to become their minister, but the Government ungenerously withheld his Regium Donum, and he was at length obliged to resign the ministry and go to Belfast, where he died in poverty in 1824.[1]

Another of the imprisoned ministers was the Rev. Samuel Barber, of Rathfriland, who had been Moderator of Synod in 1790, and whose reply to Dr. Woodward showed him to be a powerful and thoughtful controversialist.

The most cruelly treated of all the Presbyterian ministers who were accused of seditious practices at this time was the Rev. James Porter, of Greyabbey. Mr. Porter was a man of great intellectual gifts. Several of his writings were published. The most famous of these is the celebrated *Billy Bluff and Squire Firebrand*. In this amusing and clever pamphlet Mr. Porter satirizes the lord of the soil, Lord Londonderry, his agent, the Rev. John Cleland, whom he justly designated *Squire Firebrand*, and a low fellow (called by him *Billy Bluff*) who acted as a spy for Cleland, and carried him all the news of the neighbourhood. It was never proved that Mr. Porter was in arms against the Government. He was not a United Irishman. But the persons who had the control of local affairs were writhing under his faithful and clever satire, and the outbreak of the Rebellion was a good time to have their revenge. To hang a Presbyterian minister would help to overawe

---

[1] Witherow: *Presbyterian Memorials*, II., pp. 226-42.

the Presbyterian people. Accordingly, on the statement of a low informer, who swore that Mr. Porter was present when a mail was ransacked in search of some important despatches, Mr. Porter was arrested, and on this uncorroborated charge, which he utterly denied, found guilty by a court-martial and sentenced to be hung. The circumstances of his death were the very refinement of cruelty. A scaffold was erected half-way between his manse and his church, and there, in the presence of his distracted wife, the kindly and cultured Presbyterian minister died a felon's death. Professor Witherow says, "His true epitaph would have been, *Murdered by martial law for the crime of writing 'Billy Bluff.'*"[1]

The peaceful vales of county Derry were stained by actions hardly less cruel. At Maghera, for example, the Rev. John Glendy, the accomplished and eloquent Presbyterian minister, was known to sympathise with the United Irishmen. When the rebellion broke out the people of the neighbourhood were almost all on the side of the rebels. When the soldiers and yeomanry entered Maghera they took up their quarters in the Presbyterian Church, and burnt everything in it except the Bible. Professor Witherow tells us that "they burned the dwelling-houses of such of the country people as were suspected to be ringleaders, and subjected the whole neighbourhood to a severe and unnecessary chastisement. Mr. Glendy was one of those whose houses were burned, and he himself with some difficulty escaped to the United States." They hanged two persons, one of them a respectable farmer, and the

---

[1] Witherow: *Presbyterian Memorials*, II., pp. 293-302. Mr. Porter was grandfather of the celebrated Rev. Dr. Goudy, of Strabane.

other an unoffending resident in the town, who was guilty of nothing except making an unseasonable jest.

But Mr. Glendy, driven from his native land by the tyranny which he found it necessary to resist, was honoured in his new home beyond the seas. He was chosen chaplain to the House of Representatives, and amongst his personal friends were the leading American statesmen of the time—Jefferson, Monro, Madison, and John Quincy Adams. He received the degree of D.D. from the University of Maryland, and died at Philadelphia in 1832.[1]

Such were some of the incidents of the Rebellion so far as the Presbyterians were concerned. Such were some of the men whom Episcopal and landlord tyranny turned into rebels. They were no mere youthful enthusiasts. They were men of mature experience. They were men of piety and learning. Misguided they may have been, but weary years of oppression for conscience' sake were enough to drive wise men mad. They were fighting for their faith and for their freedom, for their homes and for their people. As truly as the Puritans of England who took up arms against their king, as truly as the Covenanters of Scotland who took up arms against prelatic tyranny, these Irish Presbyterian "rebels" deserve the name and the honour of Christian patriots.

---

[1] Witherow: *Presbyterian Memorials*, II., pp. 313-16.

CHAPTER XVI.

THE LEGISLATIVE UNION.

THE year 1799 was mainly occupied with those ministerial negotiations and intrigues which led to the Union between England and Ireland. The more fully one studies this subject the stronger grows the conviction that it was a forced union. Here lies, to a large extent, the secret of the perpetual Irish discontent since that time.

The Irish people, taking them as a whole, certainly did not wish for the Union. The Presbyterian people were on this point agreed with the great majority of their Roman Catholic and Episcopalian fellow-countrymen. How, then, was the Union brought about?

In the first debate on the Union in the Irish House of Commons, January, 1799, thirty members spoke for it, and forty-five against. Among the most brilliant opponents of the Union was William Conyngham Plunket, son of the Presbyterian minister of Strand Street, Dublin, and grandfather of the present Protestant Archbishop of Dublin. Mr. Plunket stated that during the past six weeks a system of corruption had been carried on within the walls of the Castle which would disgrace the annals of the worst period in the history of either country.

Plunket's words are memorable. "In the most

express manner," he added, "I deny the competency of Parliament to do this act [of Union]. I warn you, do not lay your hands on the Constitution. I tell you that if, circumstanced as you are, you pass this Act, it will be a mere nullity, and no man in Ireland will be bound to obey it. . . . You are appointed to exercise the functions of legislators, and not to transfer them. Yourselves you may extinguish, but Parliament you cannot extinguish. It is enthroned in the heart of the people; it is enshrined in the sanctuary of the constitution; it is as immortal as the island which protects it." On this occasion the Union was defeated by one hundred and eleven votes against one hundred and five.

Twenty-seven out of the thirty-two Irish counties petitioned against the Union The petition from the Presbyterian county of Down was signed by upwards of 17,000 respectable, independent men, and all the others in a similar proportion. "The persons who were in favour of the Union, possessing great influence in the country, obtained a few counter petitions; yet though the petition from county Down was signed by 17,000, the counter-petition was signed by only 415. 707,000 persons signed petitions against the measure; the total number of those who declared themselves in favour of it did not exceed 3,000, and many of these only prayed that it might be discussed."[1] The opinion of a whole nation has been seldom so decisively and unmistakably expressed.

But the Rebellion had been crushed, and the constitutional expression of a nation's will now counted for little. The Volunteers were no longer there. For

---

[1] Gilbert: *History of the City of Dublin*, II., p. 151.

the bayonets of the Volunteers there was now substituted the bribery of the Government. The question was again brought forward in January, 1800, when the Union was carried by one hundred and thirty-eight against ninety-six. There was another great debate in February, when the House of Commons went into committee on the articles of Union. On this occasion the veteran patriot, Grattan, replied to Isaac Corry, Chancellor of the Exchequer. "I will not call him *villain*," he said, "because it would be unparliamentary, and he is a Privy Councillor. I will not call him *fool*, because he happens to be Chancellor of the Exchequer. . . . I have returned to protect that constitution, of which I was the parent and the founder, from the assassination of such men as the right honourable gentleman and his unworthy associates. They are corrupt, they are seditious, and at this very moment they are in a conspiracy against their country. . . . I have returned to refute a libel as false as it is malicious, given to the public under the appellation of a Report of Committee of the Lords. Here I stand, ready for impeachment or trial. I defy the honourable gentleman. I defy the Government. I defy their whole phalanx; let them come forth. I tell the Ministers I will neither give them quarter nor take it. I am here to lay the shattered remains of my constitution on the floor of this house in defence of the liberties of my country."

Maria Edgeworth's father, Richard Lovell Edgeworth, Member for the borough of St. John's Town, stated, in his place in the House, when opposing the Union, that he had been offered 3,000 guineas for his seat during the remainder of the session.[1]

---

[1] Gilbert: *History of the City of Dublin*, III., p. 167.

The opposition to the Union was not confined to the Commons. A minority of the House of Lords protested against the Union. Their final protest, in eleven sections, dated 13th June, 1800, concluded as follows :—

"Because the argument made use of in favour of the Union, namely, that the sense of the people of Ireland is in its favour, we know to be untrue; and as the Ministers have declared that they would not pass the measure against the sense of the people, and as the people have pronounced decidedly, and under all difficulties, their judgment against it, we have, together with the sense of the country, the authority of the Minister to enter our protest against the project of Union, against the yoke which it inflicts, the disqualification passed upon the Peerage, the stigma thereby branded on the realm, the disproportionate principle of expense it introduces, the means employed to effect it, the discontents it has excited and must continue to excite; against all these, and the fatal consequences they may produce, we have endeavoured to interpose our votes; and failing, we transmit to after-times our names, in solemn protest in behalf of the Parliamentary constitution of this realm, the liberty which it secured, the trade which it protected, the connection which it preserved, and the Constitution which it supplied and fortified. This we feel ourselves called upon to do, in support of our characters, our honour, and whatever is left to us worthy to be transmitted to our posterity.

Leinster,	Belmore,	Mountcashel,
Farnham,	Granard,	Massy,
Strangford,	William, Bishop of Down and Connor,	Ludlow,
Moira,		Richard, Bishop of Waterford and Lismore,
Powerscourt,		
Charlemont,	De Vesci,	
Meath,	Riversdale,	Sunderlin."
Arran,	Lismore,	

The accusation which these Peers and which Mr. Plunket brought against the Government, of having used corrupt means to carry the Union, was only too well founded. Besides the money offered to Mr.

Edgeworth, other bribes, too numerous to recite here, were not only offered, but accepted.

But the way in which Pitt and Castlereagh attempted, only too successfully, to bribe the Churches of the people to support the Union is one of the most scandalous actions recorded on the page of history. To the Roman Catholics the prospect of immediate emancipation was held out. To the Presbyterians the allurements offered were of a most tempting character. It was proposed to found a university at Armagh, specially in their behalf, where a Presbyterian theological professorship would be endowed. And it was also agreed that the Regium Donum should be largely increased. The Regium Donum was actually increased by a further grant of more than £8,000 per annum. Along with this grant, a system of classification of ministers was proposed. The ministers were divided into three classes. Those in the first class were the ministers in cities and large towns. They were to receive from one to two hundred pounds per annum of State aid. Those in the second class were the ministers in the more populous country congregations, and they were to receive £80 per annum. Those in the third class, the ministers of the smaller congregations, were to receive £60 per annum. Strong opposition was given in the Synod to the acceptance of this classification. But the Government would not give the grant on any other terms, and the Synod thought it wiser to pocket their dignity and their scruples along with the money. In 1803 the grant and the classification were finally accepted by the Synod.

The object of the Government in both the grant and

---

[1] Reid: *History*, III., p. 400 (Killen's continuation).

the classification is now well known. The Duke of Portland, an English Minister, writing in 1799 to Lord Castlereagh, then Lord Lieutenant of Ireland, stated that "*a principal object* in increasing and remodelling their allowance was to make them more dependent and render them more amenable to Government."[1] Dr. Killen says, "It is plain that in their arrangements for the augmentation of the grant the leading statesmen of the day aimed at the political subserviency of the Presbyterian ministers of Ulster."

We have dwelt thus at length upon the means by which the legislative Union was brought about, because only in the light of that transaction can the subsequent history of Ireland be properly understood. There is a law of national, as well as individual retribution, and England has suffered for the use of methods which were unworthy of her national honour. But two questions naturally suggest themselves here.

The first is, Would it have been better for Ireland if that Union had not taken place? It is most unlikely. Justice to the Irish Roman Catholics, Parliamentary and municipal reform, the improvement of the position of the Irish tenants, and other great legislative enactments may have been slow of coming under the United Parliament, but it is likely that their advent would have been still more tardy under an Irish Parliament. Undoubtedly the history of Ireland since the Union has been a history of discontent. But it is at least probable that there would have been as much discontent under a Parliament constituted, as Grattan's was—and it

---

[1] *Memoirs and Correspondence of Viscount Castlereagh*, quoted in Reid: *History*, III., p. 405 (Killen's continuation).

would likely have continued so for years—entirely of Protestants.

The second is, Would it be for the advantage of Ireland now that the legislative Union should be repealed? Deprecating all the attempts that have been made to stir up religious bigotry and animosity, and thinking only of the interests of our country, we find it hard to see the advantage of such a change. When every grievance is redressed, and every wrong set right, Ireland's power and prosperity will be all the greater for a close alliance with the great British Empire. Statesmen of all political parties are beginning to recognise the necessity for large reforms in the administration of Irish government. It is likely that, while preserving the integrity of the Empire, a much larger share will yet be given to Ireland in the management of her own affairs. May the time soon come when Irishmen of all creeds and classes, forgetting the bitter memories of the past, or thinking of them only to learn the wisdom of a better course, shall work together for the common good of our beloved land!

CHAPTER XVII.

LORD CASTLEREAGH AND THE REV. JAMES CARLILE.

MANY years had not passed until Lord Castlereagh showed that he hoped by his grant of money to reduce the stubborn Presbyterians to subservience. There had hitherto been no public seminary in Ulster where Presbyterian candidates for the ministry could receive a college education. About the year 1809 the Belfast Academical Institution was founded, and in the year 1815 the Synod of Ulster agreed that so soon as adequate professors should be appointed, it should pay the same respect to the certificates of the Belfast Institution as to the certificates of foreign universities. In 1816 the Synod made arrangements to collect funds for the endowment of a chair of Divinity and Church History, and fixed a day for the election of a professor. But when the day came it was found that at a conference between a deputation from the Institution Board and Lord Castlereagh, his lordship deprecated the measure of connecting the Synod of Ulster with the Institution, complained of the Synod making arrangements to appoint a Divinity Professor in the Institution and to accept its certificates, without having acquainted the Government of their intention, and plainly told them that if these measures were adopted they would be regarded as acts of hostility by the Government. On account of this unforeseen difficulty, as well as the smallness of the funds that were yet forthcoming for the endowment of the chair, the Synod postponed the appointment of a professor till the following year.

Lord Castlereagh's objection to the proposed connection between the Synod of Ulster and the Institution arose from the fact that the leading Belfast people, who were the committee of management of the Institution, held political opinions of which he did not approve, and that at a public dinner at which many of them were present some objectionable political toasts had been proposed. For this reason also the Parliamentary grant to the Institution had been withdrawn.

The Synod met in 1817 amid much excitement. There was a prevailing impression, which some of the older members encouraged, that if the Synod persevered in its connection with the Institution the Regium Donum would be withdrawn. But one young Dublin minister scattered to the winds the timidity and the time-serving policy of some of the leaders of the Synod. The question clearly before the House was whether the Synod should make its own arrangements for the education of its students, or whether it should permit itself in such a matter to be dictated to by the State. The Rev. James Carlile, of Mary's Abbey, Dublin, who had been then only four years in the ministry, in brave and fearless words asserted the independence of the Synod.

"It is surely unnecèssary," he said, "to take up the time of the Synod in demonstrating that the education of our students is strictly a matter of internal arrangement. Nothing is more nearly connected with the spiritual interests of our people. There are, Moderator, some proposals which may be made to individuals or to public bodies, on which it is infamous even to deliberate. Such seems to be the nature of the proposal made to us at our late meeting in Cookstown, when, by a verbal message from an individual styling himself Lord Castlereagh, we were informed that Government may regard our electing a professor for educating our students in theology as an act of hostility, and we were required to desist from our purpose. Who or what is this Lord Castlereagh, that he should send such a message to the Synod of Ulster? Is he a minister of the body? Is he an elder? What right has he to obtrude himself on our deliberations? I revere the Government of my country. I pay it a willing obedience in matters civil. I am no cavilling politician. But I protest against government dictating an opinion as to the measures we should adopt for the interests of religion. . . . Let us tell our people that we will never permit his Majesty's bounty to operate as a bribe to induce us to desert what we believe to be their spiritual welfare. . . . This day's decision will tell whether we deserve to rank as an independent, upright, conscientious body, with no other end in view than the glory of God and the welfare of His Church, or whether we deserve that Lord Castlereagh should drive his chariot into the midst of us, and tread us down as the offal of the streets."[1]

This bold and spirited speech won the day. It saved the reputation of the Synod. It showed that Irish Presbyterian independence, despite all the ministerial tampering with it, was not dead yet. It dashed to the ground the hopes and designs of those leaders of the Synod who would have tied Presbyterianism to the

---

[1] Reid: *History*, III., pp. 425-33.

party in power, those miserable trimmers who would sacrifice principle to policy. It enlightened those who were ill-informed on the subject, it encouraged the weak, and it checked the vacillations of the wavering. The resolution that "the regulations for the education of young men intended for the ministry are strictly a matter of discipline" was carried by an overwhelming majority. The Synod asserted its independence. The threats of withdrawing the Regium Donum were never carried into effect. The Synod lost nothing, and it gained a great deal. Such was the end of Castlereagh's infamous attempt to override the religious liberty of the Irish Presbyterian Church. The great negotiator of the Union was baffled for once by the Christian manliness of a young minister from Dublin.

CHAPTER XVIII.

MISSION WORK IN THE SOUTH AND WEST.

THE political excitement of the Rebellion and the Union having to some extent calmed down, the minds of Irish Presbyterians began once more to turn to missionary effort in the South and West.

Since the early part of the eighteenth century Presbyterianism had made little progress in Ireland. New Light doctrines were not favourable to missionary effort. Even existing congregations in the South were gradually dwindling away. Arianism entered many of their pulpits, and when Arianism entered vitality began to disappear. In 1786, by the desire of the trustees of the General Fund, the Revs. Philip Taylor, of Eustace Street, Dublin, and Dr. Moody, of Strand Street, visited the congregation of Leap, King's County. They reported to the trustees that they found the "meeting-house" very much out of repair and unfit for public worship. It appeared to them, on the most careful examination, that in consequence of deaths, removals, and intermarriages with persons of the Established Church, the congregation was almost entirely dissolved, as a single person could not be found who was willing to contribute either to the repair of the meeting-house or the support of a minister. It further appeared, from conversation with those best qualified to judge, that no reasonable hope could be entertained of a revival of the Protestant Dissenting interest in that place.[1]

An English Nonconformist minister has left on record an interesting account of the condition of Presbyterianism in Dublin in 1796. In the summer of that year the Rev. Samuel Pearce, of Birmingham, came to Dublin on the invitation of the General Evangelical Society. He writes, "I found there were four Presbyterian congregations in Dublin; two of these belong to the Southern Presbytery, and are Arians or Socinians —the other two connected with the Northern Presbytery, and retain the Westminister Confession of Faith. One of these latter congregations is small, and the minister, though orthodox, appears to have but little success. The other is large and flourishing, the place of worship ninety feet by seventy, and in the morning well filled. Dr. McDowell is the senior pastor of this church—a very affectionate, spiritual man. The Doctor is a warm friend of the society at whose request I went over to Ireland. There is one congregation of Burgher Seceders, and another of Antiburghers. . . . I am at the house of a Mr. Hutton, late High Sheriff of the city, a gentleman of opulence, respectability, and evangelical piety—a Calvinistic Presbyterian, and elder of Dr. McDowell's church."[2]

In the year 1802 this Mr. Henry Hutton "served the office of chief magistrate of the city of Dublin, with high credit to himself and to the general satisfaction of the citizens. He was voted a gold box and a valuable piece of plate, and his great attention to the observance of the Sabbath is mentioned in three public addresses from the city." Mr. Hutton had only one

---

[1] MS. *Minutes of General Fund.*
[2] *Life and Times of Selina, Countess of Huntingdon*, II., p. 217.

son. This son entered the ministry, and was known as the Rev. John Hutton.

In 1804 an account of the income of the Southern ministers, as previously furnished to Government for the purposes of the classification mentioned above, was laid before the trustees of the General Fund. From this account we learn some valuable particulars regarding the Presbyterian congregations of the South. The following is a list of the congregations receiving aid from the fund, and their incomes :—

Summerhill, Co. Meath. Minister, Rev. David Trotter.
Income—
Rent-charge for ever on Rowley estate, left by Sir A. Langford	£30
House, garden, and orchard. Value per ann.	50
12 acres of land. Value (at profit rent)	20
General Fund	10
Total	£110

Rahew, Co. Westmeath. Minister, Rev. Ephraim Harper. The only income of this congregation is from General Fund, £20.

PRESBYTERY OF MUNSTER.

1. Congregation of Bandon. Minister, Rev. Edward King.

31 Subscribers give a salary of	£50
General Fund	20
Total	£70

2. Congregation of Cork. Minister, Rev. Thomas Dix Hincks. Income, £201, of which £105 is subscriptions, and £96 permanent funds. Subscribers, 44.

3. Clonmel. Minister, Rev. Dr. Campbell.

4. Tipperary. Minister, Rev. John Lister.

10 Subscribers. Subscriptions	£15
General Fund	10
Total	£25

5. Fethard. Minister, Rev. James Allen.
6. Waterford. Minister, Rev. James Marshall.

32 Subscribers. Subscriptions	£108
Permanent Fund	30
Value of House	40
General Fund	20
Total	£198

7. Limerick. Minister, Rev. Abraham Seawright.

Interest on £300	£18 0 0
House valued at	22 15 0
General Fund	15 0 0
10 Subscribers. Subscriptions	25 5 10½
Total	£81 0 10½

The congregations of Cork, Clonmel, and Fethard, though mentioned in this list, do not seem to have been then receiving aid from the General Fund, or if they were, the amount is not stated. The following list of ministers and congregations, according to the Government classification mentioned above, seems to be a complete list of all the congregations in the Southern Association:—

First Class.

The First Minister of Strand Street, Dublin; the Minister of Cork.
The Minister of Eustace Street, Dublin; the Minister of Waterford.

Second Class.

The Second Minister of Eustace Street, Dublin; the Minister of Bandon.
The Minister of Clonmel; the Minister of Limerick.

Third Class.

The Minister of Tipperary; the Minister of Rahew.
The Minister of Fethard; the Minister of Summer Hill.

Inasmuch as for many years neither the Synod of

Ulster nor the Southern Association had done much for the evangelization of the South of Ireland, a new society was formed for this purpose in the year 1814. This was the Irish Evangelical Society. Its first secretaries were Mr. Cooper, minister of the congregation of Plunket Street, Mr. Davies, minister of the congregation of York Street, and Mr. Carlile, minister of Mary's Abbey Presbyterian Church. James Clarke, Esq., a leading member of the Antiburgher (Secession) congregation, was appointed treasurer.[1]

It will be seen that the Society embraced various branches of non-episcopal Churches. Mr. Carlile represented the Presbyterians, Mr. Davies the Congregationalists. Mr. Cooper might doubtless be also classed in the latter denomination. The Presbyterian congregation of Plunket Street had in 1773 united with that of Usher's Quay. After Whitefield's visit and the beginning of Methodism in Ireland, the old Presbyterian meeting-house of Plunket Street was rented, and became one of Lady Huntingdon's chapels. The Church of England liturgy was used, and the service generally was conducted as in Lady Huntingdon's other chapels. A numerous congregation was soon raised. This was the congregation of which Mr. Cooper, Secretary of the Irish Evangelical Society, was minister. The Presbyterians were well represented in the management of the Society, for we find the names of Rev. S. Simpson, of Usher's Quay, and Rev. D. Stuart, of Mary's Abbey Secession Church, as members of committee. The newly formed society soon showed itself to be in earnest. Its report for 1816 states that "at Bray, a place of fashionable resort, about ten miles south of

---

[1] *Reports of Irish Evangelical Society*, 1815-31.

Dublin, a field of Gospel labours has lately been opened, and means are in progress to supply that place statedly." This was the origin of what afterwards became the Presbyterian congregation of Bray.

In the same year a new college was erected by the Society near Prussia Street. In this college young men were specially trained for the work of preaching the Gospel. In 1823 the Rev. David Stuart was appointed Professor of Theology. This office he held in conjunction with the pastorate of the Secession congregation of Mary's Abbey. A volume still preserved contains the manuscript notes of lectures delivered by him in the Manor Street College.

Thus once again, as was fitting, the Presbyterians and other Evangelical Protestants of Dublin led the way in the work of home missions. Soon others followed suit. Immediately after the union of the Burghers and Antiburghers in the Secession Synod in 1818, that Synod threw itself heartily into home mission work. At Drogheda, for instance, where a Presbyterian congregation had been in existence from the middle of the seventeenth to the last part of the eighteenth century, but where it had been extinct for several years, the Secession Church once more unfurled the blue banner under the energetic ministry of the Rev. Josias Wilson.

About the same time a revival of missionary spirit showed itself in the Synod of Ulster. Amongst other places, Carlow presented a sphere for its operations. In May, 1817, the trustees of the General Fund voted a grant to the Rev. Mr. Baird, minister of Stratford-on-Slaney, and expressed their hope "that he will preach as frequently as he can at Carlow, and report upon the prospect of reviving the Presbyterian congregation there." Mr. Baird, however, died in July of the same year. But about that time an unexpected opportunity arose of supplying Carlow with preaching. The Rev. Henry Cooke, though then minister of Donegore, was attending, occasionally, the classes in Trinity College, Dublin.[1] He undertook the work of preaching in Carlow and Stratford on alternate Sabbaths, leaving Dublin on Saturday by coach, and returning on the Monday. In February, 1818, the General Fund trustees voted Mr. Cooke £2 a Sabbath for the supply of Carlow, and five guineas for travelling expenses, together with their special thanks for his zealous exertion to form a congregation in Carlow. The Rev. Robert Stewart, of Broughshane, another distinguished Northern minister, preached in Carlow for several Sabbaths.

At the annual meeting of the Synod of Munster held in Dublin in 1818 the following resolutions were unanimously adopted:—

"That we contemplate with peculiar satisfaction the recent exertions made by our brethren of the Synod of Ulster to extend the Presbyterian interest in the South of Ireland.

"That we will co-operate with the Synod of Ulster in any measures they may adopt for promoting this desirable end.

"That the thanks of the Synod are due to the Rev. Mr. Cooke and the Rev. Mr. Stewart, who have recently supplied the congregation of Carlow, for the zeal, prudence, diligence, and ability exhibited by them in fulfilling the duties of their mission."

These resolutions, signed by the Moderator and Clerk, were transmitted to the Synod of Ulster, upon which that body resolved unanimously, "That we will most cordially co-operate with our brethren of the Synod of Munster in promoting the Presbyterian interest in the South of Ireland." In 1820 it was resolved to

---

[1] Porter: *Life and Times of Dr. Cooke.*

appoint annually a committee of the Synod of Ulster, consisting of eight ministers, for promoting the cause of Presbyterianism in the South and West. This committee co-operated with a committee of the Synod of Munster.[1]

The result of this new interest in home mission work was that several new congregations were formed in the South and West, and some old ones, which had become extinct, were re-erected. The efforts made at Carlow were successful, and the Rev. James Morgan was ordained there in 1820. At this time the congregation of Mullingar and Tyrrell's Pass was erected, in response to the memorial of Presbyterian residents there, and placed under the care of the Dublin Presbytery. In a similar way the congregation of Westport was erected, and that of Tipperary revived.

---

[1] *Synod's Reports*, 1820-29 (Extracts from Minutes of Synod of Ulster).

CHAPTER XIX.

ACTIVITY AND GROWTH.

IT is pleasant to notice that in some instances these efforts of Church extension and missionary work met with the sympathy and encouragement of members of the then Established Church. The Dublin Presbytery ordained Mr. Robert Creighton as minister of the new congregation of Westport on the 23rd December, 1823. On that occasion the oath of allegiance (a now obsolete feature of ordination services) was administered to him by the Marquis of Sligo and George Glendinning, Esq. The Marquis and Marchioness of Sligo and their family were attentive auditors at the ordination, and expressed their satisfaction with every part of the solemn service. The Presbytery subsequently sent letters of thanks to the Marquis of Sligo and G. Glendinning, Esq., "for their great kindness to the congregation of Westport and the ministers who had visited it on the business of the Presbytery."[1] In 1825 a memorial was presented to the Synod of Ulster from Presbyterian and other inhabitants of Kilworth and Fermoy, praying the Synod to erect them into a congregation.[2] This memorial was accompanied by a letter from Lord Mountcashel, addressed to the

---

[1] MS. *Minutes of Dublin Presbytery.*
[2] *Minutes of Synod of Ulster.*

Moderator, stating that there are many Presbyterians scattered about Kilworth and its neighbourhood, and that several individuals belonging to other Churches were favourably disposed to the erection of a Presbyterian congregation in that district of country, and would probably contribute to its support; that he himself would grant, for the use of the minister, a piece of land in perpetuity, of more than £10 clear annual value; that Lady Mountcashel would subscribe £3 per annum for a pew; and that present circumstances seemed particularly favourable to the proposed establishment. His lordship concluded with recommending the application from Kilworth and Fermoy to the attention of the Synod. The memorial was acceded to, and the thanks of the Synod were unanimously voted to Lord Mountcashel.

Steadily the work of home missions and Church extension went on. In 1826 the Committee on Presbyterianism in the South and West reported to the Synod that ministers sent by them had occasionally preached in Roscrea, Templemore, Rahue, Leap, Thurles, Littleton, Youghal, Fermoy, and Erris. In the same year was formed the Synod of Ulster Home Mission Society, "for the purpose of aiding the Presbyterian committees of Dublin and Belfast in providing Presbyterians residing in the South and West with the ordinances of religion according to the form which they prefer, and at the same time extending similar benefits to such Presbyterians in Ulster as are destitute of them." In 1827 the Presbytery of Dublin erected into a congregation the Presbyterian residents of Kingstown.

At this time the Presbytery of Dublin seems to have been, though small, a vigorous and active body. Its meetings were well attended. It was not merely a clerical meeting. The elders of the various congregations regularly attended and took part in its proceedings. Here, for instance, is a sample of the attendance in the year 1819. On the 2nd September there were present— *Ministers:* Rev. James Horner, Rev. Dr. McDowell, Rev. Hugh Moore, Rev. James Carlile, Rev. Samuel Simpson. *Elders:* Captain McLean, Mr. S. Strahan, Mr. James Ferrier, Mr. Forbes, Mr. Gilbert. There was an elder present for every minister. How seldom that happens in our Presbyteries of to-day! The Presbyterian elders and laymen of Dublin at that time, as now, seem to have been men of considerable position and influence. At the December meeting of Presbytery in the same year, amongst those present were, from the Session of Usher's Quay, Sir James Ridall and John Stewart, Esq. (afterwards called Counsellor Stewart).[1]

In 1829 the Rev. Henry Cooke, then of Killyleagh, having declined the call to Mary's Abbey, Dublin, the Rev. W. B. Kirkpatrick was ordained there as assistant and successor to the Rev. James Horner. Before his ordination he presented to the Presbytery a "Statement of my Religious Belief, drawn up at the request of the Presbytery of Dublin." This was before the present form of subscription to the Confession of Faith had become compulsory.

The Presbytery of Dublin was at that time in reality a Presbytery of three provinces. It was the only Presbytery connected with the Synod of Ulster in the provinces of Leinster, Munster, and Connaught. It threw itself heartily into the missionary work which

---

[1] *Minutes of Dublin Presbytery.*

its position involved. Mr. Horner, having now got assistance in his pastoral duties, devoted much of his time to itinerating through the three provinces, discovering scattered members of the Presbyterian family, and doing his best, where practicable, to organize them into congregations. In this he was cordially assisted by other members of the Presbytery.

In 1830 the Moderator of Presbytery, Rev. S. Simpson, of Usher's Quay, reported that in his visit to the South of Ireland, as a deputation from the Scottish Missionary Society, he had found both in Cork and Clonmel, a number of families and individuals who expressed an earnest desire to be supplied with worship according to the Presbyterian discipline. At the same meeting of Presbytery, Mr. Horner reported that he had received an application from Carnew, Co. Wicklow, and its neighbourhood, stating that several Scotch families residing in the town and its vicinity were most anxious to have the Presbyterian form of worship established amongst them, and that he had written to the applicants requesting further information to be submitted to the Presbytery.

The condition of the congregations of the Presbytery at that time may be judged from the following statistics submitted to the Presbytery in 1831 and 1832 :—

Mary's Abbey ... 220 families; 140 individuals, subscribers.
Usher's Quay ... 120 families; 500 individuals.
Kingstown ... 176 individuals.
Carlow ... 120 individuals. The attendance on Sabbath mornings was from 80 to 100.
Stratford ... 3 elders, about 25 families, about 40 communicants, and an attendance of 60-100 on Sabbath.
Lismore ... Subscribers 67, non-subscribers 53, visitors 70.
Mullingar ... (Statistics not given).

The year 1833 appears to have been one of much activity on the part of the Presbytery. A special meeting of the Synod of Ulster was held in Mary's Abbey Church, Dublin, in September, "for the purpose of considering the most efficient means of carrying forward and enlarging the operations of the Presbyterian Missionary Society." It was a memorable meeting. Sermons were preached by the Revs. S. Hanna, D.D., Belfast, H. Cooke, D.D., Belfast, R. Stewart, Broughshane, and James Morgan, Belfast, on the importance of missionary effort, and the doctrines and principles of Presbyterianism. Speeches were delivered by many eminent ministers, amongst whom were Revs. John Johnston, Joseph Denham, Robert Park, Patrick White, Dr. Horner, and two brethren from Scotland, Rev. Duncan Macfarlan, of Renfrew, and Rev. Dr. McLeod, of Campsie.[1]

The report of the Synod's mission was read by the Secretary, Rev. George Bellis. It stated that there were two missionary stations in the South, *Cork and Clonmel*, but that no minister had yet been permanently settled in them. A note, however, mentions that the Rev. Henry Wallace had since been settled in Cork. In *Longford*, through the labours of the Rev. Henry Wallace, a congregation had been organized; a church had been commenced, and subscriptions up to £200 had been received. In *Galway*, the Presbyterians there having made known their wants to the Presbytery of Dublin, were visited by deputations from the Presbytery. A place of meeting had been rented and fitted up, until a house of worship should be built. Ground had been

---

[1] *Missionary Sermons and Speeches delivered at a Special Meeting of the Synod of Ulster*, held in Mary's Abbey Church, Dublin, 1833.

obtained, on the most liberal terms, from Robert Hedges Eyre, Esq., Macroom Castle. It was further stated that the Dublin Presbytery had during the past year sent out three of their ministers to the stations in the South, and defrayed their expenses by collections taken up from the congregations under their care. It was not a bad record of a year's work.

The Rev. James Wilson, of Magherafelt, who had been engaged for some time itinerating for the Society's mission, gave a statement of his work. Some passages in this speech are of peculiar interest, as affording us a glimpse into the conditions of missionary work at that time. He says—

"My visit to *Tipperary* was made under circumstances somewhat peculiar. There are a few Presbyterians in that town, the remains of a congregation that existed there between twenty and thirty years ago. Either by the direct preaching of Arianism, or rather, I believe, by the absence of all doctrinal teaching whatever, the people became indifferent to religion, lapsed into error, and the Presbyterian congregation of Tipperary and its minister departed this life altogether."

After a conference between him and the Presbyterians of Tipperary with a committee of the Synod of Munster, the members of which committee were orthodox, and held no spiritual communion with the heterodox ministers of that body, the final resolution which the Presbyterians of Tipperary came to was " that they should continue their connection with the committee appointed by the Synod of Munster, who should take care to procure them an Evangelical minister from some orthodox body of Presbyterians, as the Church of Scotland, the Synod of Ulster," etc.

Mr. Wilson continued, "A very interesting station which I visited is Dundrum, six miles from Tipperary, where a few Scotch families reside. The minister of Fethard, fifteen miles distant, opened this station some time ago, and preaches occasionally in a spacious school-house erected by Lord Heywarden, for the tenantry of his estate. Several of our ministers from the North also preached here, whose services afforded much gratification. I will not soon forget the reception which I met from these good people, who are so seldom privileged to worship in the way they best like, and were delighted to see a Presbyterian minister; and I am well assured that the resolutions passed at this meeting, which are intended to meet the exigencies of these and others of our friends in similar circumstances, will diffuse gladness over their minds, and excite their hearts to gratitude and their tongues to praise. Nor should I omit to state here the perfect personal security which a Presbyterian missionary may feel, although he has about him few of his own denomination. The district around the last-mentioned place, Dundrum, has been one of the most turbulent in that turbulent country. It is but a few miles, on the one hand, from where the Rev. Mr. Going was shot, and on the other, from where the Rev. Mr. Whitty was stoned to death. The minister of the parish, whose life has been frequently attempted, is obliged, at this moment, to keep a party of police constantly in his house, for the protection of his person and property; and so apprehensive is he of danger that even on the Sabbath, he finds it necessary to walk between two of them with loaded firelocks, to and from the church where he officiates. And yet at this place I had a large assembly of peaceful and attentive hearers, comprehending persons of the different denominations, concluding each time with candle-light, and afterwards walked half a mile to the village without molestation and without apprehension."

Mr. Wilson thus describes the state of religion in the South at that time :—

"The religious people of the South are indeed very decided in their religion. They have no inducement to assume the profession in the absence of the reality. Religion has not yet become sufficiently fashionable in that quarter to present any temptation to this species of hypocrisy, and I hesitate not to say that I have nowhere met more serious, single-minded, or apparently more devoted Christians than some of those whom I was privileged to meet with in Munster. I am also happy to believe, upon unquestionable authority, that the number of anxious inquirers after the way of salvation is much upon the increase, and the relish for evangelical preaching quite on the advance. This was obviously the case in all the places where I preached —in Clonmel, in Enniscorthy, in Tipperary and Dundrum. I found heterodoxy totally out of repute, nay, indeed, the very name of Arian or Socinian regarded with an aversion amounting to absolute abhorrence. These heresies are evidently lost causes in the South."

Such was the great missionary meeting of the Synod of Ulster in 1833. What a pity there are not more of similar meetings in our Synods and our General Assembly of to-day!

Further particulars regarding the position of Presbyterianism in the South and West in 1835 may be gathered from statistics given by George Mathews in his account of the Regium Donum. The appendix to that pamphlet contains a list of congregations, from which we take the following :—

	Strength.	Attendance.
Mary's Abbey, Dublin	1148	600
Usher's Quay, Dublin	418	350
Kingstown	600	300
Carlow	200	55
Killala	297	90
Stratford	156	80
Longford	—	80

LIST OF SYNOD OF MUNSTER.

	Attendance.		Attendance.
Cork (2 ministers)	300	Clonmel	35
Strand Street, Dublin (2 ministers)	600	Fethard	35
		Fermoy (lapsed)	0
Eustace Street, Dublin (2 ministers)	170	Waterford	103
		Limerick	130
Bandon	80	Summerhill (Meath)	19

SECEDERS.

	Strength.	Attendance.
Dublin (Union Chapel)	1709	700
„ Mass-lane (lapsed)	—	—
„ Back-lane (lapsed)	—	—

In 1835 Dr. Horner reported to the Dublin Presbytery that he had visited *Athlone* by the instructions of the Presbytery. He stated that he had found twenty-four Presbyterian families in and around Athlone, and over eighty individuals. There were several Presbyterians also in Moate. The Presbytery resolved to establish a congregation at Athlone. In the same year the Presbytery ordained Mr. Fisher in the newly formed congregation of *Galway*.[1]

In 1836, a conversation having taken place in the Presbytery on the existing state of Presbyterianism in Dublin, it was resolved "That a committee, consisting of Dr. Horner, Mr. Dill, Mr. Ferrier, Mr. Neilson,

---

[1] *Minutes of Dublin Presbytery.*

Mr. Madden, and Mr. Greer, be appointed to inquire into the practicability of establishing a new congregation in this city, in connection with the Synod of Ulster.' This movement ultimately led to the formation of *Adelaide Road* congregation.

In 1837 a letter was read from Mr. Benjamin Digby, Mountjoy Square, requesting the Presbytery of Dublin to apply to the Synod on behalf of a number of families residing at Ballymahon, County Longford, who are destitute of religious ordinances, and are desirous of obtaining a minister from the Synod of Ulster. The Presbytery agreed to transmit the letter, with most hearty recommendations, to the Directors of the Home Mission, but no action seems to have been taken on this application.

But the Presbytery did not content itself with merely erecting new congregations, and then allowing them to shift for themselves. It sought to keep up a connection between the centre and the outposts. In 1837 the Rev. Messrs. Simpson and Kirkpatrick were appointed to visit Cork, Lismore, Clonmel, and Carlow, as a deputation from the Presbytery, accompanied by the Rev. Messrs. Poole and John Dill, and to report at next meeting on the circumstances and prospects of the Church at each of these stations. In the following year Dr. Horner and Mr. Dill were appointed as a deputation to visit the congregations of Mullingar, Athlone, and Galway. Thus the Presbytery sought to make itself acquainted with the condition of its distant congregations, in a more effective manner, probably, than by some of our modern visitations.

In 1838 the Secession Synod of Ulster formed into a Presbytery four of its Southern congregations. This Presbytery, for the short period of its existence, was known as the Secession Presbytery of Dublin, and its congregations were 1st Dublin (Union Chapel), 2nd Dublin (then D'Olier Street), Bray, and Drogheda.

But events were rapidly ripening which soon put an end to the separation between the Synod of Ulster and the Secession. On the 10th July, 1840, the memorable union of the two great branches of Irish Presbyterianism was consummated. Henceforth the two Synods were united, under the name of the General Assembly of the Presbyterian Church in Ireland. Henceforth the missionary activity which, during recent years of their existence, had been exhibited by both Synods, now flowed in a steadier and stronger stream. A Foreign Mission to the heathen in India, a Jewish Mission, a Colonial Mission, a Continental Mission, a Mission to Soldiers and Sailors, were established in quick succession.

Home Mission work was not forgotten. We have seen how actively the Presbytery of Dublin and the Synod of Ulster's Missionary Society had been labouring in the South and West. From the last report of that society for 1840, before the union of the Synods, we may take some extracts which show us something of the nature and progress of the work.[1]

Regarding *Wexford* and *Enniscorthy*, it is stated that these stations are the fruits of the labours of the Rev. Robert Knox, the Synod's missionary to the South and West. "Mr. Knox alone, of several licentiates who were invited, consented to undertake that office. He was ordained by the Presbytery of Strabane in the month of April; since then he has been doing the work of a pioneer."

---
[1] *Reports of the Home Mission and Schools of the Synod of Ulster*, 1832-40.

Mr. Knox's own account of his work is full of interest. He says, "No part of the South has been so much neglected as the county of Wexford and the whole of that extensive and beautiful country southeast of Dublin. There is not a Presbyterian minister in the county. It cannot be argued, in palliation of the neglect which this melancholy state of affairs manifests, that this county is destitute of a Presbyterian population. We can point to one town in that county that contained, but a few years ago, twenty-five families, at the lowest calculation. We can point to another, in which there are at this moment some twenty families, including the surrounding neighbourhood, and to a third, in which there are four or five families, yet not one minister to watch for their souls." In the town of Wexford he found very few Presbyterians. The attendance at the service which he conducted for two months was never more than twenty. But, he adds, "there are at present about twenty-five Presbyterian families in the town and neighbourhood who profess their willingness to assist."

Of Enniscorthy he says, "In this place there was a Presbyterian minister and congregation so late as 1833. At that time the minister died, and the congregation became extinct. Above thirty families were connected with, or at least subscribed to, the support of the late minister. . . . I preached in the market-house on a Tuesday evening, to about one hundred and thirty persons, most of whom had been at one time Presbyterians. Regular services have since been kept up every Friday evening." He adds, however, that recent interference of the Episcopal clergy had clouded the prospects there. In November, 1840, the Dublin Presbytery organized the congregation of Wexford, the

Presbyterian people there promising a stipend of £23 a year.

The old historic town of Bandon was another important sphere of missionary effort. The Rev. Robert Gault, of Killyleagh, visited it as a deputation in the spring of 1841, and has left a record of the state of matters there in a letter to the *Downpatrick Missionary Herald*. He says of Bandon, "Presbyterianism is reduced to the shadow of what it formerly was. Mr. Knox, the Assembly's missionary to the South and West, told me, what he ascertained to be a fact, that at one time a large Presbyterian meeting-house was filled to overflowing, not merely with the people residing in the town, but with those who came from the adjoining parishes.

"The old place of meeting was thrown down, and at a time when Arianism came in a new meeting-house was erected, and even it, though smaller than the other, was numerously attended. . . . But as the coldness of spiritual death gradually paralyzes the energies of both minister and people, the congregation slowly and silently fell away, until when, one day during my stay at Bandon, the numbers attending on a pleasant Sabbath in spring were reckoned : *twenty-nine* persons alone, of all ages and sexes, were found the *remnant* of the once happy and flourishing Presbyterian Church of Bandon." The writer then goes on to show that this is the natural result of the Arian error.

"There is one circumstance which I think worth recording. The preacher who first propagated false doctrine among his people in Bandon was the man who occupied the pulpit immediately before its present possessor. He did so in a very guarded manner, and not till after he had been in the place a considerable time. The first day when he broached the opinion that the Lord Jesus is a mere creature, and that His atonement is a mere fancy of interested, ignorant men, there sat in the front seat of the gallery one of the elders of the congregation. He was a man now grown grey in the service of his Master; he leant upon his staff as he walked, but his soul still beat responsive to the tale of a Saviour's incarnation and dying love. When he heard a professed minister of Christ deny our Saviour's Divinity, and make light of His work of passive obedience, he was fired with holy indignation at the insult thus openly and for the first time offered to the name, and dignity, and death of Him upon whom all his hopes of present and eternal happiness were founded. He could not restrain the overwhelming emotions that at that moment struggled in his bosom, and in the audience of the assembled people, he loudly protested against this overt act of rebellion, and shouting 'Treason, treason!' he hurried out of that house where he had heard his Saviour's name dishonoured, and never could be induced to enter it more."

In another letter Mr. Gault concludes his narrative. He says, "Mr. Knox, then the only ordained missionary in connection with our Church to the people of our native land, was invited to visit Bandon by a Scotch gentleman from Annandale, a near relative and once school companion of the lamented Edward Irving, and who then resided in Bandon. This request was seconded by a native of the town, a descendant of the original English Presbyterian settlers, and son to the faithful elder who publicly protested against the introduction of error into the congregation.

"Mr. Knox says of the difficulties he encountered at first, '. . . I was feared and avoided. Many came to hear me through curiosity. They were astonished to hear a Presbyterian minister preach the doctrines of the *Atonement* and the Deity of Christ, and during my first sermon some of them whispered to the others that surely I was not a *Presbyterian.*'

" The site of a new church was obtained in the very heart of the town, and subscriptions cheerfully entered into for its erection."

This letter shows the difficulties which the new apostles of Evangelical Presbyterianism had to encounter as they went everywhere preaching the Word. Arianism had done serious damage to Presbyterianism, especially in the South and West, and as the Arians still continued to use the name of "Presbyterians" after their separation from the Synod of Ulster, outsiders could hardly be expected to know the difference. The present writer himself has been more than once asked by intelligent and educated Episcopalians if Presbyterians believed in the Divinity of Christ.

A remarkable accession to the Presbyterian Church took place in the year 1839. The Rev. William Crotty, parish priest of Birr (or Parsonstown), and the greater part of his congregation, seceded from the Church of Rome, and applied to the Presbytery of Dublin to supply them with the ordinances of religion. The Presbytery acceded to the request, and at its annual meeting the Synod of Ulster formally received Mr. Crotty and his congregation under its care. The Rev. Dr. Carlile, minister of Mary's Abbey, who had just resigned the Resident Commissionership of the Board of National Education, resolved to devote himself to missionary labour in the promising field of Birr. His colleague, Dr. Kirkpatrick, carried on the ministerial duties of Mary's Abbey, and Dr. Carlile, without being loosed from his charge, was, at his own request, sent by his generous and spirited congregation to labour as their missionary at Birr. There Dr. Carlile spent the remaining years of his busy and useful life, and there he and his wife are buried.

CHAPTER XX.

INTOLERANCE AGAIN.

IN the year 1839 an Irish Presbyterian minister received a very unusual honour. The freedom of the city of Dublin was conferred upon the Rev. Dr. Cooke, of Belfast, by the Corporation, "in consideration of the zeal which he has so long manifested in support of pure religion." He had previously, in 1837, received the degree of LL.D. from Trinity College, Dublin.[1]

But it is not to be imagined that the feelings of Episcopalians—who were then the reigning power in the land—were friendly to Presbyterians in general. Dr. Cooke was honoured by them rather as a political champion than as a Presbyterian minister. Even he himself experienced more than once something of their intolerant spirit.

"Soon after his settlement in Killyleagh," says his biographer, "while yet a young man, he was asked to take part in a meeting at Downpatrick on behalf of the Bible Society, under the presidency of Lord Roden, and in company with the leading men of the county. Dr. Daly, afterwards Bishop of Cashel, in his speech, referred to Dr. Cooke, and expressed his delight at having the countenance and aid of his 'Dissenting brother.' When Dr. Cooke rose, he too, in graceful sentences, gave thanks to God that Christian men of

---

[1] Porter: *Life and Times of Dr. Cooke.*

different communions could thus meet for a common object on a common platform. He congratulated Dr. Daly on his liberal sentiments and Christian charity. 'But,' he said, 'for myself I repudiate the name Dissenter. I am no Dissenter. The Presbyterians of Ulster were never connected with the Episcopal Church of England or Ireland. The Presbyterian Church of Ireland is a branch of the Church of Scotland. From it I hold my orders, and as one of its ministers I stand before you this day.'"

Many years later some of the Episcopal clergy were highly indignant at the brotherly relations between certain of their brethren and Dr. Cooke. In the *Irish Ecclesiastical Journal* for November, 1848, the following letter appears:—

"A PRESBYTERIAN PREACHER IN A PARISH CHURCH.

"DEAR SIR,—I enclose you a handbill which has been distributed in the neighbourhood to which it relates, and which strikes me to be so passing strange as to deserve the more extended publicity which your pages can confer. It is desirable that the Church at large should be aware of the growth and progress of *liberal sentiments* in that branch of it which is comprised in the diocese of Derry and Raphoe.

'CHARITY SERMON AT KNOCKCLOGHRIM.

A SERMON

Will be preached by the

REV. HENRY COOKE, D.D., LL.D.,

in the Parish Church of Termoneeny,

On Thursday, the 19th day of October inst.,

At Twelve o'clock precisely,

After which a Collection will be made to assist in the Purchase of a Religious, Moral, and Agricultural Library, for the use of the inhabitants of that Neighbourhood.'

"This handbill speaks for itself; but it may be necessary to add that the 'Rev. Henry Cooke, D.D.,' is really and truly the celebrated Presbyterian divine; and that the 'parish church of Termoneeny' actually is the consecrated edifice in which the rites and ceremonies and public ministrations of the United Church of England and Ireland are, or ought to be, conducted, as by law directed; and furthermore that there are a resident incumbent and curate." . . . He adds that the transaction "has excited as much surprise among Dissenters as indignation among Church-people.

"Your obedient Servant,
"ARMACHANUS."

But the matter did not rest there. In the same journal for December, 1848, appears a letter entitled "A Presbyterian *Teacher* in a Parish Church," and signed " A Clergyman of the Diocese of Derry," in which the writer says, with reference to Dr. Cooke at Termoneeny, that "as soon as the Bishop's attention was called to the matter, he immediately communicated to the incumbent his disapprobation, calling his attention to the infringement of canon law which such a course would entail. The incumbent did not receive the Bishop's communication, I believe, till a few days before the sermon was to be preached, according to the printed notice. He thought it then too late to withdraw the permission he had already given, but he has since, I have good reason to believe, signified to his Lordship his sorrow that he had been induced to act in any way contrary to the usages or laws of the Church."

Other articles and letters in the *Irish Ecclesiastical Journal* about that time show the bitter spirit by which the Episcopalians were actuated. In July, 1845, a correspondent "M," writing on the new Marriage Act, criticises a letter of the Registrar General, and finds fault with it on the ground that it "*is addressed to the clergy of the Church and to Presbyterian ministers indiscriminately.*" He adds that " whatever religious persuasion the writer may belong to, or whatever may be his private views upon such a subject, he may be supposed to be aware that *the Church does not recognize Presbyterian teachers as ministers of religion.*" Evidently there was still the same hatred of the Presbyterians as there was in the days of Bishops Echlin and Knox and in the time of Dean Swift.

CHAPTER XXI.

THE GENERAL FUND LAW-SUIT.

IT was in the year 1840 that the celebrated law-suit began which rescued the valuable property of the General Fund from Arian hands and restored it to its rightful Presbyterian owners. " Mr. George Mathews, at that time a clerk in Dublin Castle, and largely employed in Government confidence, but whose previous and subsequent history is more like a romance than truth, sent a letter to the then trustees, stating that he was a non-subscribing Presbyterian, and that in accordance with the Trust Deed he enclosed £100 late Irish currency, with a view of becoming a trustee. The trustees resolved to take the opinion of two learned counsel on this application, and were informed by them 'that they had a discretionary power as to the appointment of trustees,' in accordance with which opinion they unanimously resolved not to receive Mr. Mathews' subscription." [1]

A suit in Chancery was then instituted on April 18th, 1840, by the Rev. Robert Quinn, of Fermoy, Mr. George Mathews, Mr. William Sheriffs, architect, of Fermoy, and Mr. John Black, nurseryman, also of

---

[1] *Report of Chancery Proceedings* (1850). Dr. Frazer's MS. *Account of the General Fund.*

Fermoy, as elders of that congregation, against the trustees. The chief charges were—

Misapplication of the funds to Unitarian purposes.

Expenditure in support of Summerhill congregation, which was asserted to be "Unitarian and nearly extinct."

Refusal of the trustees to make grants to the Fermoy Presbyterian Trinitarian Church.

It was also urged that the original trustees had all been Trinitarian in their doctrine, and that they had excluded Emlyn from communion with them for entertaining Unitarian opinions.

In November, 1843, judgment was given by the Lord Chancellor. He decreed that "Unitarian ministers, students, and congregations were not entitled to participate in the Fund." He further removed the following trustees:—

Representing Strand Street congregation:—

Rev. W. H. Drummond.
Rev. Geo. A. Armstrong.
Thomas Wilson.
John Barton.
John Strong Armstrong.
Brindley Hone.

Representing Eustace Street congregation:—

Rev. Joseph Hutton.
Rev. Jas. Crawford Ledlie.
William Drennan.
Nathaniel Hone.
Robert Moore Peile.
William Biggar.

Representing Mary's Abbey:—

James Ferrier.

Representing Usher's Quay:—

Rev. Samuel Simpson.
Dr. William Madden.
William Wilson Jameson.

These four were Trinitarians, but were removed for having joined the Unitarians in their pleading and defence.

He also referred it to Edward Litton, Esq., Master in

Chancery, to appoint proper trustees in their room. This left

Rev. Dr. Horner.
Rev. Dr. Carlile.
George Proctor.
William Johnston.
Joseph Henry.
} Residuary Trustees, all belonging to St. Mary's Abbey Church.

Two of the trustees thus removed, Rev. W. H. Drummond and Rev. J. C. Ledlie, appealed to the House of Lords, but their appeal was dismissed with costs, judgment being given July 31st, 1849.

The five trustees who were retained had meanwhile pressed the Attorney General to have new trustees appointed as decreed, but he filed another information (at the relation of George Mathews and John Black) against them on the 27th February, 1846, praying that all ministers and members of congregations subscribing the Westminster Confession or any other formula should be declared not fit objects of said charity, and that all such should be excluded from the trusteeship. Mr. Mathews had ejected the Unitarians from the Fund, but he now endeavoured to obtain it for those ministers and congregations of the Synod of Munster who, though orthodox, were non-subscribing.

At the time when this information was filed four of the residuary trustees had died, leaving Dr. Carlile sole surviving trustee. In November, 1850, he obtained a decree from the Lord Chancellor " that the information of February, 1846, be dismissed with costs." A strong bar was engaged on both sides of this case. For the relators (George Mathews and John Black) the counsel were the Attorney General, Mr. Brewster, Q.C., Mr. Whiteside, Q.C., and Mr. Edward Wright; solicitor, Mr. Adam John Macrory. For the defendant (Rev. Dr. Carlile) counsel were Mr. Christian, Q.C., Mr. Francis Fitzgerald, Q.C., and Mr. James Peebles; solicitors, Mr. Matthew Anderson and Mr. William Findlater.

Dr. Carlile hereupon applied to the Master to appoint trustees under the original decree, but again the Attorney-General, to defeat the claims of the congregations in connection with the General Assembly, filed a charge to exclude subscribing churches, and to elect trustees exclusively from the Presbytery of Munster.

Dr. Carlile, in reply, stated that the question of subscription or non-subscription was not contemplated when the Fund was formed, but that any of the Dublin congregations of Orthodox Presbyterians would be entitled to participate in the charity, and consequently entitled to be represented in the trusteeship.

He proposed, therefore, that the places of the sixteen trustees removed by the decree of November, 1842, and the four subsequently removed by death, should be filled up by an equal number from the five orthodox congregations in Dublin. In this view the Master acquiesced, and appointed the new trustees, as proposed by Dr. Carlile. This appointment was confirmed by the Lord Chancellor. The following were the new trustees appointed:—

For Mary's Abbey, in connection with the General Assembly.
- Rev. W. B. Kirkpatrick, D.D.
- Mr. Robert Orr.
- Mr. William Neilson.
- Mr. Thomas Drury.

For Ormond Quay, in connection with the General Assembly.
- Rev. Richard Dill.
- Mr. James Henry.
- Dr. William Frazer.
- Mr. James Bryce.

For Lower Gloucester Street, in connection with the General Assembly.	Rev. William Wilson. Dr. James Foulis Duncan. Mr. William Bell Herron. Mr. John Hamilton Reid.
For Adelaide Road, in connection with the General Assembly.	Rev. Joseph Weir Hunter. Mr. William Todd. Mr. Thomas Heiton. Mr. John Lang.
For Abbey Street Congregation, in connection with Presbytery of Munster.	Rev. Simpson G. Morrison. Mr. David McDowall. Mr. Frederick Wells. Mr. Adam Robertson.

From this time the General Fund entered on a new period of its existence and administration, more in harmony with the spirit and intentions of its early founders.

CHAPTER XXII.

THE MARRIAGE QUESTION.

ANOTHER important legal discussion arose at this time, which caused widespread excitement and, for a time, indignation amongst the Presbyterians of Ireland. This was the discussion on the marriage question. A man belonging to the Episcopal Church had married a Presbyterian wife. The marriage took place in the Presbyterian church. While his wife was still alive, he was again married to an Englishwoman, according to the rites of the Church of England. He was arrested and tried for bigamy. The defence was that the first marriage, having been celebrated by a Presbyterian minister and not by a priest in holy orders, was invalid. The case was taken to the Queen's Bench, and finally to the House of Lords. The result was that the Presbyterian marriage was declared invalid because the minister who performed it was not in priest's orders, that is because he was not episcopally ordained. The Irish Chief Justice, in giving his decision in the Court of Queen's Bench, stated that *" the law of this country does not recognize the orders of the Presbyterian Church, because it is not episcopal and conformable to what the Act of Uniformity had before made the law."* [1]

---

[1] *Life of the Rev. A. P. Goudy, D.D.*, pp. 95, 96.

"Seldom of late years," says Professor Witherow, "have the feelings of Presbyterian people been so deeply touched. They felt aggrieved that the agency of the law courts should be used to affix an unmerited stigma on their ministers, and that they themselves were to be compelled by law to face the alternative of a marriage now pronounced legally invalid, or to affront their own ministers by accepting in the Established Church a form of marriage service, which some regarded then, as they regard it now, unscriptural, unreasonable, and superstitious. The ground taken in the courts that Presbyterian ministers have no right to marry, because they are not 'mass-priests,' and are not episcopally, that is prelatically ordained, they considered to be an insult. Their ministers did not profess to be ordained by prelates or to be mass-priests; they never sought nor wished for any higher orders than those which Barnabas and Saul got from the 'prophets and teachers at Antioch,' or which Timothy received 'with the laying on of hands of the Presbytery.' . . . Further, if a mixed marriage was not valid on the ground that the officiating minister was not episcopally ordained, they could not see that their ordinary marriages, though sanctioned by law, could be free from the same objection; and the inference which they drew from the decision of the law courts was that in the eye of British law they and their wives were regarded by the State as living in fornication, and their children in bastardy. Not only so, but the decision touched them to the quick in the matter of religion. If the marriage performed by their ministers was not valid, what could be thought of the baptism, or communion, or any other rite received at their hands?"

Everywhere throughout the country great indignation

meetings of Presbyterians were held. A meeting held in Mary's Abbey Church, Dublin, was attended by all the influential Presbyterians of the city. It is fully reported in the newspapers of the day.[1] Particular condemnation was given to the action of the Episcopalian bishops and clergy. It was no wonder. They were at the bottom of the whole matter. The Primate himself paid the cost of the law-suit against the Presbyterians, which it was said amounted to £6,000. The Bishop of Exeter denied in the House of Lords that "there was any Presbyterian Church in Ireland at all, and that if any body was so called it was in violation of the canons."

But the Presbyterians had shown before now that they were not exactly persons to be trifled with. They were now thoroughly roused, and if the British Parliament had supported the British judges and the bigoted bishops it is hard to say how it might have fared with British rule in Ireland. It was wise policy to conciliate a body which even then numbered in its membership almost half the Protestants of Ireland. The result was that in 1844 a Bill was brought in and passed, legalizing Presbyterian marriages and authorizing Presbyterian ministers to celebrate marriage between Presbyterians and Episcopalians.

---

[1] See *Saunders's Newsletter*, April 10th, 1844.

CHAPTER XXIII.

CHURCH EXTENSION.

THE year 1842 was the Bi-centenary year of the Irish Presbyterian Church. The first Irish Presbytery had met at Carrickfergus in 1642. Then there were only five Presbyterian ministers in Ireland; now there were more than four hundred. The Presbyterian Church might well rejoice on the occasion of its two-hundredth anniversary. It had spread itself as a power for good over the land. Its Arian controversy was happily at an end, and the Arian influence gradually dwindling away. Its two divided branches had been blended into one, and it had entered on a new era of progress, activity, and missionary enterprise.

To commemorate this memorable year a Bi-centenary Fund was established. It shows how thoroughly the missionary spirit had taken possession of the Church at this time when we find that this fund was devoted entirely to mission work, including erection of churches, in the South and West. The fund reached the splendid sum of £14,000.[1]

The Dublin Presbytery continued its missionary activity during these years of law-suits and excitement. In 1841 the Rev. Mr. Boyd, of Drogheda, reported to the Presbytery that he and Mr. Wilson, of D'Olier Street,

---

[1] Reid: *History*, III., p. 485.

had preached occasionally at *Balbriggan*, that about one hundred persons had occasionally attended, and that there was a favourable prospect of establishing a missionary station in that place, there being twenty families in the neighbourhood who have expressed themselves favourably disposed to that object. Mr. Boyd was requested to visit Balbriggan at his earliest convenience, and report to the Presbytery. This effort, however, was not prosecuted further. At a subsequent meeting Mr. Boyd reported that he had not visited Balbriggan, as he had learned that ministers of the Established Church were at present officiating there.

In the same year the new Presbyterian church of Adelaide Road was erected in Dublin, at a cost of nearly £3,000. The collection at the opening services amounted to about £150.

In 1846 Messrs. Hunter and Kirkpatrick reported to the Presbytery that they had visited Dalkey at the request of the Presbytery, and that it was their decided opinion that an effort should be made to establish, if possible, a congregation in a place where the population is so rapidly advancing and likely to advance. They were reappointed, with other members of Committee, to inquire what amount of local encouragement can be given to the erection of a church at Dalkey. Nothing more seems to have been done in this matter.

In 1852 the congregation of Athy, which had been extinct for fully a century, was revived, and the Rev. John Hall became its first minister. In succeeding years were erected, under the Dublin Presbytery, the congregations of Sandymount, Naas, Duncannon, Rathgar, Wicklow, and Belview.

The congregations under the care of the Dublin Presbytery had been gradually growing so numerous that it became necessary to form new Presbyteries. The Athlone Presbytery, formed in 1842, took charge of the Western congregations, and the Cork Presbytery was formed in 1843 for the oversight of the Southern Churches.

During the sittings of the General Assembly at Dublin in 1845 a pleasant incident took place. The Rev. Dr. Henry presented to the Assembly, as a gift from the Archbishop of Dublin (Whately), fifty copies of his Grace's work on "The Kingdom of Christ," for the use of the Presbyteries of the Church. The hearty thanks of the Assembly were accorded to the Archbishop.[1]

---
[1] *Minutes of General Assembly.*

CHAPTER XXIV.

*THE GENERAL ASSEMBLY OF 1850
AND THE LAND QUESTION.*

IN the early part of the nineteenth century, Daniel O'Connell was the most prominent figure in Irish history. His name still lives in the hearts of the Irish people, who fondly call him "the Liberator." A magnificent statue of him adorns the principal street of the metropolis, facing the bridge which bears his name. O'Connell won Catholic Emancipation in 1829, that gift which Pitt had promised, to induce the Roman Catholics to support the Union, but which he never gave. But the great energy of his life was thrown into the Repeal movement. The Union, up to that time, had never been accepted by the great mass of the Irish people. At first Protestants were as anxious as Roman Catholics for its repeal. The movement for Repeal of the Union was really begun in 1810, by a requisition from the Grand Jurors of Dublin (all Protestants) to the High Sheriffs, Sir Edward Stanley and Sir James Riddall, calling upon them to convene a public meeting of the freemen and freeholders of Dublin, "for the purpose of petitioning Parliament to repeal the hateful and injurious Act." At this meeting, held on the 18th of September, 1810, the Protestant merchants and gentry of Dublin launched the movement which O'Connell, thirty years after, made his own.[1] The story of the Repeal movement we need not repeat here. When it seemed to be at its height, O'Connell summoned a monster meeting to be held at Clontarf, where Brian Boroimhe defeated the Danes in the celebrated battle of 1014. The very evening before the meeting was to be held the Government issued a proclamation forbidding it. Not only so, but they arrested O'Connell and his son, Charles Gavan Duffy, of the *Nation*, Dr. Gray, of the *Freeman*, and others. That was the end of "Repeal." O'Connell died at Genoa on his way to Rome, three years afterwards.[2]

Following the Repeal movement, and arising out of it, came the Young Ireland movement, ending in the rising of 1848, headed by Smith O'Brien. The feeling which fostered these insurrectionary movements was greatly intensified by the poverty of the people, and especially by their sufferings in the famine year, called ever since "the Black Forty-seven." The wretchedness and poverty of the people had taught the landlords no mercy, and wholesale evictions took place.[3] Thousands of people emigrated to America, and thousands of them died of typhus and cholera on the way.

The spirit of the country was at last thoroughly awakened. Insurrection had failed, and the people

---

[1] A. M. Sullivan : *New Ireland*, p. 21.
[2] O'Keeffe : *Life and Times of Daniel O'Connell*.
[3] Mr. Froude, speaking of Irish absentee landlordism, says, "The absentee landlords of Ireland had neither community of interest with the people nor sympathy of race. They had no fear of provoking their resentment, for they lived beyond their reach. They had no desire for their welfare, for as individuals they were ignorant of their existence. They regarded their Irish estates as the sources of their income; their only desire was to extract the most out of them which the soil could be

now resolved to have recourse to constitutional agitation. For once North and South were united! Presbyterian and Roman Catholic farmers alike felt the common burden of an oppressive landlordism. All over the country public meetings in favour of land reform were being held, and Tenant Protection Societies were being formed. The agitation penetrated even the General Assembly. On the motion of the Rev. John Rogers,[1] of Comber, the Assembly in 1850 resolved "That the Assembly do petition Parliament that whatever measure they may adopt to adjust the relations of landlord and tenant in Ireland, such measure shall secure to the tenant-farmers of Ulster, in all its integrity, the prescriptive usage of that province known by the name of tenant-right." Notwithstanding the strenuous opposition of the veteran orator and leader Dr. Cooke, the motion was carried by a large majority. The Rev. Dr. Kirkpatrick, of Dublin, was Moderator of the General Assembly this year.[2]

In the same year a conference of the Tenant Societies of the four provinces was held in Dublin. The circular summoning it was signed by Dr. Gray, of the *Freeman's Journal*, Samuel McCurdy Greer, barrister, a respected member of Ormond Quay Presbyterian Church, and Frederick Lucas, of the *Tablet*. When the conference assembled, Dr. Macknight, the Presbyterian editor of the *Banner of Ulster*, took the chair. At this conference the principles of land reform were laid down which

---

made to yield; and they cared no more for the souls and bodies of those who were, in fact, committed to their charge, than the owners of a West Indian plantation for the herds of slaves whose backs were blistering in the cane-fields."—*English in Ireland*, Vol. II., pp. 22, 23.

[1] Afterwards the Rev. Professor Rogers, D.D., of the Assembly's College, Belfast.

[2] *Minutes of General Assembly; newspaper reports*, etc.

were afterwards known as "the three F's," viz :—*fair rents, fixity of tenure,* and *freedom of sale.* John Bright said of this conference, in the House of Commons, "Instead of the agitation being confined, as heretofore, to the Roman Catholics and their clergy, Protestant and Dissenting clergymen seem to be amalgamated with Roman Catholics at present; indeed, there seems an amalgamation of all sects on this question, and I think it time the House should resolutely legislate on it." The conference separated after it had formed the "Irish Tenant League," and elected a council of one hundred and twenty representatives from the four provinces.

In 1855 the Presbyterians took a further step towards the securing of their civil rights and privileges. During the meeting of the General Assembly in Dublin that year, the "Irish Presbyterian Representation Society" was formed, the object of which was to secure Parliamentary representation, and a recognition of their claims to public offices and appointments, for the Presbyterians of Ireland. Among the speakers at this meeting were Dr. Peebles, Rev. A. P. Goudy, D.D., of Strabane, G. W. Slator, Esq., Rev. Clarke Huston, D.D., Macosquin, Rev. J. Barnett, D.D., Moneymore, Rev. Joseph Macdonell, Coleraine, etc. Since that time three Irish Presbyterian ministers have been members of the British House of Commons. These were Rev. Richard Smyth, D.D., Professor of Theology in Magee College, Derry, Rev. John Kinnear, D.D., minister at Letterkenny, and Rev. Isaac Nelson, minister of Donegall Street Church, Belfast. Several Irish Presbyterian laymen, such as the late Samuel McCurdy Greer, Sir Thomas McClure, of Belfast, Sir James P. Corry, of Belfast, Thomas A. Dickson, of

Dungannon and Dublin, W. P. Sinclair, of Belfast and Liverpool, and Daniel Taylor, of Coleraine, have also represented important constituencies in the House of Commons.

The very mention of a similar movement for Presbyterian representation had caused Dr. Cooke to withdraw from the Assembly some years before. In 1843 the following resolution was passed: " That the difficulty which has been often experienced in having the wishes and interests of Presbyterians efficiently represented in Parliament—a difficulty powerfully manifested during the recent struggles of the Scottish Church—and the serious injury which, from the aspect of the times, we have reason to fear may arise from a similar course, warrant this Assembly in recommending the adoption of measures for securing a more adequate representation of the principles and interests of Presbyterians in the Legislature of the country." At that time there was only one Irish Presbyterian member in Parliament, though the Presbyterians numbered almost one-half of the Protestant population of Ireland. Yet Dr. Cooke, though himself a most ardent politician, took exception to any attempt to remedy this state of things. When the resolution was passed he entered his protest against it, then withdrew from the Assembly, and did not enter it again until, four years later, the resolution was rescinded.

CHAPTER XXV.

THE MAGEE COLLEGE CONTROVERSY.

THE Magee College controversy was one of the fiercest ecclesiastical contests ever waged in the Irish Presbyterian Church. Though it was chiefly carried on in the meetings of the General Assembly at Belfast, and in the newspaper press of Ulster, yet it had a considerable connection with Dublin Presbyterianism. The innocent cause of much of the controversy was the generous benefactress whose name is perpetuated in Magee College, and who was for some years before her death a member of Usher's Quay (now Ormond Quay) congregation in Dublin. One of the most prominent leaders in the controversy was the Rev. Richard Dill, the able and eloquent minister of Usher's Quay.

The Belfast Academical Institution, prior to the establishment of the Queen's College and of the Assembly's College, Belfast, was a college with professors both in arts and in divinity. There most of the Presbyterian students for the ministry were educated, some, however, attending divinity classes in Edinburgh and Glasgow. The Institution is now a very efficient and well-equipped high school, preparatory to entering college.

The appointment of Arian professors to theological

chairs in the Institution, and the general disregard shown by its governing board to the views of the Synod of Ulster, and subsequently of the General Assembly, caused the General Assembly at last to relinquish all connection with it. In 1844 it was unanimously resolved—

1. "That this Assembly considers it to be one of the most important duties of the Christian Church to provide a sound literary, as well as theological, education for the young men intended for the office of the holy ministry, and over which it shall have complete control.

2. "That the total failure of all negotiations with the Managers and Visitors of the Belfast Institution to effect a satisfactory arrangement with that seminary demonstrates the impracticability of obtaining a safe and suitable education there.

3. "That the College Committee be empowered to take such steps as to them may appear expedient for the erection and endowment of a college for this Assembly."

One of the prominent advocates of these resolutions, and the necessity for a complete college, with classes in Arts and Theology, under the control of the Assembly, was the Rev. James Morgan, D.D., minister of Fisherwick Place Church, Belfast. Amongst other things, Dr. Morgan reminded the Assembly that in the history of all Churches it will be found that the education of candidates for the ministry has been kept under their own exclusive direction and control. No Church, he said, has a right to commit its students to any man on whom it is not ready to put the seal of its approval. "In my humble judgment," he added, "we have erred in ever consenting to place our students in another position to obtain their education." He expressed the determination of the Assembly to carry out this project either with the help of the Government or without it.

To the College Committee, as we have seen, was

entrusted the work of raising subscriptions for the erection and endowment of the college, and the money was beginning to flow in. But the high ground taken at the Assembly of 1844 was soon abandoned. At that very time the Government of Sir Robert Peel were preparing their plan for the establishment of the Queen's Colleges. Then began the first mutterings of the approaching storm. The cleavage began to show itself between the two great parties of the Assembly—the Belfast party, and what might be called the country party. On the one side the leaders were Rev. Dr. Cooke, Rev. Dr. Edgar, and Rev. Professor Wilson, of Belfast, and Rev. Dr. Stewart, of Broughshane. On the other side were Rev. Richard Dill, of Dublin, Rev. Dr. Goudy, of Strabane, Rev. John Rogers, of Comber, Rev. Dr. Brown, of Aghadowey, Rev. Dr. Huston, of Macosquin, Rev. S. M. Dill (then of Ballymena, afterwards Professor in Derry), Rev. N. M. Brown, of Limavady, and Rev. Matthew Wilson, of Derry. The Belfast party thought that the Assembly should accept, or at least give a fair trial to, the Queen's College in Belfast, for the undergraduate course of its students for the ministry, and seek from the Government an increase in the number and in the salaries of the Belfast theological professors. The "country party," if we may call them so, thought that the Assembly should hold by the position it had taken up at its meeting of 1844, and whether the Government would help it or not, that it should proceed with the establishment of a college in which both a literary and a theological education should be given to its students for the ministry.

At this time the struggle became unexpectedly intensified. Mrs. Magee, the widow of Rev. William Magee, of Lurgan, had for some time resided in Dublin, where she was a member of Usher's Quay congregation, under the ministry of Revs. S. Simpson and Richard Dill. Her two sons, one an ensign, and the other a surgeon in the Army, had both been cut off in early youth. Shortly after their death, her two brothers, both officers of high rank in the Army, died, leaving her the possessor of a vast fortune. During her lifetime, while living in a plain and quiet way in Dublin, she gave large sums to religious and charitable objects. She died in June, 1846. By her will she left upwards of £60,000 for various objects connected with the Irish Presbyterian Church. These objects were the Foreign Mission in India and elsewhere, the Home Mission, the Female Orphan School in connection with Usher's Quay congregation, and the erection and endowment of a Presbyterian College. Besides a large sum which she had already given to the building of a new Presbyterian church on Ormond Quay, she also left a sum of £1,350 for the benefit of that church. For the building of the college she left the handsome sum of £20,000.

In a speech of great eloquence and beauty, Mr. Dill announced these bequests to the General Assembly at its meeting in July, 1846. A committee was appointed to prepare a record of the Assembly's veneration for Mrs. Magee's memory, and its gratitude for her munificence. But the question immediately arose, How was the bequest to be applied? The majority, headed by the Belfast leaders, thought that as the Government were about to erect a Queen's College in Belfast, and had consented to endow additional Presbyterian Professors of Theology, as well as to increase the salary of the existing professors, the Magee bequest might be devoted to the erection of a theological college and providing bursaries for it, while its students could receive their literary training in the Queen's College. The minority held that the Queen's College arrangement was no better than that of the old Belfast Institution, inasmuch as the Assembly would have no voice in the selection of the professors from whom its students for the ministry were to receive part of their training. They reaffirmed the declaration of 1844 in support of the establishment of a college, literary as well as theological. And finally, they fell back on the terms of Mrs. Magee's will, and the undisputed fact that she had given her bequest in response to the resolutions of 1844 and the appeal made in connection with those resolutions.

The words of Mrs. Magee's will in this connection are—

"I give and bequeath to the Rev. Richard Dill, of Dublin, and the Rev. John Brown, of Aghadoey, and James Gibson, barrister-at-law, the sum of £20,000, in trust, to apply the same to the building and endowment of a college for the education of young men in preparation for the ministry in connection with the General Assembly, the same to be built where the said trustees or a majority of them shall determine, and to be subject to such rules, regulations, and discipline as they shall determine, subject to the advice and direction of the General Assembly in the first instance, and from time to time, as there may be occasion for altering the same."

The trustees were willing to build the college on whatever site the Assembly might determine, on condition that the college would have a full curriculum in Arts and Theology. The Assembly, however, would not bind itself to appoint forthwith all the professors required for such a curriculum. The trustees, therefore, declined to give the bequest for the purpose desired by the majority of the Assembly, namely, the building of a college in Belfast. The majority then proposed an amicable suit in Chancery for the purpose of settling, first, whether, in terms of the will, the college on which the Magee bequest was to be expended was to be a complete college, with a literary and scientific as well as a theological department, or to be a mere theological institution; and secondly, whether the right of selecting the site should belong to the trustees or to the General Assembly. "What began as an amicable suit," says Professor Witherow, "proved to be anything but amicable before it ended." The suit was not ended till April, 1851, when Master Brooke gave his judgment. He decided that by the true construction of the will the trustees were authorized—having sought for the advice and direction of the General Assembly—to determine themselves the rules, regulations, and discipline of the intended college; that the determination of the site belonged to them exclusively; and that the testatrix intended her bequest to be devoted to the establishment of a college in which a literary as well as a theological training should be given. Finally, with the assistance of representatives of both sides, Master Brooke drew up a scheme for the government of the college, and this scheme became in due time a decree of court.

Meanwhile the college question continued to agitate the Assembly from year to year. In 1850 the majority passed a resolution that a scheme should be drawn up for the Magee College, fixing the site in Belfast. But soon after the meeting of Assembly, eighteen of the Presbyteries of the Church passed resolutions condemning the choice of Belfast as the site for the proposed college, most of them recommending Derry, and the Coleraine Presbytery recommending Coleraine, for the intended site. In the meetings of Assembly of 1851, 1852, and 1853, excited debates took place, mainly on the question of the test of orthodoxy to be required from professors in the Magee College, but many side issues were raised from time to time which did not help to cultivate a judicial frame of mind. One particularly exciting day in 1851 was known as "Fighting Friday." There have been a good many "Fighting Fridays" since that time.[1]

The end of the matter was that the Assembly, after the judgment in Chancery and the determination of the trustees, saw the uselessness of waiting any longer for the Magee bequest. They were bound by their arrangement with Government to erect a theological college in Belfast. What is now known as the Assembly's College was erected in the vicinity of the Queen's College, which had been opened in 1849. The Assembly's College was opened in 1853, an address being given on the occasion by Dr. Merle D'Aubigné, the historian of the Reformation.

The trustees of Mrs. Magee's bequest chose Derry as the site of the college which was to be erected by her munificence. There, on a commanding site overlooking the Foyle, stands Magee College, opened in 1865, one of the most beautiful buildings to be seen in Ireland, calm and tranquil as if its establishment had not been the occasion of one of the hottest controversies ever waged.

Now the controversy is over, and our two colleges are both doing a good work. There is ample room for both. In both of them we have professors of whom any Church might well be proud. Many of our pro-

---

[1] Dill: *Prelatico-Presbyterianism*; Witherow: *Life of Dr. A. P. Goudy*; Reid: *History*.

fessors have enriched our theological, historical, and general literature. In the Assembly's College, Belfast, such works as the *Ancient Church, The Old Catholic Church,* and *The Ecclesiastical History of Ireland* have proceeded from the pen of the learned and now venerable President Killen; the late Professor Henry Wallace was the author of *Representative Responsibility;* Professor J. G. Murphy, D.D., LL.D., has written *Commentaries* on Genesis, Exodus, Leviticus, Psalms, and Revelation, and a work on *The Human Mind.* Professor Watts, D.D. LL.D., has written *The Newer Criticism* and *The Reign of Causality;* Professor Todd-Martin, D.Lit., is the author of *The Evolution Hypothesis,* a criticism of the new Cosmic Philosophy; while Professor Heron, M.A., one of the latest additions to the Professorial staff, has written a book on *The Church of the Sub-Apostolic Age.* The other Professors in Belfast are Rev. Professor Leitch, D.D., Rev. Professor Robinson, D.D., and Professor Walker, M.A.

In Magee College, Derry, the late Professor Croskery, D.D., wrote a book on *Plymouth Brethrenism,* but his principal writings were contributions to the *Pulpit Commentary,* and to the leading theological and other reviews and magazines. The late Professor Witherow, D.D., LL.D., was one of our most voluminous writers. His principal works are: *Historical and Literary Memorials of Presbyterianism in Ireland; The Boyne and Aghrim; Derry and Enniskillen; The Form of the Christian Temple;* and pamphlets on *The Apostolic Church, Three Prophets of our Own,* and other subjects. The late Professor Given, D.D, Ph.D., besides contributing to the *Pulpit Commentary,* wrote also a work on *Revelation, Inspiration and the Canon.* Professor Leebody, M.A., D.Sc., has recently written *Religious*

Teaching and Modern Thought. The other Professors in Magee College are Rev. Professor Petticrew, D.D., Rev. Professor Bigger, M.A., B.D., Rev. Professor Graham, M.A., Rev. Professor Dougherty, M.A., and Professor MacMaster, M.A., D.Lit.

Dublin Presbyterianism has borne a leading share in the establishment and endowment of both colleges. If, as we have seen, it was the money bequeathed by a member of a Dublin congregation that established Magee College, the Assembly's College, Belfast, is hardly less indebted to the liberality of members of our Dublin Churches. The late Mr. Adam S. Findlater, a member of Kingstown congregation, gave, anonymously, the large sum of £10,000 for the enlargement of the college buildings, and afterwards another £1,000; and Mr. William Todd, a member of Adelaide Road congregation, also gave £1,000 for that purpose.[1] Scholarships were also founded in connection with the Assembly's College by Mr. Findlater and Mr. Todd.

Besides Mrs. Magee's bequest, Magee College has received other benefactions from Dublin. The Rev. Richard Dill bequeathed money sufficient to endow permanently two professorships and to found two bursaries. Bursaries bearing the names of Findlater and Todd are also among the treasures of Magee College.

But rich as both our colleges are in men of intellect and power, it is not to be supposed that they are rich in pecuniary resources. There is quite insufficient provision for the annual maintenance and repair of the college buildings, not to speak of the salaries of the professors, which are far below what

---

[1] Hamilton: *History of the Irish Presbyterian Church*, p. 172 n.

they ought to be. In Derry, at least, more bursaries or scholarships might with great advantage be provided.¹ Wealthy members of our Church, whether in Dublin and the South, or in Belfast and Derry and the North, might do much good by the foundation of scholarships for the help and encouragement of our students for the ministry.

---

¹ Every donor of £50 to Magee College is entitled to the free education of one student through the Literary and Scientific course; every donor of £100 to the free education of one student through the entire curriculum (Arts and Theology); and every donor of £200 to a similar privilege in perpetuity.

CHAPTER XXVI.

THE ULSTER REVIVAL.

THE year 1859 is memorable as the year of the Ulster Revival—"the year of grace," as it was called. It began in a quiet work of spiritual awakening in the congregation of Connor, near Ballymena, under the ministry of Rev. J. H. Moore, afterwards minister of Elmwood, Belfast. Gradually it spread over the whole of Ulster, and even extended to Dublin, and parts of the South. Never was there such a universal interest in religious matters. Not only on the Sabbath, but on week days, the churches were crowded with multitudes of people, eager to hear the word of life. Revival meetings were even held on board the packet-steamers between Kingstown and Holyhead. Many of the most eminent ministers and most earnest laymen of the Irish Presbyterian Church trace their conversion to the Revival of 1859. The effect upon the morals of the people was most marked. An astonishing diminution took place in all kinds of crime. Even the presiding barristers at quarter sessions attributed the decrease in crime to the influence of the religious revival, and at some quarter sessions there was no criminal business at all. The annual party demonstrations, for which Ulster is unhappily so notorious, were for the time spontaneously repressed. "Even in Sandy Row," says Dr. Killen, "a portion of Belfast long noted as the grand theatre for the orgies and broils of Orangeism, that day passed away without disturbance. No drums were heard; no drunken Protestants were seen staggering through the street cursing the Pope and breathing out threatenings and slaughter against Romanists; but in many of its dwellings were heard the notes of grave sweet psalmody and the voice of prayer."[1]

In that year the General Assembly held its annual meeting in Dublin. Resolutions were passed expressive of thankfulness to God for the outpouring of His spirit upon the Church, and at the same time guarding against the abuses and errors which might arise in such a time of excitement. Brownlow North, the celebrated Scotch evangelist, addressed the Assembly, and a resolution was passed, recommending ministers to avail themselves of his evangelistic services.[2]

In 1860 the total number of ministers of the Irish Presbyterian Church was 566, of congregations, 525, licentiates, 64, and 45 had been sent as missionaries to the colonies. Thus the Presbyterian Church was steadily continuing to grow in numbers and in power.

In 1867 the General Assembly again met in Dublin. In that year the Lord Mayor of Dublin and the Lady Mayoress "honoured the Assembly with their presence," and invited the Moderator and members of Assembly to an entertainment at the Mansion House, which invitation was accepted.

---

[1] Reid: *History*, III., 513 (Killen's continuation).
[2] *Minutes of General Assembly.*

CHAPTER XXVII.

DISESTABLISHMENT.

THE social and political state of Ireland at this time was far from satisfactory. No measure of land reform had yet been introduced. Some of the leaders of the Tenant League had been bought off. They obtained important positions of trust and emolument under the Government. This was perhaps a politic way of dealing with the leaders, many of whom were mere place-hunters. But for the peace and prosperity of the country, for the credit and security of British rule in Ireland, it was a very impolitic and unstatesmanlike way of dealing with the grievances and poverty of the people. The perpetual Irish discontent which had existed ever since the Union, the attempts at insurrection, repeated every few years, were the natural result of such methods of governing a country.

The Irish people had tried constitutional agitation when the Tenant League was formed. But with what success? Year by year passed by; evictions were continuing; depopulation of the country was continuing; and yet nothing was being done. The more desperate spirits resolved once more to have recourse to arms. From about 1859 to 1867 the Fenian conspiracy spread itself over the country. For a long time its movements were kept secret. But about 1865 the Government began to get information by means of spies. In that year they seized and suppressed the *Irish People*, the newspaper established by James Stephens, and of which John O'Leary, Charles Kickham and T. C. Luby were the editors. They arrested at the same time O'Donovan Rossa, O'Leary, Luby and others. It was two months later before the arrest of James Stephens was effected. He bore the title of C.O.I.R. (Central Organiser of the Irish Republic), but was generally spoken of as the Head Centre. It was the 11th November when Stephens was arrested. After being brought before the magistrates, he was committed for trial, and imprisoned, meantime, in Richmond Prison, Dublin. On the 25th November, the news flashed through the city of Dublin that Stephens had escaped. It subsequently transpired that some of the prison officials had been long before sworn in as members of the Fenian Brotherhood, and they facilitated the escape of the Fenian leader.

"At no time probably since Emmet's insurrection," says Mr. A. M. Sullivan,[1] "were the Irish executive authorities thrown into such dismay and confusion as on this occasion. They now realised what it was to deal with a secret society. Whom could they trust? How could they measure their danger? Very evidently the ground beneath them was mined in all directions. Uncertainty magnified every danger. Meantime the most desperate efforts were made to secure Stephens. Cavalry scoured the country round. Police, scattered all over the city, particularly in suspected neighbourhoods, ransacked houses, tore down wainscoting, ripped up flooring, searched garrets, cellars, coalholes.

---

[1] *New Ireland*, p. 269.

Telegrams went flying all over the kingdom; steamers were stopped and the passengers examined. Gunboats put to sea and overhauled and searched fishing-smacks and coasters. Flaming placards appeared with 'One thousand pounds reward' in large letters, announcing the escape and offering a high price for the lost one. The 'C. O. I. R.' was all this time, and for a long period subsequently, secreted in the house of a Mrs. Butler of Summer Hill (Dublin), a woman of humble means. She knew her peril in sheltering him. She knew what would be her reward in surrendering him. She was poor, and could any moment earn £1,000 by giving merely a hint to the authorities. Stephens confided himself implicitly into her hands, and he did not trust her in vain.

"One Sunday evening about three months afterwards, a handsome open carriage-and-four drove through the streets of the Irish metropolis, two stalwart footmen seated in the dickey behind. Two gentlemen reclined lazily on the cushioned seat within. They proceeded northwards through Malahide and towards Balbriggan. Near the latter place, close by the sea, the carriage stopped. One of the occupants got out, walked down to the shore, where a boat was waiting. He entered and was pulled off to a lugger in the offing. The carriage returned to Dublin. The 'coachman,' 'postilion,' 'footmen,' and companion were all picked men of the 'I. R. B.', and were all armed to the teeth. The gentleman placed on board the lugger, now speeding down Channel with flowing sheet for France, was James Stephens, the 'Central Organiser of the Irish Republic.'"

But this arrest of the leaders did not put an end to the conspiracy. The most important incidents in the subsequent history of the "Fenian rising" were the attempted raid on Chester Castle (foiled through secret information supplied to the authorities), the attack on Kilmallock police-barrack, County Limerick, and the so-called "Battle of Tallaght" near Dublin. The spring of 1867 saw the end of the actual insurrection in Ireland itself. The severity of the weather did more to quell it than even the want of training and discipline among the insurgents, or the extensive military preparations made by the Government. In September of the same year took place the rescue of the Manchester prisoners and the murder of Sergeant Brett, who was in charge of the prison van. For this three of the rescuing party, Allen, Larkin and O'Brien, were afterwards hanged. In November took place the Clerkenwell explosion. A Fenian prisoner was confined in Clerkenwell Prison, London, and some of his friends, to rescue him, exploded a barrel of gunpowder against an outer wall, through which they hoped he would then effect his escape. But the explosion was the means of shattering several poor houses on the opposite side of the street, killing twelve persons and wounding a large number of others. Such were the closing incidents of what, we may sincerely hope, was the last attempt to take up arms in Ireland against British rule.

At last the eyes of English statesmen began to be opened to the necessity of doing something to redress the real grievances of Ireland. True, National Education had been and is a great boon, but it only made the Irish people more sensible of the wrongs under which they still laboured. Reforms for which North and South, Roman Catholic and Presbyterian, had been asking in vain, so long as they asked them in a constitutional way, were now about to be granted as the result of incessant insurrection.

In 1869 Mr. Gladstone introduced his Bill to disestablish the Irish Church. It was an act of simple justice. For centuries the Episcopalians had been the dominant party in Ireland, though only a small minority of the people. We have seen how they used their power. They monopolised, so far as they could, not only ecclesiastical but civil privileges. They persecuted those who ventured to worship God in a different way from theirs. Presbyterians and Roman Catholics they looked upon as alike the enemies of the "Protestant" faith. Indeed they sometimes regarded the Presbyterian, or "dissenter" as they inaccurately and contemptuously called him, with an intenser hatred than that with which they hated the "Papist." There were honourable exceptions, no doubt, but this was the rule.[1] But the day of retribution came. They had misused their power; now it was about to be taken from them. On the 26th July, 1869, the Irish Church Act received the Royal assent.

It cannot be said that the Presbyterian Church has suffered by the Irish Church Act. True, it was disendowed. But hitherto it had occupied an anomalous position. From its very entry into Ireland Presbyterianism had been endowed by the State. Presbyterian ministers for a time received the tithes, and then, when these were taken away, the Regium Donum was conferred in lieu of them.[2] Thus on the one hand it was recognised by Government; on the other hand it was treated as an intruder. Its ministers had more than

---

[1] See Froude: *English in Ireland*, Vol. I., 83, 237; II., 2, 3, etc.
[2] Mr. George Mathews, a well-informed authority, says that "The Regium Donum was in the first instance given on account (as the

once been imprisoned for preaching, and inhibited from doing so for the future. Its people, up to the present century, were debarred from holding the smallest office under the Crown unless they conformed to the Established Church. Henceforth all Churches in Ireland were to be put on the same footing so far as their civil rights and privileges are concerned. This is the law. But old ascendancy does not like to lower itself. Old monopolies are hard to break down. The old spirit of ascendancy is not dead yet, and the monopoly of place and power is still largely retained in the hands of the favoured few. Presbyterians are not unduly solicitous of state patronage and favour. They have before now existed without either. But it is their just demand that under a Government professing civil and religious liberty—a liberty which Irish Presbyterians have done so much to defend and maintain—no man shall be disqualified for holding positions of honour and emolument simply because of his religious opinions.

The ministers of the Irish Presbyterian Church acted nobly in the time of disendowment. They might have retained their endowments so long as they lived, or they might have commuted them in their own interest. But they chose rather to take the more self-denying course of commuting in the interests of the Church. The endowment thus created, called the Commutation Fund, amounted to £587,735, and yields an annual interest of about £25,000. At the same time the laity of the Church agreed to form a Sustentation Fund. They put £30,000 per annum before them as the amount to be aimed at, but it has actually realised about £25,000

---

patent bears) of the losses sustained by the Presbyterian clergy in being deprived of the tithes with which they were originally invested."—*Account of the Regium Donum.*

per annum. Financially, the Presbyterian Church is better off since the disendowment than before it.

Shortly after the Irish Church Act, Mr. Gladstone brought in his Irish Land Bill of 1870. The main provision of this Act was to grant compensation to tenants for improvements effected by them on the farms they occupied. In 1881 he brought in another Land Bill, granting the provisions for which the Tenant League had sought in vain thirty years before, but which the agitation of more recent years had shown to be a necessity—the famous "Three F's," *fair rents, fixity of tenure,* and *freedom of sale.* Conservative as well as Liberal Governments have had a share in the settlement of the Irish Land Question, and by the Ashbourne Act and other subsequent legislation, tenants have been empowered to obtain aid from the State in purchasing their farms. In the year 1888 the judicial rents fixed by the Land Courts had effected a diminution of nearly £1,000,000 on the former rents paid in Ireland.[1]

---

[1] Thom's *Official Directory*, 1890, p. 743.

CHAPTER XXVIII.

THE PRESENT OUTLOOK.

THROUGH these years of unrest and agitation the Irish Presbyterian Church has quietly held on its way. It has now 554 congregations under its care, and 636 ministers, as compared with the five ministers of 1642 and the 400 of 1840. For the most part it has held aloof from political controversy, though at the introduction of Mr. Gladstone's Home Rule Bill in 1886, the General Assembly unanimously passed resolutions deprecating the establishment of a separate Parliament for Ireland or any legislation tending to imperil the Legislative Union or to interfere with the unity and supremacy of the Imperial Parliament.

It is a gratifying fact that the Presbyterians of the South and West have, through all these years, lived on friendly terms with their Roman Catholic fellow-countrymen. Over and over again it has been reported at the meetings of the Synod of Dublin, which extends over the three provinces of Munster, Leinster and Connaught, as well as part of Ulster, that none of our ministers or missionaries or colporteurs have been molested or interfered with in the discharge of their duty. This is sufficient proof that the agitation of recent years is not a movement inspired, to any perceptible extent at least, by religious fanaticism or bigotry. So far as the Irish Presbyterians of the South and West are concerned, they hold tenaciously by their Presbyterian faith, they are strongly opposed to what they regard as the errors of Rome, many of them differ politically from their Roman Catholic neighbours, yet their uniform testimony is, that they, a small minority, have been treated with kindness by the great mass of the population among whom their lot is cast.

A great change has undoubtedly taken place in the attitude of the Irish people towards their priests. There have been not merely indications, but many strong manifestations, of revolt against priestly and even Papal authority. Fulminations from Rome against the Land League and recent agrarian movements produced little effect upon the Irish Roman Catholics, except to draw out a spirit of insubordination to the ecclesiastical power. Whether this will prove an unmixed good remains yet to be seen. There is a danger of revolt against all authority, of casting-off all religion, and of utter infidelity and lawlessness as the result.

The Irish Roman Catholic clergy, headed by Archbishops Walsh and Croke, are at the present time actively engaged in promoting a great temperance crusade, in commemoration of the labours of Father Mathew. Much good is being done by administration of the temperance pledge, and for many years flourishing temperance societies—sodalities and confraternities —have been in existence in connection with Roman Catholic churches. "The League of the Cross" is now extending its temperance work into all the parishes of the country. At the same time, it seems to us that temperance work in this country is hardly as practical as it might be. Temperance reformers, both Protestant and Roman

Catholic, should do more to provide counter-attractions to those afforded by the public-house. Farmers who visit country towns on fair-days and market-days, working men in our towns and cities as well as in country districts, and the fishermen in our sea-board towns, have often no other place of resort but the public-house. The Irish Temperance League has indeed done good work by its cafés, workmen's taverns, and cabmen's shelters, in Belfast at least. In Ballymoney, Co. Antrim, a company has been organised, by whose enterprise a place has been provided, mainly in the interests of the farmers, where good and substantial food and temperance refreshments can be obtained, and where clean and comfortable stables can also be secured. This example might be followed in every country town in Ireland. Why should not Protestants and Roman Catholics work together in philanthropic work of this kind? Intemperance is still Ireland's greatest curse.

The Protestant Episcopal Church of Ireland is perhaps as vigorous as ever it was. Many of its own best people assert that it has gained, rather than lost, by disestablishment. It may have lost in a financial way, and may still lose, as the landlord class is further reduced in wealth and numbers. But it has gained in a deepening of its spiritual life, in the increased activity and earnestness of its clergy, in the increased liberality of its people, and in the growing interest which they are taking in the Church's work, in proportion as they have been admitted to a larger share in its administration and government. In recent years it has numbered among its prominent leaders Biblical scholars like Archbishop Trench, Bishop Alexander and Dr. Charles H. H. Wright; preachers like John Gregg, Bishop of

Cork, Achilles Daunt, Dean of Cork, and Dr. Reichel, Bishop of Meath; theologians like Dr. Jellett and Dr. Salmon, the late and present Provosts of Trinity College; and ecclesiastical historians like Dr. Reeves and Professor Stokes; while in the present Archbishop of Dublin, Lord Plunket, it has a man whose great desire, like that of Archbishop Ussher, is to draw closer together the divided branches of Irish Protestantism.

At a recent meeting of the General Synod of the Protestant Episcopal Church, resolutions in favour of union with other Protestant Churches were heartily adopted. On the part of Irish Presbyterians such a desire has long been felt. The advances have hitherto, however, been from the Presbyterian side. Episcopalian ministers have been free to occupy our pulpits, and some of them have done so. But Presbyterian ministers are shut out of Episcopalian pulpits by the theory of "apostolical succession" and "holy orders." How far the resolutions adopted by the Synod will go towards breaking down this old exclusiveness still remains to be seen. There are few Presbyterians, at any rate, who are not willing to hold out the right hand of fellowship to their Episcopal brethren, and to co-operate with them in the service of their one Great Master.

The Irish Methodist Church is also an energetic body, though much smaller in numbers than either the Episcopalian or Presbyterian Churches. Wesley and his followers helped by their coming into Ireland to check the tide of moderatism and indifference which was flowing over the Churches in the close of the eighteenth century. Ever since, the labours of Irish Methodist ministers, particularly in the South and West, have been greatly blessed. All denominations were aroused and helped by the work of such devoted evangelists as Gideon Ouseley and Graham Campbell. The history of Irish Methodism has recently been written by one of its own ministers, Rev. C. H. Crookshank.

The Congregational and Baptist Churches have never made much progress in Ireland, though to the former belonged one of the most eloquent preachers and most ardent workers which Irish Protestantism has ever had, the Rev. William Urwick, D.D., of Dublin.

What the future may have in store for us in the domain of political changes—who can tell? But we look forward hopefully to the religious future of our country. Education has done much for Ireland. Intercourse with the great Republic across the Ocean has prompted a spirit of independence and inquiry. We are already in a "new Ireland." There is a loud call to Christian men of every creed to do all that in them lies to guide, affectionately and wisely, the forces of the people's will and power. In the great work of national progress and spiritual reformation, we may hope that the Presbyterians of Ireland, holding by their time-honoured principles of civil and religious liberty, maintaining their high standard of public and social morality, and sympathising with every fair and legitimate aspiration of their countrymen, will take an active and honourable part.

END OF PART I.

PART II.

HISTORY OF CONGREGATIONS OUTSIDE ULSTER.

I.

PRESBYTERY OF ATHLONE.

[The Presbytery of Athlone was formed in the year 1841. The congregations first constituting it were Galway, Mullingar, Athlone, Birr, and Moyvore, all of which had previously belonged to the Presbytery of Dublin.]

ATHENRY.

IN April, 1872, the Presbyterians in and around Athenry sent a memorial to the Presbytery of Athlone, asking to be supplied with ordinances. The first minister was Rev. Archibald Henderson, ordained there September 25th, 1874. Mr. Henderson resigned in 1876, and was for a time minister in Canada, but returned to Ireland, and has been minister at Malin, Co. Donegal, since 1878. The Rev. Samuel Walker was ordained at Athenry, September 17th, 1878, but removed to Donaghadee in 1882. He was succeeded by the present minister, Rev. T. H. Burkitt, installed there May 4th, 1882. Mr. Burkitt had previously been missionary in the Southern Highlands of Donegal for about seventeen years. During his ministry at Athenry the present ornamental iron church was erected, and a manse procured and fitted up, both standing on about two acres of ground on the outskirts of the town.

ATHLONE.

In 1704 Major Thomas Handock supplicated the

Synod of Ulster to send supplies of preaching to Athlone.[1] In 1706, the Rev. George Lang of Newry, writing to the Rev. Robert Wodrow, minister at Eastwood, near Glasgow, says, " Ye small congregations of Gallway and Athlone have of Late submitted to our Genl. Synod."[2] The first ordained minister of the Presbyterian congregation at Athlone was the Rev. Samuel Dunlop, who was settled there in 1708. He resigned in 1722. The congregation then became extinct, but was revived in 1835, by the Rev. Dr. Horner of Dublin, who visited Athlone by instructions of the Dublin Presbytery, and found about twenty-four Presbyterian families (over eighty individuals) in and around the town. The Rev. E. H. Allen was installed there by the Presbytery of Dublin in 1837. Its subsequent ministers have been Rev. James Mawhinney (1851-1861); Rev. S. E. Brown, M.A. (1861-1878), now minister of Clough, Co. Antrim ; and Rev. Robert Waston, B.D., the present minister, ordained there in 1879.

BALLINASLOE.

In 1844 the congregation of Ballinasloe was organised, largely through the efforts of Rev. John Edmonds, who had been appointed to the itinerating department of the General Assembly's Home Mission. Soon after this, a church and manse were erected. Considerable delay took place in procuring a suitable site, as the Earl of Clancarty was most unwilling to afford facilities for the erection in "his town" of what he called a "Separatist" place of worship. But the members of the infant congregation were firm and resolute, and

---

[1] Killen: *History of Congregations of the Presbyterian Church in Ireland*, Belfast, 1886.

[2] *Woodrow MSS.*, Letters, IV., No. 59.

they succeeded at last in obtaining a valuable and suitable site. The contractor unfortunately failed when the walls were ready for the roof, but a member of the congregation, the late Mr. James Campbell, J.P., of Galway—then a young man—lent £200 to put on the roof. A minister was called, but difficulties arose about his ordination, and he went to America. The congregation dwindled away during the time of the famine until scarce a fraction of it remained. At length, on the earnest solicitation of Dr. Edgar, the present minister, Rev. James W. Whigham, was induced to come and "try to raise the fallen tabernacle in Ballinasloe." Mr. Whigham had early shown a missionary spirit, and had been invited by Dr. Morgan, the first Convener of our Foreign Mission, to go as missionary to India. But he had concluded that he was better fitted for work at home. He was ordained at Ballinasloe in November, 1851. It was then the day of small things in that now flourishing Western congregation. His call was signed by six persons. But under his faithful ministry, and with an increase of Scotch and North of Ireland residents in the neighbourhood, the work grew and prospered. The church had to be enlarged by the addition of the manse, which was previously a separate part of the same building, and the present commodious manse was built a little outside the town. This enterprise, which cost £1,146, was finished without a penny of debt—all giving and all working—in the year 1860. Dr. Whigham has been successively Convener of the Continental Mission, the Church Extension Mission, and now of the Sustentation Fund. He was Moderator of the General Assembly in the year 1885-1886. He is author of the *Presbyterian Map of Ireland*, an ornamental map on which the Presbyterian congregations and mission-stations all over Ireland are marked in red, with a picturesque border containing historic scenes in Presbyterian history and much interesting information. He received the degree of D.D. in 1888 from the Irish Presbyterian Theological Faculty.

CREGGS AND ROSCOMMON.

The congregation of Creggs was organised in 1863. Its first minister was the Rev. Robert Kennedy, who was ordained there on the 31st March, 1863. In 1867 Mr. Kennedy resigned the pastorate of Creggs, and was designated by the Athlone Presbytery to the Colonial Mission. He was succeeded by the Rev. Samuel Lyle Harrison, licentiate of the Route Presbytery, who was ordained at Creggs, November 19th, 1867. Mr. Harrison removed to Clogher, in the Connaught Presbytery, in 1872, thence to Dromore West, and afterwards to Castlebellingham, where he now labours. In 1873 the General Assembly united the two congregations of Creggs and Roscommon.

The congregation of Roscommon was organised in 1867. After the union of Creggs and Roscommon, the first minister of the united congregations was the Rev. Wm. Smyth, who was installed there on the 5th August, 1873. Mr. Smyth removed to Loughgall in 1880, and was succeeded by the Rev. A. Ferguson (previously of Corboy), who was installed at Creggs and Roscommon, June 21st, 1881. Mr. Ferguson accepted a call to Kilkinamurray, near Rathfriland, in 1882. He was succeeded by the present minister, Rev. Joseph McCorkell, licentiate of the Presbytery of Derry, who was ordained to the pastorate of Creggs and Roscommon, August 1st, 1882.

Corboy.

A detailed account of Corboy congregation is given in Dr. Killen's *History of Congregations*. Its first minister, whose name has not been preserved, was settled there about 1675. The subsequent ministers have been

Rev. John Mairs (1697-1706).
Rev. William Hare (1708-1720).
Rev. James Bond (1723-1762).
Rev. Joseph Martin (1765-1767).
Rev. William Fleming (1767-1784).
Rev. Robert Rodgers (1785-1791).
Rev. Joseph Osborne (1792-1799).
Rev. James Wilson (1801-1816).
Rev. Thomas Kennedy (1817-1839).
Rev. John Henry (1839-1843).
Rev. John McCubbin (1843-1847).
Rev. Robert W. Fleming (1848-1860).
Rev. Alexander Ferguson (1860-1881).
Rev. William Burke (1881).

Ennis.

Ennis is the first Presbyterian congregation which was organised in the county of Clare, in the present century at least. In Cromwell's time there were Puritan ministers (whether Presbyterian or Independent we cannot now definitely ascertain) in Ennis and Six-Mile-Bridge, midway between Ennis and Limerick. There was an interesting Moravian settlement for some years near Corofin, eight miles north of Ennis. Two Clare gentlemen, Messrs. Burton and Blood, joined the United Brethren, or Moravians, towards the end of last century, and settled a pastor and colony from Germany, giving land for church and parsonage, and letting small farms to the settlers. All flourished till 1798. The congregation then numbered at least a hundred, when the Rebellion burst upon them and, like many of our Presbyterian congregations throughout the South and West at that time, the little community was dispersed.[1]

The first efforts to gather together the Presbyterian residents at Ennis in this century were made by the Rev. Dr. Wilson of Limerick, who reported to the Presbytery of Munster in 1845 that he had visited Ennis, and would recommend it being taken up as a station. For a time the Rev. Archibald Lowry faithfully laboured there as missionary, and other supplies were sent, but chiefly through lack of funds nothing permanent was done.

About 1853 Dr. Brown of Aghadowey wrote to Rev. J. W. Whigham, then recently settled at Ballinasloe, requesting him to go to Ennis, find out the number and circumstances of the Presbyterians there, and report to the Mission Board. Dr. Whigham did so, and as the result of his visits and representations a congregation was organised. Just about that time an old college friend of Dr. Whigham's arrived on a visit to him at Ballinasloe. This was the Rev. Thomas Warren, who had been licensed by the Belfast Presbytery in 1850, and after spending nearly three years as minister of a church in the city of Baltimore, in the United States, had returned to Ireland in ill-health. Dr. Whigham induced his friend to settle in Ennis. The first services were held in the Wesleyan chapel, and afterwards in the Record Court, the use of which was most kindly granted by three successive high sheriffs. One of the local priests, however, complained

---

[1] Letter of Rev. T. Warren to the author.

to the Grand Jury, and the Presbyterian congregation deemed it prudent to withdraw. They then resolved to build a church of their own. Mr. Warren was formally installed by the Presbytery of Athlone, June 6th, 1854, and the church, a neat Gothic structure, was opened by Rev. Dr. Cooke of Belfast on May 16th, 1856. Church and manse were erected at a cost of £1,100 and left free of debt, mainly through the exertions of Mr. Warren, by whom also, before his resignation, funds were collected and used for the purchase of the ground (upwards of half-an-acre) on which the church and manse stand, and it is now rent free for ever.

Besides his services in Ennis, Mr. Warren conducted services, in the early years of his ministry, at Kilrush and Miltown Malbay. The erection of Kilrush into a congregation relieved him of this portion of his work, but he also held services at Carhue, eight miles from Ennis, which still remains in connection with the congregation, and at Clare Castle, a military station, two and a half miles from Ennis.

On October 2nd, 1885, the Rev. Richard Scott, licentiate of the Glendermot Presbytery, was ordained as assistant and successor to Mr. Warren in the pastorate of Ennis congregation. Far from the centre of Presbyterianism, labouring in much isolation, the minister of Ennis deserves the sympathy and encouragement of the Irish Presbyterian Church.

Galway.

Galway is a historic congregation. Its foundations were laid in persecution. The first Presbyterian minister who preached there was imprisoned for presuming to "divide the Protestant interest, at a time when the Papists were rapidly conforming."[1] This was the Rev. William Biggar of Limerick, who came to preach in Galway in 1698 at the request of some Presbyterian residents in that city. But persecution did not crush the spirit of the people, for the Rev. Thomas Hooks was ordained as minister of the Presbyterian congregation in Galway in 1700. The subsequent ministers were Rev. Nathaniel Orr (1707-1710) and Rev. Alexander Hamilton (1710-1722). The congregation had become so weakened, that no Presbyterian minister was settled there for a hundred and ten years. The Rev. Joseph Fisher was ordained there in 1835. He resigned in 1845, and was succeeded by Revs. William Adair (1846-1882), Dr. W. Ross Hamilton (1872, died 1873), John C. Moore (1875-1879), Dr. J. G. Robb (1879-1881), and the present minister, Rev. John C. Clarke, M.A., who was installed in 1882. Mr. Clarke is Convener of the General Assembly's Church Extension Mission. The late James Campbell, Esq., J.P., Mrs. Wilson, sister of the late Rev. William Adair, and John Miller, Esq., have been among the most active and generous members of the Presbyterian Church in Galway in recent years.

Longford.

The congregation of Longford owes its origin to the zealous missionary labours of the Rev. Henry Wallace, afterwards minister at Cork and Derry, and finally Professor of Christian Ethics in the Assembly's College, Belfast. As the result of Mr. Wallace's labours, a congregation was organised at Longford, in 1833, and its first minister, the Rev. Samuel McCutcheon, was ordained there in 1834. Mr. McCutcheon died, after a

---

[1] See above, page 16.

faithful ministry, in 1875, and was succeeded by the Rev. Alexander Rentoul, M.A. (1875-1881), afterwards minister of Sandymount, and by the present minister, Rev. Alfred H. Rentoul, M.A., who was ordained there in 1882.

MOYVORE.

The congregation of Moyvore was organised by the Dublin Presbytery in the year 1838. The church was built in 1840. The first minister was the Rev. John Fisher, ordained there March 30th, 1841. He was succeeded by Rev. John Boyd, licentiate of Belfast Presbytery, who was ordained there February 7th, 1844, by the Presbytery of Athlone. On that occasion the Presbytery were entertained at dinner by Benjamin Digby, Esq., of Mountjoy Square, Dublin, and Moyvore. Mr. Boyd was succeeded by Rev. Mr. Watson (previously of the Belfast Town Mission), in 1855. The manse was built in 1869 by the efforts of Mr. Watson. Mr. Watson died September 17th, 1873, and the present minister, Rev. John Topping, M.D., was ordained there in February, 1874.

MULLINGAR.

The congregation of Mullingar was organised in 1821, mainly by the labours of Rev. James Horner of Mary's Abbey, Dublin. Mr. Horner visited Mullingar in 1820 and 1821, and preached to the Presbyterians there. In January, 1821, he gave the Dublin Presbytery a report of his visit and a list of the Presbyterians in and near Mullingar who were disposed to favour the establishment of a congregation there. In August, 1821, he read to the Presbytery a letter from Colonel Armstrong, agent of the Earl of Granard, granting a site for a

Presbyterian church at Mullingar. The church was built soon after, and its first minister, Rev. Alexander Gibson, was ordained there in 1823. He was succeeded by the Rev. R. H. Harshaw (1858-1859) now of Mountmellick, and the present minister, Rev. Matthew Murphy, who was ordained there in 1862. When the Athlone Presbytery was formed in 1841, the congregation of Mullingar was transferred to it from the Presbytery of Dublin.

TULLY.

The congregation of Tully was organised by the Presbytery of Athlone in December, 1844, in compliance with a memorial from Presbyterian families in the neighbourhood of Coolarty and Tully. The first minister was the Rev. Thomas J. Patteson, who was installed there March 21st, 1845. Mr. Patteson resigned in August of the same year, having accepted a call to a congregation of the Free Church of Scotland. He was succeeded by the Rev. John Edmonds, who had previously been labouring as itinerant missionary in County Longford and other midland counties, and who was installed at Tully, September 16th, 1846. Mr. Edmonds, after a faithful ministry of more than twenty years, died on the 8th November, 1867. The next minister was the Rev. William Moore, M.A., who was ordained at Tully, November 3rd, 1868. In December, 1869, Mr. Moore went as missionary to Spain, at the call of the Board of Missions. He was succeeded by Rev. Walter Anderson, ordained at Tully, April 17th, 1871. Mr. Anderson died in 1873 and was succeeded by the Rev. William Moore, who had returned from Spain and was installed as minister of Tully for the second time, May 26th, 1875. In 1879

Mr. Moore removed to Dublin, where he became minister of Jervis Street Mission church, and afterwards of Gloucester Street, whence he once more removed to Spain. Mr. Moore was for some years editor of *Daybreak*, the children's magazine of the Irish Presbyterian Church. He is now principal of the training college for Spanish pastors in connection with the Presbyterian Church.

On the 10th February, 1880, the Rev. William Burke was ordained minister of Tully. In 1881 the congregation of Corboy having become vacant, the two congregations were united, and Mr. Burke became minister of the joint charge. This arrangement, however, did not prove satisfactory in its working, and the union of the two congregations was dissolved by the Assembly of 1886, Mr. Burke remaining minister of Corboy. The present minister, Rev. James Mitchell (previously of Newcastle, Co. Down), was installed as minister of Tully, April 12th, 1887.

Tully Presbyterian Church is about three miles from Edgeworthstown, a station on the Midland Railway to Sligo. It takes its name from the townland Tully, the property of J. W. Bond, Esq., D.L., whose father, Captain Willoughby Bond, was an elder of the congregation till the time of his death, and whose great-grandfather, Rev. James Bond, was Presbyterian minister of Corboy. The only elder now in connection with the congregation of Tully is G. W. Wilson-Slator, Esq., D.L., who takes an active part in the proceedings of the General Assembly.

The church is a neat Gothic building of dressed stone. It was built in 1855, the services having previously been held in a hired house. The manse, which has four acres of land as a glebe, was built about 1860.

It is two miles from the church, on the road to Castlepollard, where the minister conducts public worship on the afternoon of every alternate Sabbath. This station is also ministered to by the Rev. John Rainey of Killucan.

II.

PRESBYTERY OF BAILIEBOROUGH.

KELLS, CO. MEATH.

KELLS, in the County Meath, is one of the mos ancient and interesting towns in Ireland. Sir William Wilde speaks of it as "one of the most memorable places in early Irish ecclesiastical history." It abounds with valuable architectural remains, such as sculptured crosses, ancient inscriptions, a round tower, etc., and is closely associated with the early labours of Columbkille, the Apostle of Iona and of Scotland.

Two of the most ancient books in the world are closely associated with Kells. One of these is the "Book of Kells," which may be seen in the Library of Trinity College, Dublin, where it is an object of great interest to visitors and scholars. It is a Latin manuscript of the Gospels, beautifully illuminated. It was written in the sixth century, was discovered in the Abbey of Kells, and is generally attributed to Columbkille and his disciples.[2]

The other book is called the "Cathac." It is believed to be the identical Latin Psalter copied from the original by Columbkille in 560. The Cathac may be seen in

---

[1] All the congregations of this Presbytery, with the exception of Kells, are in the province of Ulster. Their history is therefore not given here.

[2] See Gilbert on the National Manuscripts of Ireland. See also Stokes: *Ireland and the Celtic Church.*

the Royal Irish Academy, Dublin. It was enclosed in a bronze shrine, mounted with silver. On this shrine or casket is an Irish inscription stating that it was made in the town of Kells by one Litric MacAedha, who worked in the house of the Abbot, Donal O'Rafferty. This fixes the age for us, as O'Rafferty died in 1098. This shrine (or *Cumdhach*) is thus about 800 years old, and is a beautiful specimen of artistic skill and excellent workmanship.[1]

It is only in recent years that a Presbyterian congregation has been established at Kells. It was organised by the Presbytery of Bailieborough in 1869, having been for several years previous conducted as a mission station. The first minister was the Rev. James Maconaghie, M.A. (now of Fortwilliam Park Church, Belfast), who was ordained at Kells in 1869. During Mr. Maconaghie's ministry a neat and substantial church was built in 1871. Mr. Maconaghie was succeeded by Rev. Patrick W. White (now of Stonebridge), who was ordained in 1872. The next minister was Rev. Alex. McClinchie (now of New South Wales), who was ordained in 1879. Mr. McClinchie was succeeded by the Rev. H. H. Moore, M.A., who was ordained in 1883. Mr. Moore removed to Hilltown, Rathfriland, in 1885, and was succeeded by the present minister, Rev. William Fearon, B.A., who was installed at Kells, September 2nd, 1885. By Mr. Fearon's energetic efforts, a manse has recently been erected in connection with the congregation. Besides his services at Kells, Mr. Fearon preaches also on alternate Sabbaths at Navan, where there is a flourishing station.

---

[1] *Kells and its Books.* By Rev. W. Fearon, B.A., of Kells, in *Daybreak*, Feb., 1889.

III.

PRESBYTERY OF CONNAUGHT.[1]

[The Presbytery of Connaught was formed in 1825.]

BALLINA.

BALLINA congregation was for some years maintained as a mission station in connection with Killala. The first services were commenced there in 1835 by the Rev. David Rodgers, minister of Killala. In 1844 the Rev. Archibald Lowry, afterwards minister of 1st Donegal, was appointed to take sole charge of the station. He removed to Roundstone, County Galway, in November, 1845.

The next minister was the Rev. Thomas Armstrong, licentiate of the Presbytery of Monaghan. Mr. Armstrong came in November, 1845, and was ordained May 6th, 1846. The Presbytery of Connaught had in 1844 recommended the erection of a Presbyterian church in Ballina, the average attendance of Presbyterian worshippers at the service there being then about forty. For some time the services were held in a schoolroom, but at last by the exertions of Mr. Armstrong a church was erected. It was opened in July, 1851, by the

---

[1] Most of the particulars regarding the congregations of this Presbytery have already been given by Dr. Killen in his *History of Congregations*. Some of the additional facts here stated are from the minutes of the Connaught Presbytery.

Rev. Dr. Cooke of Belfast. Subsequently a manse and school were also erected.

Mr. Armstrong's ministry at Ballina was commenced in trying times. Soon after his settlement there the terrors of the Irish famine swept over the land, and nowhere were its ravages more severely felt than in Connaught. Mr. Armstrong took an active and prominent part in the measures which were adopted to alleviate the distress and sufferings of the people. He was a member of the Ballina Relief Committee, on which were to be found the leading ministers and members of all denominations, who, laying aside their sectarian differences, worked together for the help of their starving fellow-creatures. The chairman was Colonel, afterwards Sir Arthur Knox Gore, Bart. Other members, besides Mr. Armstrong the Presbyterian minister, were the Rector, Rev. Joseph Verschoyle, his curate, Rev. Joseph Kinkead, and the Rev. Hugh Conway, then Roman Catholic administrator of the parish and now Bishop of the diocese. Of that committee of 1846, Bishop Conway and the Rev. Thomas Armstrong are now the only survivors.[1]

Mr. Armstrong's labours and experiences at this time were very similar to those of the Rev. Samuel Craig, which are related below in an account of Summerhill congregation, Presbytery of Munster.

Terrible poverty and desolation followed the famine and the fever which accompanied and succeeded it. Emigration then became the resort and refuge of many. The poverty of those who remained led to wholesale evictions from their small holdings. Of this Mr.

---

[1] "My Life in Connaught." By Rev. Thomas Armstrong. *Missionary Herald*, 1889, 1890.

Armstrong says: "There would have been wisdom in this course if carried out with kindness and care. Provision should have been made for these humble people to enable them to emigrate with comfort to another land where their toil would be repaid by prosperity and comfort. But, as a rule, this was not done. Entire families were turned out on the roadside without a shelter, sometimes even in the cold and rain of the winter time. 'The Crowbar Brigade' unroofed the houses and broke down the walls, so that the poor creatures had nothing to protect them from the weather, even in the ruins of their old homes. . . . The mode of carrying out clearings was such as to leave a sting of bitterness in the hearts of the evicted, which they carried to other lands, and still rankles in their breasts. I have seen crowds of peasantry, as they were about to take their seats on the long Bianconi car, kneel down in the open street of Ballina, and invoke the direst curses on those who had forced them into exile."

At the visitation of Ballina congregation by the Connaught Presbytery in 1862, the representatives of the congregational committee were: David Baird, Henry Cummings, William Little, J. W. Chisholm. There were then thirty-six families and sixty-one communicants connected with the congregation.

The Rev. Dr. Edgar of Belfast, who visited Connaught about the beginning of the famine time, was so touched by the destitution of the people, both spiritual and temporal, that he appealed to the Presbyterians of Ulster for practical help. The result was not only a large contribution of pecuniary relief for the starving people, but also the establishment of the Connaught Scriptural and Industrial Schools. Of these schools, with their headquarters at Ballina, the Rev. Robert

Allen, previously of Stewartstown, was appointed the first superintendent.

Mr. Allen died in 1865. At his death Mr. Armstrong was appointed Superintendent of the Connaught schools, and resigned the pastorate of Ballina, April 8th, 1868. Mr. Armstrong in this new sphere has done a great and good work. The Ballina Orphanage, watched over with such care by him and Mrs. Armstrong, has afforded a shelter, a home, and an education to hundreds of orphan children, many of whom are now occupying positions of honour and usefulness.

The next minister of Ballina congregation was the Rev. Robert Duff, M.A., who was ordained there on December 30th, 1868. Mr. Duff resigned, January 31st, 1877, having accepted a call to St. George's Presbyterian Church, Liverpool. He was succeeded by the Rev. T. R. Cairns, previously minister of Moy, who was installed in Ballina, October 24th, 1877, but resigned in August, 1879, having been appointed to the Colonial Mission in New Zealand.

The present minister, Rev. John Cairns, previously of Turlough, in the same Presbytery, was installed in Ballina, October 29th, 1879. There are now fifty-five families and eighty-two communicants connected with the congregation.

BALLINGLEN.

The first minister of Ballinglen was the Rev. Michael Brannigan. Mr. Brannigan was a Roman Catholic by birth, a native of Co. Tyrone. The study of the Bible in the Irish language led him to question the teachings of the Church of Rome. He sought counsel from the Rev. Robert Allen, then of Stewartstown, and finally resolved to enter the Presbyterian ministry. He was ordained in 1845 as itinerant missionary in Mayo and Sligo in connection with the Students' Missionary Association of Belfast College. By his indefatigable labours, twelve new mission stations were established before the end of 1846. Among these was Ballinglen, over which district Mr. Brannigan was appointed minister after the appointment of Rev. Robert Allen as superintendent of the Connaught schools. In 1848 the congregation of Ballinglen was formally organised, and the funds were collected by Mr. Brannigan for the erection of a church, which was opened free of debt in 1850 by the Rev. Dr. Cooke of Belfast. In 1864 both church and manse were burned down, but were rebuilt in 1865. Mr. Brannigan died in November, 1874.

He was succeeded by the Rev. William Fearon, B.A., now of Kells, Co. Meath. Mr. Fearon was ordained at Ballinglen, January 26th, 1876, and resigned in 1879. The present minister, Rev. James Wilkin, M.A., was ordained on April 10th, 1879.

BALLYMOTE.

The congregation of Ballymote dates from about the year 1760. The first ministers were successively Rev. Hugh Nesbit, Rev. Joseph King, and Rev. Booth Caldwell, who were ministers of Sligo and Ballymote. Mr. Caldwell died in 1810. Rev. Jacob Scott was the next minister. After labouring in the joint charge of Sligo and Ballymote, he was appointed in 1823 as minister of Ballymote exclusively. When the Connaught Presbytery visited the congregation in 1826, during Mr. Scott's ministry, there were two elders, thirty families and fifty communicants. The elders were William Cunningham and Robert Orr, and the representatives of the congregation were Russel Hunter and James Orr. Mr. Scott was succeeded by the Rev. James Fleming, licentiate of the Tyrone Presbytery, who was ordained at Ballymote, January 22nd, 1829. Mr. Fleming died on May 9th, 1850.

The present minister, Rev. John Dewart, was ordained there October 9th, 1850.

In April, 1856, it was reported to the Presbytery that there was a debt on the manse at Ballymote of over £100, that the church was in need of extensive repairs, almost equivalent to re-building, and that the landlord, Sir Robert Gore Booth, had resolutely and obstinately refused to grant a lease in perpetuity, and that thus the congregation were cut off from the possibility of obtaining a grant from the Church and Manse Fund. It was also reported that Jemmett Duke, Esq., of Newpark, had spontaneously offered a suitable site for church and manse in perpetuity, and that the congregation were in favour of accepting this offer and erecting a new church and school. The Presbytery approved of this proposal, expressing at the same time their regret at Sir R. G. Booth's action and their thanks to Mr. Duke. On this site church, manse and schoolhouse, with teacher's apartments, have since been built.

Mr. Dewart becoming infirm, the Rev. Joseph Northey, licentiate of the Presbytery of Derry, was ordained as his assistant, March 3rd, 1886. Mr. Northey removed to Turlough and Castlebar in 1888, and was succeeded by the Rev. Hugh Montgomery Knox, who was ordained in Ballymote, October 9th, 1888, as assistant and successor to Rev. John Dewart.

BOYLE.

The congregation of Boyle is associated with the

early labours of the Rev. John Hall, D.D., now the distinguished minister of Fifth Avenue Presbyterian Church, New York. When he was labouring as missionary at Camlin, he preached fortnightly in the Wesleyan church at Boyle. On Mr. Hall's removal to 1st Armagh, he was succeeded by the Rev. James Robinson. Under Mr. Robinson's ministry the congregation of Boyle was formally organised, February 10th, 1857. Mr. Robinson resigned, owing to ill-health, and died June 27th, 1858. He was succeeded by the Rev. R. A. Caldwell. During Mr. Caldwell's ministry a church and manse were built at a cost of £955, on a site kindly presented by Captain Robertson. The church was opened in May, 1859. Mr. Caldwell removed to Australia in October, 1863. He was succeeded by the Rev. David McKee, afterwards minister at Ballywalter, Rutland Square, Dublin, and Christchurch, New Zealand. After Mr. McKee's removal to Ballywalter, the present minister, Rev. John Watson, was ordained at Boyle, November 13th, 1866. There are now thirty-three families and forty communicants in connection with the congregation.

CASTLEBAR.

[See Turlough.]

CLOGHER.

Presbyterian services were commenced in Clogher, at the request of residents there, in 1848. For three years services were held every alternate Sabbath by Revs. T. Y. Killen, John Hall, and John Dewart, then missionaries in Connaught. In 1851 the Rev. John Barnett was appointed permanent missionary at Clogher, in connection with the Students' Missionary

Society of Belfast. Mr. Barnett removed to Carlow in 1856, and subsequently to Katesbridge. He was succeeded by the Rev. James Megaw, who left for Australia in 1858. The next minister was the Rev. Samuel Johnston, who was appointed in June, 1858. He was succeeded by the Rev. S. L. Harrison, afterwards of Dromore West and now of Castlebellingham, who came to Clogher in January, 1873. The present minister, Rev. James Strothers Smith, was ordained in Clogher, July, 1879. The congregation owed its origin to the interest and liberality of the late Miss Elizabeth Holmes, who died on June 9th, 1877.

CREEVELEA.

The first Presbyterian services at Creevelea (Drumkeeran, Co. Leitrim) were conducted on week-days by the Rev. James Heron of Sligo. The first minister of the congregation was the Rev. John Ashmore, who was ordained there December 15th, 1852, and still labours in the sphere of his early ministry. In addition to his work at Creevelea, Mr. Ashmore conducts services at the stations of Manorhamilton, Dromahaire, and Collooney.

DROMORE WEST.

This congregation was first organised as a mission station by the Rev. Michael Brannigan in 1846. Mr. Brannigan conducted regular services there as well as at Ballinglen, until the year 1848, when the Rev. Matthew Kerr was appointed to labour at Dromore West. The congregation was formally organised in July, 1848, and Mr. Kerr was ordained by the Presbytery of Connaught on the 8th August, 1849, the Rev. Hamilton Magee (now D.D.) being ordained at the same time to labour at Mullafarry (Killala). By Mr. Kerr's efforts a church was erected, and opened in May, 1850, and a manse and schoolroom were subsequently added. Mr. Kerr resigned in July, 1862, on accepting a call to labour as itinerant missionary in Tipperary. He is now minister of Queen Street, Cork.

Mr. Kerr was succeeded by Rev. Silas E. Wilson, who was ordained in Dromore West, April 5th, 1864. Mr. Wilson resigned in October, 1872, having accepted a call to Parsonstown. He is now minister of 2nd Armagh.

The next minister was the Rev. Thomas Armstrong, who was installed May 28th, 1873, and resigned November 10th, 1875. He was succeeded by the Rev. David S. K. Coulter, now of Gilnahirk, near Belfast, who was ordained at Dromore West, May 17th, 1876, and resigned in 1878. The next minister was the Rev. S. L. Harrison, previously of Clogher, who was installed March 6th, 1878. Mr. Harrison resigned on May 17th, 1883, having accepted a call to Jonesboro and Castlebellingham, where he still labours. He was succeeded by the present minister, Rev. William Stuart, who was installed in Dromore West, September 5th, 1883.

HOLLYMOUNT.

The first Presbyterian services were held at Hollymount by the Rev. John Hamilton of Turlough, after the settlement of some Scotch and Northumbrian families in the year 1851. In October, 1852, the Rev. D. Adair of Westport reported to the Presbytery that he had preached in Hollymount on the preceding Sabbath to about thirty people, and that the people were anxious to have a missionary settled among them.

The Rev. James Love was ordained the first minister of the congregation in August, 1883. For some time the services were held in a schoolroom, kindly granted by Mrs. Lindsay, of Hollymount House. But a church and manse were soon erected at a cost of £1,200, and the church was opened for public worship in 1856.

At a visitation of Presbytery held in Hollymount in 1858, the elders were Francis Laurie and James Simpson, and the commissioners from the congregation were John Anderson and George Rutherford. There were at that time twenty-seven families and forty-seven communicants connected with the congregation.

In 1862 Mr. Love removed to Brisbane, Queensland, and was succeeded by the Rev. Samuel Wilson, ordained at Hollymount, June, 1862. Mr. Wilson's pastorate there was a short one, for in consequence of ill-health he removed to Australia in January, 1863.

He was succeeded by the Rev. Andrew Brown, previously of Turlough, who was installed at Hollymount February 17th, 1863. Mr. Brown was not only a faithful minister, but had considerable literary gifts. He published a number of small works, chiefly of a devotional character. On account of failing health, Mr. Brown retired from active duty, and the present minister, the Rev. Samuel E. Caldwell, was ordained as his assistant and successor, October 5th, 1887. Mr. Brown removed to America to reside with some relatives there, but died on the 14th May, 1888.

KILLALA.

The congregation of Killala or Mullafarry is one of the oldest in Ireland. It was originally associated with Sligo. The first minister of whom we have any record was the Rev. Samuel Henry, who was ordained to the joint charge of Sligo and Moywater (Killala) in 1695. Killala became a separate congregation about 1698. The Rev. James Pringle was the first minister after its separation from Sligo. He was previously minister of Ballindrait, and was installed in Killala in June, 1700. Mr. Pringle died on the 1st January, 1707. The next minister was the Rev. James Wallace, who laboured there from August, 1709, to June, 1720, when he removed to Moville, Co. Donegal. After a protracted vacancy, the Rev. William Wilson was ordained in Killala in 1733. He was minister there for nearly fifty years. It is likely that the emigration of that time told heavily on the congregation, for we find that in 1746 Sir Arthur Gore wrote a sympathetic letter to the Synod, "representing the melancholy situation of the people." Mr. Wilson died in 1781, and was succeeded by the Rev. Isaac Barr, previously minister of Ray, Co. Donegal. Mr. Barr resigned about 1792, and was succeeded by the Rev. Alexander Marshall, previously of Turlough, who was installed in December, 1795. Mr. Marshall died February 28th, 1819. The next minister was the Rev. David Rodgers, who was ordained there September 11th, 1820.

At a visitation of Presbytery held in Killala in 1826, the representative elders were William Duncan and Samuel Eakins, and the commissioners from the congregation were James Baird and James Ramsay. There were at this time sixty families, seventy-nine communicants, and six elders connected with the congregation. It was reported that "the meeting-house is in a state of forwardness, but unfinished for want of a lease." In 1829 the representative elders at a visitation were James Ramsay and William Duncan, and the commissioners from the congregation were Joseph Alexander and W. Watson. In 1841 the minister of Killala conducted a service every Sabbath in Ballina as well as in his own church of Mullafarry (Killala). This he had been doing for some years, and continued it until 1844, when the Rev. A. Lowry was appointed to minister to the congregation at Ballina. In 1847 there were eight elders, forty families, and eighty communicants in connection with Killala.

Mr. Rodgers, after a ministry of nearly thirty years became infirm, and the Rev. Hamilton Magee (now D.D.) was ordained as his assistant, August 8th, 1849. Mr. Magee removed to Dublin in 1854, and was succeeded by the Rev. John Wilson, who was ordained at Killala, March 14th, 1854. Mr. Rodgers died in June, 1859.

At a visitation of Presbytery held there in 1861 the representative elders of Killala were Dr. Neilson and Robert Eakins, and the representatives of the committee were James Massy and Thomas Carson. There were then thirty families and fifty-two communicants connected with the congregation.

Mr. Wilson was appointed to the Colonial Mission in Queensland, and was succeeded by his namesake, Rev. John Wilson, who was ordained in Killala, December 31st, 1862.

In March, 1872, the Presbytery passed a resolution, expressing their regret at the death of Dr. Neilson, an elder of the congregation of Killala. Mr. Wilson was married to Dr. Neilson's daughter.

At a visitation held in 1872 the representative elders of Killala were Robert Eakin and Joseph Alexander, and the representatives of committee were Robert Massey and Joseph Alexander, jun. Services were then held every Sabbath at Mullafarry at 12 noon, and at

Lisglennan schoolhouse at 5 p.m., and at Fortfield once a month. It was also reported that a commodious manse had been secured for the minister.

Mr. Wilson removed to Lecumpher, and the Rev. George Clarke Love was installed as his successor April 1st, 1885. Mr. Wilson was the fourth of the family who ministered in Lecumpher, his family being connected with that congregation for a period of ninety-five years. He died on March 28th, 1890.

Mr. Love removed to Killeter, and was succeeded by the present minister, Rev. Thomas Edwards, a licentiate of the Presbytery of Derry, who was ordained at Killala, February 3rd, 1886.

NEWPORT.

The congregation of Newport was formally organised August 11th, 1857. The Presbyterians there had been previously ministered to by Rev. David Adair of Westport, and subsequently by the Rev. George S. Keegan, who began to labour there in October, 1853. He was ordained as missionary by the Presbytery of Connaught in March, 1854.

On August 5th, 1856, a memorial was presented to the Presbytery from the Presbyterians of Newport, asking to be formed into a separate congregation. This memorial was signed by John Johnston, James Aitken, and others. The request was granted in 1857.

The services had been held for four years in the court-house, kindly granted by Sir Richard A. O'Donnel, but a church was built soon after the date of the memorial above referred to. The church was opened for public worship by the Rev. John Macnaughtan of Belfast, June 3rd, 1857. Since then a manse has been erected. Mr. Keegan's ministry in Newport extended over a period of more than thirty-six years. He died on May 10th, 1890. He was much beloved, and his knowledge of the Irish language gave him ready access to many who were not connected with his own church.

SLIGO.

Sligo is an old congregation. Its first minister appears to have been Rev. Samuel Henry, who was ordained to the joint-charge of Sligo and Moywater (Killala) in May, 1695. Mr. Henry resigned in 1727, and settled at Abbeyfoile. He was succeeded by the Rev. Luke Ash, son of Captain Ash, one of the defenders of Derry during the siege. Captain Ash wrote a *Journal of the Siege*, the original manuscript of which is in possession of H. Tyler, Esq., of Limavady, one of his descendants. This Journal was reprinted in 1888 with introduction and notes by Professor Witherow.[1]

The Rev. Luke Ash was ordained at Sligo, August 9th, 1732. He died there in 1742, and was succeeded by Rev. Hugh Nesbit, who was ordained there May 5th, 1756. Ballymote congregation was united with Sligo in 1760. Mr. Nesbit died in 1778, and was succeeded by Rev. Joseph King, who was ordained there August 4th, 1784. Mr. King resigned in 1797, and was succeeded by Rev. Booth Caldwell. Mr. Caldwell died on the 24th October, 1810. He was succeeded by Rev. Jacob Scott, who was ordained, March 19th, 1811, to the joint-charge of Sligo and Ballymote. In 1823 Mr. Scott was appointed by the Synod of Ulster to labour exclusively in Ballymote.

---

[1] *Two Diaries of Derry in* 1689. Being Richards' Diary of the Fleet, now first printed from the original MS., and Ash's Journal of the Siege. Londonderry: William Gailey. 1888.

The next minister of Sligo was the Rev. James Heron, who was ordained there March 18th, 1824. At a visitation of Presbytery held in 1826 the representative elders of Sligo were Adam Guthrie and Robert Ramsay, and the representatives of the congregation were Donald McDougal and Robert Barclay. There were then sixty families, seventy communicants, and four elders connected with the congregation, and the stipend paid to minister was £50.

At a visitation held in 1834, it was reported that a new church had recently been erected at a cost of upwards of £780. In 1844 the commissioners from the congregation at a visitation of Presbytery were Henry Lyons, Mr. Balfour, and Mr. Campbell. Mr. Heron preached at this time in Drum once a fortnight, having an attendance there of about forty.

On April 11th, 1855, the Rev. Moffatt Jackson, A.M., was ordained as assistant and successor to Mr. Heron. Mr. Heron died July 28th, 1860. In 1870 the Presbytery passed a resolution expressing their regret at the death of Henry Lyons, Esq., J.P., who for more than thirty years had been an active and generous elder of the Presbyterian Church in Sligo. Mr. Jackson continued in Sligo till his death, November 17th, 1887. His son, the Rev. W. J. Jackson, M.A., is the popular minister of Duncairn, Belfast.

The present minister, Rev. Francis O. M. Watters, M.A., previously of Kilrea, was installed in Sligo on May 16th, 1888.

Turlough and Castlebar.

The origin of the Presbyterian congregation at Turlough is somewhat interesting. Towards the close of the eighteenth century a number of Ulster families settled on the estate of Colonel Robert Fitzgerald. They found, after coming there, that there was no Protestant place of worship in the immediate neighbourhood. A deputation accordingly waited on Colonel Fitzgerald and requested his counsel and assistance in obtaining a minister to labour amongst them. As the colonists consisted of Presbyterians and Episcopalians, each party wished for a minister of their own denomination. The colonel said that, as one minister would be sufficient for both, he would put it to the vote, and give his vote with the majority. On the vote being taken the Presbyterians had the majority.

The first minister who preached to them was the Rev. Henry Henry, a licentiate. After he had been there for some time, the people of Turlough called him to be their minister. But he accepted a call to Garvagh, Co. Derry, where he was ordained, May 13th, 1788. In the same year he removed to Connor, Co. Antrim, where he remained till his death in 1840. Mr. Henry was a man of much ability. He took a prominent part in the Synod of Ulster in opposing the system of classification in the distribution of the Regium Donum. He was one of those who obtained a hearing for the Rev. Dr. Waugh of the London Missionary Society, at the meeting of the Synod in 1812, when missions to the heathen were in their infancy, and there was strong opposition to hearing a deputation on that subject. He sympathised with the United Irishmen, and was imprisoned for his opinions.[1] Professor Croskery says "he was one of the finest spirits in the Synod, with a truly patriarchal influence."[2]

---
[1] Witherow: *Presbyterian Memorials*, II., 287-292. Reid: *History*, III., 424.

[2] Croskery and Witherow: *Life of Rev. A. P. Goudy, D.D.*, p. 44.

After Mr. Henry's removal to Garvagh, the Rev. Alexander Marshall became minister of Turlough. He removed to Killala in 1795. He was succeeded by Rev. James Hall, who laboured there from 1795 until his death in 1824. The next minister was the Rev. John Hamilton, who was ordained there in 1824.

At a visitation of Presbytery held in 1825, the commissioners from the congregation were James Leister and John McAdam. There were then about thirty families connected with Turlough. In 1834 the congregation was represented at a visitation by Samuel McAdam and John McClean, elders, and by John Mulloy, James Keenan, Matthew Cochrane, and Joseph Rankin, commissioners. There were then forty families, forty communicants, and seven elders in connection with the congregation. At this meeting the thanks of the Presbytery were given to St. Clair O'Malley, Esq., of Castlebar, for his kind services in securing for the Rev. Mr. Hamilton of Turlough, as chaplain of the jail in Castlebar, a salary equal to that of the other chaplains. Mr. Hamilton died in May, 1854.

The next minister was the Rev. Andrew Brown, who was ordained at Turlough, September, 1854. Soon after his coming to Turlough, he commenced to hold a service in Castlebar every Sabbath evening. The service was first held in the court-house and afterwards in a schoolroom; in 1861 a site was acquired for the erection of a church.

Mr. Brown removed to Hollymount, in the same Presbytery, in 1863, and was succeeded by the Rev. John Cairns, who was ordained at Turlough, June 2nd, 1863. During his ministry a church and manse were erected at Castlebar. The church at Castlebar was opened in November, 1863, by the Rev. Dr. Edgar of

Belfast. The congregations of Turlough and Castlebar have since then been united as a joint-charge.

Mr. Cairns removed to Ballina in 1879, and was succeeded by the Rev. James Steen, previously of Drum, who was installed as minister of Turlough and Castlebar in May, 1880. Mr. Steen removed to Wexford in May, 1888, and was succeeded by the present minister, Rev. Joseph Northey, previously of Ballymote, who was installed as minister of Turlough and Castlebar, July 19th, 1888.

Westport.

Towards the close of the eighteenth and at the beginning of the present century, occasional services were held in Westport by the Presbyterian minister of Turlough. In 1821 a deputation from the Presbytery of Dublin, consisting of the Rev. James Horner and John Birch, visited Westport. As the result of their inquiries the Rev. Henry Cooke, afterwards the celebrated Dr. Cooke, was sent to officiate for a few Sabbaths. The service was held in a room in the market-house, granted by George Glendinning, Esq. After Mr. Cooke left, the congregation was favoured with the services of such men as Rev. John Bleckley of Monaghan, Rev. John Johnston of Tullylish, and Rev. Henry Dobbin of Lurgan. In 1823 the congregation was formally organised by the Synod of Ulster.

The first minister was the Rev. Robert Creighton, licentiate of the Tyrone Presbytery, who was ordained at Westport by the Presbytery of Dublin, December 23rd, 1823. The officiating ministers were Rev. James Horner (Dublin), James Morgan (Carlow), and James Hall (Turlough). The oath of allegiance was administered to Mr. Creighton by the Marquis of Sligo and George Glendinning, Esq. The report made to the Dublin Presbytery states that the Marquis and Marchioness of Sligo and family were attentive auditors at the ordination, and expressed their satisfaction with every part of the solemn service. The Presbytery resolved to send letters of thanks to the Marquis of Sligo and George Glendinning, Esq., for their great kindness and attention to the congregation of Westport and the ministers who had visited it on the business of the Presbytery.[1]

In 1830 the Marquis of Sligo granted a site for the erection of church and manse, and these buildings were completed soon after.

Mr. Creighton died October 31st, 1834. In the interval between his death and the settlement of his successor, the congregation enjoyed once more the services of some ministers who afterwards became well known. Among these were Rev. William Graham of Dundonald, afterwards missionary to the Jews at Damascus and at Bonn, D.D., and author of *Commentary on the Ephesians* and other works ; Rev. John Dill, Rev. Richard Dill, and Rev. J. K. Leslie (now of Cookstown).

The next stated minister was the Rev. James Smith, who was ordained at Westport, June 4th, 1837. At a visitation held in 1838 the elders of Westport were James Pinkerton and Joseph McCreery, and the commissioners from the congregation were Joseph McCreery, jun., and Patrick Louth. Mr. Smith removed to Scotland in 1845. He was succeeded by Rev. David Adair, who was ordained there May, 1846, and died of smallpox in 1854.

The next minister was one who afterwards took a high

---

[1] *Minutes of Presbytery of Dublin.*

place in the Irish Presbyterian Church—Rev. Richard Smyth. He was ordained at Westport, June 20th, 1855. He removed to the pastorate of 1st Derry in 1857, and was subsequently D.D., Professor of Theology in Magee College, and Member of Parliament for County Derry. He took an active part, along with the late A. M. Sullivan, Esq., M.P., in promoting the Irish Sunday Closing Act. He died in 1878.

Mr. Smyth was succeeded by the Rev. John James Black (now LL.D.), who was ordained at Westport, September 8th, 1857. Mr. Black accepted a call to Ormond Quay Church, Dublin, in 1859, whence he afterwards removed to his present pastorate, the Free High Church of Inverness, Scotland.

The Rev. William F. White was the next minister. He was installed at Westport, August 2nd, 1859. During his pastorate schoolhouses were built at Leenane, on Killery Harbour, and at Clogher. In the latter building a school is still maintained, and in the former a mission service is held once a month by the minister of Westport. The manse was also enlarged, and the church fenced in. Mr. White resigned in 1874, and became minister of Lucan, near Dublin, where he died in June, 1887.

The next minister was the Rev. Joseph McKinstry, who was ordained at Westport, January 6th, 1875. Mr. McKinstry removed to Randalstown, Co. Antrim, in 1881, and was succeeded by the Rev. S. G. Crawford, who was ordained at Westport, October 5th, 1881. Mr. Crawford was appointed on the colonial mission in 1887, and was succeeded by the Rev. Samuel Andrews. After a brief pastorate Mr. Andrews removed to America, and was succeeded by the present minister, Rev. David Wark, M.A., who was ordained at Westport, November 27th, 1888.

IV.

CORK PRESBYTERY.

[The Presbytery of Cork was formed in 1843.]

BANDON.

THE congregation of Bandon is one of the oldest in Ireland. Bandon itself is a historic town.[1] It was originally colonized by Protestant settlers from the south and west of England in the time of Queen Elizabeth and James I., and up to the close of the eighteenth century it maintained its character as a Protestant town. Being strongly walled and fortified, it offered more than once a successful resistance to attack in times of conflict, and was hence called "the Derry of the South." Dean Swift is said to have written on one of its gates as he entered the town—

> "A Turk, a Jew, or an Atheist,
> May enter here, but no Papist."

But his servant-man, who followed him, and who, it is to be presumed, was a Roman Catholic, was equal to the occasion, and wrote beneath—

> "Whoever wrote this wrote it well,
> For the same is written on the gates of hell."

The first Presbyterian minister of Bandon seems to

---

[1] See Bennett's *History of Bandon.*

have been the Rev. Mr. Harding, who was ordained there in 1679. In that year the minutes of Presbytery[1] state that "Mr. William Cock writes from Tipperary, whether he ought to join with Mr. Wood and Mr. Bernard in ordaining Mr. Harding to a congregation near Cork. He is advised to try Mr. Harding's abilities and qualifications for our ministry, and his agreeing to our Confession and Catechisms, and so, after satisfaction in these, to concur." This entry proves the Trinitarianism of Bandon, as well as of Mr. Cock of Tipperary, who was afterwards minister of Waterford.

In 1689 Mr. Harding was unanimously called to preside over a meeting whose object was to close the gates of the town against the troops of James, and to declare in favour of William.[2] This was carried into effect; but on Sabbath, April 30th, 1690, the garrison was surprised at the entrance of Colonel McCarthy into the town, and into the very church in which Mr. Harding was preaching. The text for the day was: "Let not your hearts be troubled; ye believe in God, believe also in Me"; and the minister, faithful to the trust committed to him, and nothing daunted by the presence of McCarthy and his troops, proclaimed the divine precepts with the same earnestness for the spiritual welfare of his hearers as he had done for the years preceding.

The ministers who followed Mr. Harding were Mr. Millet, Mr. Clugston, Mr. Hazlitt, Mr. King and Mr. Hunter.

---

[1] Appendix to Matthews' *Account of Emlyn's Trial*.
[2] *Evangelical Witness*, edited by Rev. John Hall, July, 1864. Paper on the History of Bandon Congregation, by B. Hayes. Mr. Hayes was for many years a staunch supporter of the Presbyterian Church in Bandon.

Mr. Hazlitt was father of William Hazlitt, the well-known historian and critic.

The history of the Presbyterian congregation of Bandon in the beginning of the present century is well described in a letter by the Rev. Robert Gault, then minister of Killyleagh. Mr. Gault visited the South of Ireland as a missionary deputy from the General Assembly, and gives his experiences in a letter to the *Downpatrick Missionary Herald*[1] of August, 1841. Speaking of Bandon, he says:[2]

"Presbyterianism is reduced to the shadow of what it formerly was. Mr. Knox [afterwards the Rev. Robert Knox, D.D., of Belfast] the Assembly's missionary to the South and West, told me, what he ascertained to be a fact, that at one time a large Presbyterian meeting-house was filled to overflowing, not merely with the people residing in the town, but with those who came from the adjoining parishes.

"The old place of meeting was thrown down, and at a time when Arianism came in, a new meeting-house was erected, and even it, though smaller than the other, was numerously attended. . . . But as the coldness of spiritual death gradually paralyses the energies of both minister and people, the congregation slowly and silently fell away, until when, one day, during my stay at Bandon, the numbers attending during a pleasant

---

[1] *The Downpatrick Missionary Herald* was the pioneer of missionary literature in the Irish Presbyterian Church. Its promoters were the Revs. Andrew Breakey and James A. Canning, and Archibald Hamilton Rowan, Esq., the latter of whom resided at Downpatrick. It lasted from 1837 to 1842, when it gave place to the *Missionary Herald of the Presbyterian Church in Ireland*.

[2] The following extracts have already been given above, pp. 113-115, but are reproduced here to preserve the continuity of the congregational narrative.

Sabbath in spring, were reckoned; *twenty-nine* persons alone, of all ages and sexes, were found the remnant of the once happy and flourishing Presbyterian church of Bandon."

[The writer then goes on to show that this is the natural result of the Arian error.]

"There is one circumstance which I think worth recording. The preacher who first propagated false doctrine among his people (in Bandon) was the man who occupied the pulpit immediately before its present possessor. He did so in a very guarded manner, and not till after he had been in the place a considerable time. The first day when he broached the opinion that the Lord Jesus is a mere creature—that His atonement is a mere fancy of interested ignorant men—there sat in the front seat of the gallery one of the elders of the congregation. He was a man now grown grey in the service of his Master—he leant upon his staff as he walked, but his soul still beat responsive to the tale of a Saviour's incarnation and His dying love. When he heard a professed minister of Christ deny our Saviour's divinity, and make light of His work of passive obedience, he was fired with holy indignation, . . . and in the audience of the assembled people he loudly protested against this overt act of rebellion, and shouting 'Treason, treason,' he hurried out of that house where he had heard his Saviour's name dishonoured, and never could be induced to enter it more."

In the November number of the same year, Mr. Gault continues the subject. He says:

"Mr. Knox, then the only ordained missionary in connection with our church to the people of our native land, was invited to visit Bandon by a Scotch gentleman from Annandale, a near relative and once school-companion of the lamented Edward Irving, and who then resided in Bandon. This request was seconded by a native of the town, a descendant of the original English Presbyterian settlers, and son to the faithful elder who publicly protested against the introduction of error into the congregation. . . .

"Mr. Knox, says of the difficulties he encountered at first : . . . 'I was feared and avoided. Many came to hear me through curiosity. They were astonished to hear a Presbyterian minister preach the doctrine of the *Atonement* and the Deity of Christ, and during my first sermon some of them whispered to the others that surely I was not a *Presbyterian.*' . . .

" The site of a new church was obtained in the very heart of the town, and subscriptions cheerfully entered into for its erection."

I have not been able to ascertain the name of the elder who thus protested against error. In 1818 the elders of the Presbyterian congregation were Francis Allman and William Dowden. Their families have long been, and still are, connected with the town of Bandon, where they have always been highly esteemed. It is highly probable it was one of these who thus lifted up his voice against erroneous doctrine in the pulpit. We find Richard Dowden one of those present at a meeting of the congregation in 1842, and he was sent as delegate to Cork to raise subscriptions for their new church.

The new church, spoken of above, was built for the orthodox (Trinitarian) Presbyterian congregation under the ministry of the Rev. R. McEwen, who was ordained in 1842. The Arian (Unitarian) congregation held the old church or meeting-house, where the Rev. Mr. Hunter continued to officiate till his death. Since then the congregation has been so small that it was not able to maintain a stated pastor, and occasional services have been supplied by Unitarian ministers from Cork. The Presbyterian congregation, on the other hand, has grown strong and flourishing. Mr. McEwen removed to Saintfield, Co. Down, in 1847, and was succeeded by Rev. William Hogg (1847-1848), Rev. J. White (1848-1854), Rev. W. Irwin, now D.D., of Castlerock (1855-1874), Rev. R. S. Coffey, now of Bradford, England (1875-1879), Rev. James Bingham, M.A., now of Dundonald (1879-1883), and the present minister, Rev. Thomas Brown, M.A., who was ordained there on the 2nd October, 1883. During the ministry of Mr. Irwin, a manse and schools were built at a cost of about £1,600, and the schools have proved a valuable assistance to the life and work of the congregation. By the efforts of the Rev. Thomas Brown the site of the church has been purchased and is now the property of the General Assembly.

Castlemartyr and Aghada.

The mission stations of Castlemartyr, Aghada, and Middleton, County Cork, were first ministered to by the Rev. R. McClelland, who was appointed to labour there in 1863. He was succeeded by the Rev. Hugh Hunter (previously of Queen Street, Cork), who was installed at Castlemartyr and Middleton in 1865. Mr. Hunter removed to England in 1867. He was succeeded by the Rev. J. A. Smith, M.A. (previously of Tartaraghan), who came to Middleton in 1868. The sphere is known as that of the Itinerant Mission, and covers a large portion of the eastern side of County Cork. For some years Mr. Smith resided in Middleton, but finding the city of Cork more central for his work, he removed thither. He holds regular Sabbath services in Castlemartyr, Middleton and Aghada, with occasional services at Blarney, Youghal, and elsewhere. Few Irish Presbyterian ministers have so laborious a sphere as Mr. Smith's, and he is a faithful and welcome visitor in the Presbyterian families scattered over his extensive district.

CLONAKILTY.

The congregation of Clonakilty was organised by the Presbytery of Cork in November, 1859, after having been conducted as a mission station for about four years by the Rev. William Irwin of Bandon. Its first minister was the Rev. Dr. E. M. Dill, who was ordained there March 27th, 1860. Dr. Dill died on the 23rd November, 1862. He was succeeded by the Rev. Thomas Croskery, previously minister of Creggan, who was installed there March 24th, 1863. Mr. Croskery (afterwards D.D.) was a man of great ability, combined with rare gentleness and modesty of character. He wrote a valuable book on *Plymouth Brethrenism*, and contributed largely to the *Pulpit Commentary*, but most of his literary work appeared in the great Reviews. Between 1862 and 1886 he wrote fifty-four articles for the leading magazines. Of these two were published in the *Eclectic*, four in the *Princeton Review*, six in *Fraser's Magazine*, seven in the *London Quarterly Review*, eight in the *British Quarterly*, fourteen in the *British and Foreign Evangelical Review*, eleven in the *Edinburgh Review*, and two in the *Presbyterian Review*. There have been few Irish Presbyterian ministers who worked so hard as Dr. Croskery. In 1866 he resigned the pastorate of Clonakilty, having accepted a call to Waterside, Derry. He was subsequently appointed Professor of Logic, and afterwards Professor of Theology, in Magee College. He died in 1886 amid universal sorrow for a distinguished and loyable minister.

Mr. Croskery was succeeded in Clonakilty by the Rev. J. H. Charlton, who was installed there in 1866. In 1869 Mr. Charlton accepted a call to Maguiresbridge, and is now minister of Clonduff, near Rathfriland. The next minister of Clonakilty was the Rev. William Reid, who was ordained there July 24th, 1869. Mr. Reid removed to 1st Moneymore in July, 1873, and was succeeded by the Rev. Robert Cowan, who was ordained in Clonakilty, December 2nd, 1873. Mr. Cowan accepted a call to St. Andrew's Church, Nottingham (previously ministered to by Rev. Professor Dougherty, now of Derry), in 1880. The present minister, Rev. Edward Kimmitt (previously of Loughgall), was installed in Clonakilty, June 1st, 1880.

The church is one of the neatest in the Assembly, and the manse, a commodious building overlooking the town, was built during the ministry of Rev. William Reid. The late George Ronaldson, Esq., was for many years one of the most respected and liberal members of this congregation, and the late Mr. Shiels and Mr. Law were always among its most zealous and energetic supporters.

FERMOY.

The beginnings of Presbyterianism at Fermoy would seem to have been under Arian influences. The Rev. T. D. Hincks became tutor of the Fermoy Academy in 1818.[1] The Synod of Munster having procured him Royal Bounty, he preached in Fermoy, until he removed to the Belfast Institution in 1825.

---

[1] Appendix to Matthews' *Account of Emlyn's Trial.*

His removal probably caused the orthodox Presbyterians of the district to desire some one more evangelical. At the meeting of the Synod of Ulster in 1825, a memorial was read from Presbyterian and other inhabitants of Kilworth and Fermoy, praying the Synod to erect them into a congregation. This memorial was accompanied by a letter of recommendation from Lord Mountcashel, containing a most generous gift from that nobleman.[1] The Synod granted the request, and from this time supplies of preaching were regularly sent.

In 1837 the Rev. Robert Quinn became minister at Fermoy. The congregation was formally taken under the care of the Presbytery of Munster in 1841. On September 28th, 1841, Rev. Mr. Kerr, licentiate of the Ballymena Presbytery, was ordained in Fermoy. Mr. Kerr gave a statement of "his belief in the leading parts or heads of the Christian religion, and his future intentions of the mode in which he should discharge his duties as the pastor of that congregation."[2] He also declared his adhesion to his belief in the Confession of Faith, which he had signed. The following were present at the meeting :—Rev. Mr. Ferris (Fethard), Moderator ; Rev. Dr. Sloane (Cork), Clerk ; Rev. Mr. McCance (Waterford) ; Rev. Mr. McCorkle (Limerick) ; Rev. Mr. Alexander, missionary at Tipperary ; Rev. Mr. McGavan, missionary at Portlaw ; and three members of the General Assembly [with which the Presbytery of Munster was not yet formally connected], Rev. Dr. Dill (Cork) ; Rev. John Dill (Clonmel) ; and Rev. Mr. Poole (Lismore). The following were the elders of Fermoy congregation, who

---

[1] See above, Chapter XIX., p. 103.
[2] *Minutes of Munster Presbytery.*

were also present : Mr. George Mathews, Mr. Sheriffs, and Mr. Richie.

An interesting glimpse of Presbyterian practice in the South of Ireland fifty years ago is afforded by the fact that at a meeting of the Presbytery of Munster held in Fermoy, May 24th, 1842, two hymns were sung. Yet in 1851 we find the same Presbytery recommending the congregation of Fethard " to substitute the Psalms of David in the stead of the hymns at present in use."[1] Perhaps there were some objectors to hymn-singing among the congregation of Fethard, and the Presbytery may have thus thought to promote peace.

In 1846 the congregation of Fermoy consisted of twenty families, and the average attendance of communicants at the Lord's Supper was thirty-two. Mr. Kerr died July 12th, 1853, and on April 25th, 1854, the Presbytery of Cork (with which the congregation had become connected in 1851) installed the Rev. Joseph Donaldson in the pastorate. Mr. Donaldson laboured there faithfully and zealously till his death, December 1st, 1880. He was much respected by all denominations in and around Fermoy. During his ministry a commodious manse was built. The present minister, Rev. J. King Clarke, was installed in the pastorate of Fermoy, February 22nd, 1882.

LISMORE.

The first minister of the congregation of Lismore was the Rev. John Poole, who was ordained there by the Dublin Presbytery, May 18th, 1828. The church was built in 1827 at a cost of £205, on the property of the Duke of Devonshire, who gave a lease on very liberal terms. The property, including manse, was

---

[1] See below, p. 289.

purchased in 1853 by the trustees of the General Fund. Mr. Poole was succeeded by the Rev. W. J. Gill, who was ordained by the Presbytery of Cork, January 20th, 1852. Mr. Gill removed to Edinburgh in 1857, and was succeeded by Rev. John Ashwood, ordained at Lismore, September 1st, 1857. Mr. Ashwood resigned in 1863, and was succeeded by the present minister, Rev. John MacKeown (previously of Beresford Street Church, Waterford), who was installed in Lismore, September 27th, 1864. At the time of Disestablishment the Duke of Devonshire generously gave a grant of £10 per annum to Mr. MacKeown, so long as he should remain minister of Lismore.

MALLOW.

The first ministers of Mallow were Mr. Lorrimer and Mr. B. Smith. For a time the congregation was supplied with preaching by the Irish Evangelical Society. The Rev. C. B. Gibson became minister of Mallow, in connection with this society, in 1834. The society having become denominational and Independent, instead of undenominational as it had been at first, the congregation left it and joined the Presbyterian Church in 1848.[1] Mr. Gibson was loosed from Mallow in 1856, having been appointed government chaplain to the convicts at Spike Island. Mr. Gibson was the author of a romance called, *The last Earl of Desmond*, and subsequently wrote a volume entitled, *Philosophy, Science, and Revelation*.[2] He was succeeded in

---

[1] *The Spike Island Chaplaincy and the Mallow Congregation*, by Rev. Charles B. Gibson, M.R.I.A., Cork, 1860.

[2] *Philosophy, Science, and Revelation*. By the Rev. Charles B. Gibson, M.R.I.A., Lecturer of St. John's, Hoxton. 2nd Ed. London: Longmans, 1874.

Mallow by Rev. John Baird. During Mr. Baird's ministry the present church and manse were built. Mr. Baird retired from the active duties of the ministry in 1883, and on October 6th, 1884, the Rev. Robert Jeffrey, M.A. (previously of the Free Church of Scotland, Bombay), was installed as his assistant and successor. Mr. Jeffrey resigned Mallow in 1887, and was succeeded by the Rev. Thomas Dysart (previously of 1st Newtownhamilton), who was installed in Mallow, July 11th, 1887.

QUEEN STREET, CORK.

Some time after the erection of Trinity Church, Cork, a new congregation was organised in the old church of Queen Street, previously occupied by the Trinity Church congregation. This was in 1862. The first minister was the Rev. Hugh Hunter, who was installed there January 6th, 1863. Mr. Hunter resigned in June, 1864, having accepted a call of the Mission Board to labour as itinerant missionary in the Castlemartyr district. He was succeeded by the Rev. Robert McCheyne Edgar, M.A., who was ordained there March 7th, 1865. Mr. Edgar removed to Adelaide Road Church, Dublin, in August, 1866.[1] The next minister of Queen Street Church was the Rev. George Magill (previously minister of 1st Antrim), who was installed May 7th, 1867. Mr. Magill removed to 2nd Donaghready, near Derry, in 1874, and is now minister of Cliftonville Church, Belfast. He is known as a thoughtful preacher, and an able speaker in debate. He was succeeded in Queen Street by the present minister, Rev. Matthew Kerr, who was installed there on June 16th, 1874. Mr. Kerr, who had previously done

---

[1] See under *Adelaide Road*, Presbytery of Dublin

a good work in Connaught and in Tipperary, has had a successful ministry in Cork. For many years he devoted much of his time to visiting the ships at the quays, and inviting the sailors to the house of prayer on the Lord's Day. During his ministry the church has been repaired and renovated at considerable expense, and the congregation, previously assisted by the Mission Funds, has become self-supporting.

QUEENSTOWN.

Rev. James Gailey was installed there in 1845, and resigned in 1850 to become minister of the Free Church congregation at Annan, Scotland. The present minister, Rev. William Simpson, was ordained there in February, 1851.

TRALEE.

The congregation of Tralee was organised in 1846. It had previously been conducted as a mission station under the care of the Rev. William Chestnut, who was ordained there as missionary in 1843. He was installed as minister on March 23rd, 1846. During his ministry the church and manse were built. Mr. Chestnut was universally respected as a faithful and amiable minister of the gospel, and had friendly and pleasant relations with the ministers and members of other denominations in Tralee. After labouring in Tralee for forty-five years, Mr. Chestnut, on account of failing health, retired from active duty in 1888, and died on July 29th of that year. He was succeeded by Rev. Albert Gailey, B.A., who was ordained there December 11th, 1888. Mr. Gailey resigned in the following May, owing to serious illness, and on September 26th, 1889, the present minister, Rev. John

Keers, licentiate of the Presbytery of Route, was ordained to the pastorate.

Trinity Church, Cork.

The first Presbyterian minister of Cork of whom we have any account was the Rev. Mr. Brinkley. There is a letter from Mr. Cock of Tipperary, written in 1675, respecting Mr. Brinkley's settlement in Cork.

Mr. Brinkley was succeeded by Mr. Lowthian, settled there in 1706, Mr. Tweed, Mr. Cuthbert, and Mr. Hutchinson, who was ordained there in 1757. It is on record that Mr. Hutchinson assented to the Westminster Confession. The ministers succeeding Mr. Hutchinson were Mr. Kiddell, Mr. Perrett, Mr. Jeffries, Mr. N. Shaw, Mr. T. D. Hincks, Dr. Willis, Mr. Moore, Mr. W. Hincks, Mr. Hart, and Dr. Sloane.

In the case of the Attorney-General (for George Matthews and others) against Rev. Joseph Hutton and Rev. J. C. Ledlie, D.D. (ministers of Eustace Street), and others,[1] the Rev. Thomas Dix Hincks deposed:

"I was for many years minister of the congregation of Prince's Street, Cork, belonging to the Presbyterian Association in the South of Ireland, formerly known as the Presbytery of Munster. I was such minister from 1790 to 1815. . . . I have been present at, and took part in, three ordinations of ministers into congregations connected with said Presbytery of Munster, viz.—Mr. Wilson at Youghal in room of Mr. Crooks; Mr. Pinkerton, assistant and successor to Mr. Seawright of Limerick; and Dr. Willis as my own successor in Cork. . . . At the period of my admission into said Presbytery of Munster, said body maintained

---

[1] See pamphlet, *Report of Proceedings*, Dublin : 1844.

a friendly intercourse with the Presbyterian Association in Dublin, formerly known as the Southern Presbytery of Dublin ; the said last-mentioned Presbytery at that time consisted of Strand Street, Eustace Street, and Summerhill congregations, as I best recollect and believe."

Dr. Sloane, though a non-subscribing minister, was a Trinitarian. He became a member of the orthodox non-subscribing Presbytery of Munster in 1840, when it asserted its claim to independence of the Arian Synod of Munster. His colleague, Mr. Hart, appears to have been an Arian. Dr. Sloane resigned the active duties of the ministry in 1844. His congregation was then known as Prince's Street congregation.

The Presbyterian congregation of Cork, like so many others in the South of Ireland, suffered from the prevalence of New Light or Arian views. Many who were attached to the Presbyterian form wished for more evangelical doctrine in their pulpits. Accordingly, at the meeting of the Presbytery of Dublin held in June, 1830,[1] the Moderator, Rev. Mr. Simpson, reported that in his visit to the South of Ireland as a deputation from the Scottish Missionary Society, he had found both in Cork and Clonmel a number of families and individuals who expressed an earnest desire to be supplied with worship according to the Presbyterian discipline. The Presbytery acceded to this desire, and sent several ministers to preach, with the result that a new congregation was organised, and the Rev. Henry Wallace of Holywood was installed there in 1832. Mr. Wallace gave up a large and flourishing congregation in the North to take charge of this infant

---

[1] *Minutes of Dublin Presbytery.*

church at Cork. In 1835 he reported that he had sixty communicants, and that their place of meeting was quite filled. But ill-health obliged Mr. Wallace to relinquish his faithful labours in the South, and he resigned his charge in Cork in 1837.

Mr. Wallace was succeeded by the Rev. Edward M. Dill, M.D., who was installed there in 1838. During Dr. Dill's ministry the present church of Queen Street was built, and until the building of Trinity Church it was the only (orthodox) Presbyterian church in the city of Cork. Dr. Dill resigned the charge in 1846, having been appointed General Itinerant Missionary Agent of the Home Mission. He was succeeded by the Rev. William Magill, who was installed in 1847. For thirty-seven years Dr. Magill honourably upheld the interests of Presbyterianism and the cause of religion in the city of Cork. He is an eloquent and powerful preacher and a zealous pastor. In 1874 he was Moderator of the General Assembly. During his ministry the congregation built for itself a beautiful new church, known as Trinity Church, which is an ornament to the city. Dr. Magill retired from active duties in 1884 and was succeeded by the Rev. Samuel Law Wilson, M.A., who was installed there in the same year. Mr. Wilson resigned in December, 1889, having accepted a call to the congregation of York Street, Belfast. The Rev. J. H. Murphy, M.A., previously of Cavan, has been installed in Trinity Church, June, 1890.

During the present century many prominent merchants of the city of Cork have been identified with the Presbyterian Church, such as Messrs. Carmichael, Coldbeck, Dale, Dobbin, Dowden, Ferguson, Lunham, McOstrich, Ogilvie, Sutherland, etc.

V.

PRESBYTERY OF DUBLIN.

Abbey Street, Dublin (Union Chapel).

THE congregation of Union Chapel, Lower Abbey Street, Dublin, takes its name from a union of two Seceding congregations which existed in Dublin toward the close of the last century. These were the Burgher and Anti-burgher congregations. The latter previously worshipped in the old Tailors' Hall, Back Lane. The former had for a long time worshipped in a church which had an interesting history. This was the church of Mass Lane or Lucy Lane. This lane has now disappeared, but was about the spot now called Chancery Place, near the east end of the Four Courts.

The church of Mass Lane was originally the chapel of a Dominican friary. After the suppression of the friary by Henry VIII. the Benchers of the King's Inns obtained the building and used it as their chapel. James II. restored it to the Jesuits and heard mass in it during his stay in Dublin. After the Revolution William III. presented it to a congregation of French Huguenots, and the King himself attended services in Mass Lane after the battle of the Boyne. Some years later the Huguenots of Mass Lane joined the French church in Peter Street, which was in existence until the beginning of the present century.[1]

At length the church of Mass Lane came into possession of the Seceders. In 1796 we find in Dublin two congregations of Seceders, divided by the controversy about the burgess oath into Burghers and Anti-burghers.[2] They do not appear to have been very numerous. In 1818 the two congregations only numbered 140 persons.[3] Mass Lane was the more important, as it received a grant of £70 a year Regium Donum, while the congregation of Back Lane received £50 a year.[4] The Rev. Mr. Hutcheson was up to this time minister of Mass Lane, and the Rev. David Stuart was minister of Back Lane. About this time the congregation of Back Lane removed to a new church which they had built in Mary's Abbey, not far from the Synod of Ulster church of Mary's Abbey (which since removed to Rutland Square). This Secession church was built on the site of the old Bank of Ireland, and is now used as the Jewish synagogue. James Clarke, Esq., was a wealthy member of the congregation, and it was largely by his liberality that the new church was built. He was Treasurer of the Irish Evangelical Society (1814).

In 1818 the Rev. Thomas Hutcheson retired from the pastorate of Mass Lane, owing to ill-health, and shortly after this his congregation united with that of Mary's Abbey (Secession Church). It was in this

---

[1] "Presbyterianism in Dublin," by Dr. William Frazer, in the *Evangelical Witness* (edited by Rev. John Hall, Dublin), April, 1863.

[2] *Life and Times of the Countess of Huntingdon*, II., 217.

[3] Warburton, Whitelaw, and Walsh: *History of Dublin.*

[4] Mathews: *Account of Regium Donum.*

year that the two Synods of Burghers and Anti-burghers united and formed the Secession Synod. Wm. McAuley, Esq., was at this time a leading member of Mass Lane congregation, and appeared before the Synod on its behalf. It was the united sessions of Mass Lane and Mary's Abbey who, about the year 1819, overtured the Secession Synod to undertake home mission work in the South and West of Ireland.[1]

The Rev. David Stuart, who thus became minister of the united Secession congregation at Mary's Abbey, was a man of great ability. He preached a sermon at the opening of the Secession Synod in Cookstown in 1820, on "The call of God to Irish Christians on behalf of their perishing countrymen, and the guilt and danger of neglecting to hear it." The sermon is still preserved,[2] and is a very earnest and powerful discourse. Other published sermons of his which are preserved in the same volume are on *The Death of Judas*, and two sermons on *Unitarianism another Gospel*, a reply to Rev. Dr. Armstrong's *Vindication of Unitarian Christianity* (1838). He also published a small pamphlet on the *Doctrines of the Trinity and the Incarnation and Atonement of our Lord Jesus Christ* (Dublin : 1834).

In 1823 Mr. Stuart, still retaining his pastorate, was appointed Professor of Theology in the Theological Training College or Academy of the Irish Evangelical Society at Manor Street, near Prussia Street. A manuscript volume of notes of his lectures on Theology is preserved in the library of Magee College.

Under Mr. Stuart's ministry, the Secession congregation of Mary's Abbey became so large that, in seven

---

[1] *Minutes of Secession Synod.*
[2] *Miscellaneous Sermons by Ministers of the Secession Synod*, 1799-1839.

years after the erection of its church and its union with Mass Lane congregation, it was necessary to erect a new building. A new church was then erected in Lower Abbey Street in 1825, and was called, in commemoration of the union of the congregations—and perhaps, also, of the Synods—" Union Chapel."

In 1837 the Secession Synod organised another congregation in Dublin. This was the congregation of D'Olier Street (afterwards Gloucester Street). Union Chapel congregation then became known as " First Dublin " on the minutes of the Secession Synod. After the union of the Secession Synod with the Synod of Ulster, the congregation of Union Chapel became part of the Presbytery of Dublin in connection with the General Assembly. In 1841 Mr. Stuart's connection with Union Chapel ceased.

He was succeeded by the Rev. S. G. Morrison. Mr. Morrison had been ordained by the Independents at Armagh in August, 1838, Rev. Mr. Edgar and Rev. Mr. McAlister, Presbyterian ministers, assisting. He continued to labour in the Tabernacle, Armagh, till 1843, when he removed to the Independent congregation of Plunket Street, Dublin, where he was installed by Rev. Dr. Urwick, Rev. Mr. Hands, and Rev. Mr. Cooper. About the close of 1844 Mr. Morrison received an invitation from the congregation of Union Chapel to become their minister, and both he and the congregation of Plunket Street then joined Union Chapel.

In 1846 Mr. Morrison and the congregation of Union Chapel applied to be received into connection with the Presbytery of Munster. After inquiry by a committee of Presbytery the request was granted, and Mr. Morrison was formally installed in Union Chapel, December 30th,

1846. At that time Mr. Morrison's reputation as a preacher had already attracted a large congregation. The average attendance on Sabbath was seven hundred; there were one hundred and fifty communicants, and seventy in attendance at Sabbath-school.[1] In 1861 there were two hundred communicants on the roll, and one hundred families in connection with the congregation.

In 1869 the Munster Presbytery ordained the following gentlemen as elders and deacons in Union Chapel: *Elders*—David Bryan, Adam Kirkpatrick, John Adams, James Baird; *Deacons*—Benjamin Patterson, James M'Robbie, Alexander McKay, Samuel Bouchier, Henry Cochrane,[2] John Orr Miller, and Frederick Winder. The congregation subsequently became once more connected with the Presbytery of Dublin.

Mr. Morrison having retired from active duty, the Rev. William Tait, LL.D. (previously of Castleblayney), was installed as his assistant and successor on the 1st November, 1881. Dr. Tait resigned the pastorate in February, 1890.

ADELAIDE ROAD, DUBLIN.

The increasing strength of Presbyterianism in Dublin in 1840 led to the formation of a new congregation. The foundation-stone of Adelaide Road Church was laid in this year. The first minister of the congregation was the Rev. Charles Nairne, ordained there in 1842. Mr. Nairne resigned the pastorate in 1844, having accepted a presentation to the parish of St. John's, Glasgow, in connection with the Church of Scotland. In May, 1844, the Rev. William Arnot of Edinburgh

---

[1] *Minutes of Munster Presbytery.* [2] Now Sir Henry Cochrane.

conducted the anniversary services in Adelaide Road Church, and the names given in an advertisement o the services in *Saunders' Newsletter*, as connected with the church, are Wm. Todd, Alexander McCook, Dr. Paterson, Wm. McIntosh, Andrew Risk, Frederick C. Ferguson, Samuel Morewood, J. T. Mackay, Thomas Heiton, Kenneth Chisholm, John Johnston, Thomas Peile, jun., and John Lang.

The Rev. J. W. Hunter, previously of Terrace Row, Coleraine, was installed here in January, 1845. When the new Trustees of the General (Eustace Street) Fund were appointed by the Lord Chancellor in 1850, the first trustees representing Adelaide Road were Rev. J. W. Hunter, and Messrs. William Todd, Thomas Heiton, and John Lang.

In 1865 Mr. Hunter obtained leave for his congregation to choose an assistant and successor to him, in consequence of infirmity.[1] In September of that year, the Rev. R. A. Carden, D.D., was installed as assistant-minister. Dr. Carden had been minister of the Episcopal Church of America, but sought admission into the Presbyterian Church of Ireland, and was received by the Assembly. In 1866 Dr. Carden was called to 1st Ballymena, but declined the call.

Dr. Carden's career in Adelaide Road was a brief one. He declined the call to Ballymena in March, 1866. In April of the same year he was reported to the Dublin Presbytery by the Session of his congregation for his method of administering baptism, using some form of prayer and the Apostles' Creed, bowing at the name of Jesus, and making the sign of the cross on the forehead of the child in baptism. He explained

---

[1] Mr. Hunter died in 1879.

that he had not read the directions in the Presbyterian Book of Discipline, and had used principally the forms with which he had been familiar. His explanation was accepted, the Presbytery expressing regret that he had not previously acquainted himself fully with Presbyterian order and discipline. Dr. Carden doubtless chafed under his own hastily-imposed burden of Presbyterianism, for in the month of May, 1866, he resigned the pastorate of Adelaide Road and his connection with the Presbyterian Church, intimating his intention of returning to the Episcopal Church.

In August, 1866, the present pastor, Rev. R. McCheyne Edgar, M.A., previously of Queen Street, Cork, was installed as assistant-minister in Adelaide Road. Mr. Edgar's has been a faithful and laborious pastorate. During his ministry a commodious manse has been built, a fine lecture-hall and suite of rooms have been added to the church, and the church itself has been completely renovated. Amid all the labours, pastoral and public, of a city minister, Mr. Edgar has found time to contribute largely to the theological literature of the day. His best-known works are *The Philosophy of the Cross; Does God answer Prayer?;* and homiletic contributions to several volumes of the *Pulpit Commentary.*

Adelaide Road is an active and flourishing congregation. The pastor is ably assisted by an excellent staff of elders and members of committee.

ATHY.

The congregation of Athy is one of those which had an early existence in the history of Irish Presbyterianism, which for a time became extinct, and were afterwards revived.

Its first ministers were Revs. Dr. Thralkeld and Mr. Walker. The Rev. Mr. McGachin (or McGachy) was ordained there in 1720. His was a lengthened pastorate. He was still minister in 1770, though beginning to feel the infirmities of age, for we find it reported in that year to the Trustees of the General Fund that " Mr. McGachin is no longer capable of preaching at Ballybrittas." Ballybrittas was a congregation in Queen's County, to which Mr. McGachin ministered, as well as to the congregation of Athy, in County Kildare. The troublous times toward the close of the eighteenth century had probably the effect of scattering some of the members, and the growth of moderatism had probably exercised its destructive influence on the internal life of the congregation, for soon after this it became extinct.

In November, 1851, the Presbytery of Dublin organised the Presbyterian families of Athy into a congregation, under very promising circumstances. The Rev. John Hall (now of Waterford) was the first minister of the revived congregation. He was ordained there in 1852. In 1861 Mr. Hall resigned the charge of Athy, having been appointed to the work of the Colonial Mission in British Columbia. Mr. Hall was succeeded by the Rev. Robert Wallace (previously of Glennan, Co. Monaghan, and now of New Row, Coleraine), who was installed there in 1861. Mr. Wallace was succeeded by the Rev. T. R. White (previously of Loughmorne, now of Bailieboro'), who was installed there in 1865.

The present minister is the Rev. J. G. Clarke, who was installed in 1874, and is universally respected and beloved. The congregation of Athy is a strong and generous one. Its large contributions to missionary objects are specially noteworthy.

BALLACOLLA.

Ballacolla congregation was organised in 1858. Its first minister was the Rev. Alexander Milligan, ordained there in 1860. Mr. Milligan removed to Corlea in 1882, and was succeeded by Rev. A. Mogee, B.A., ordained there in August, 1882. Mr. Mogee resigned, to go to Canada, in 1889. Further particulars are given in Killen's *History of Congregations*. The present minister, Rev. W. S. Montgomery, B.D., was ordained there on April 30th, 1890.

BIRR, OR PARSONSTOWN.

The story of Birr congregation is unique in the history of the Irish Presbyterian Church. In 1839 the Rev. William Crotty, Parish Priest of Birr, renounced the doctrines of the Roman Catholic Church, and he and his congregation were received, on their own application, into connection with the Synod of Ulster,[1] under the care of the Presbytery of Dublin. The two congregations of Mary's Abbey and Usher's Quay contributed liberally for the assistance of this newly-formed and novel Presbyterian congregation, and a joint committee, consisting of the ministers and leading members of these two city churches, was appointed to look after its financial interests. The Rev. Dr. Carlile of Mary's Abbey, who had Mr. Kirkpatrick for his assistant, devoted the remainder of his days to the work at Birr, where he lived and laboured till his death in 1854. The Presbyterian Church, which had been thus unexpectedly called to labour in spiritual matters in Birr, was not unmindful

---

[1] See above, Chapter XIX., p. 117.

of the bodily and temporal needs of the people, and in 1848 Dr. A. W. Wallace (M.D.) came there as the representative of the Edinburgh Medical Missionary Society. Dr. Wallace's medical skill was the means of alleviating much distress and suffering in the dark days of the famine and the cholera.

Dr. Carlile was succeeded, as minister of Birr, by the Rev. W. H. Horner, who was installed there in April, 1854. Mr. Horner resigned in 1855, and was succeeded by Rev. E. Kimmitt (now of Clonakilty), ordained there in 1856. The next minister was the Rev. John Chambers, ordained there in September, 1857. Mr. Chambers resigned owing to ill-health, and was succeeded by Rev. J. Brady Meek, ordained there on July 13th, 1869. Mr. Meek accepted a call to 1st Larne in 1872, and was succeeded in Birr by Rev. Silas E. Wilson (previously of Dromore West), who was installed there December 4th, 1872. Mr. Wilson accepted a call to 3rd Armagh in 1876. He was succeeded by Rev. D. H. McMurtry.

During Mr. McMurtry's ministry the present manse was purchased for the congregation. Mr. McMurtry resigned Birr in December, 1881, having accepted a call to 2nd Castleblayney. He was succeeded by Rev. John M. Simms, B.A., who was ordained there on May 16th, 1882. During the ministry of Mr. Simms the present beautiful new church was built. It was opened for public worship in 1886 by the Rev. James W. Whigham, D.D. (Ballinasloe). The foundation-stone was laid by Rev. Jackson Smyth, D.D. (Armagh). Mr. Simms, having been appointed Chaplain to the Forces, resigned the pastorate, and was succeeded by Rev. J. Melville Irwin (previously of Cavanaleck), who was installed at Birr, May 24th, 1887.

BRAY.

The congregation of Bray owes its origin to the Irish Evangelical Society. This was an undenominational society, founded in 1814, for the purpose of carrying on mission work in Ireland. Its first secretaries were Revs. Mr. Cooper, minister of Plunket Street (Independent), Mr. Davies, minister of York Street (Independent), and Mr. Carlile, minister of Mary's Abbey (Presbyterian).[1] James Clarke, Esq., a leading member of the Anti-burgher Society (Presbyterian), was treasurer. The report of the Society for 1816 states that "at Bray, a place of fashionable resort, about ten miles south of Dublin, a field of gospel labours has lately been opened, and means are in progress to supply that place statedly." Several ministers of the Presbyterian Church had already preached there. For some years before 1816 the Rev. S. Simpson of Usher's Quay had been in the habit of preaching there twice a week. The services at first were held in the house of Mr. Beggs, now Wilde's coach factory, in Little Bray. Mr. Beggs used to go round and announce the preachers. The Rev. Dr. Urwick often preached there. After the Irish Evangelical Society took charge of the work, the students from their theological college in Prussia Street preached there for a considerable time in the court-house. The attendance at these services was so encouraging that in 1817 a plot of ground was taken, and "a plain but neat place of worship was built." The population of Bray "and its vicinity" is said to have been at this time about 5,000 souls.

In 1827 the Rev. C. E. Paul was settled as the

---

[1] *Reports of the Irish Evangelical Society*, 1815-1831. Library of Assembly's College, Belfast.

Society's minister at Bray. He was succeeded by the Rev. J. B. Grey. Mr. Grey was succeeded by the Rev. D. H. Creighton. In 1834 Mr. Creighton and the congregation of Bray were received into connection with the Secession Synod, under the care of the Monaghan Presbytery. At that time Mr. Creighton came from Dublin every Sabbath on the mail-car, but about 1836 he began to reside in Bray. Mr. Creighton was an able and earnest preacher.[1] In 1840, however, his health gave way; the congregation fell off considerably; and in 1841 he obtained leave for the congregation to choose an assistant and successor. In 1838 the congregation had already been transferred from the Presbytery of Monaghan to the new (Secession) Presbytery of Dublin. The union of the Synods in 1840 of course resulted in the congregation of Bray coming under the care of the General Assembly.

In 1841 the Presbytery of Dublin met at Bray. Mr. George Matthews, who appears to have been, temporarily at least, a member of the congregation, was present. He stated that there were about twenty persons then in attendance on public worship, and sixteen communicants, and that there were altogether only six Presbyterian families in connection with the congregation, some of whom resided at a great distance. Mr. Matthews, coming out to Bray, and finding the church almost deserted, had himself procured the services of Mr. Bennett, a licentiate, Mr. Matthews paying his expenses. The place of worship, Mr. Matthews stated, belonged to the Evangelical Society. The station of Bray, he added, was most unpromising.

---

[1] See *Redemption Consummated*. A discourse on the death of Simon Christie, Esq. By the Rev. D. H. Creighton, 1837. The text is Hosea xii. 14. Magee College Library.

Presbyterian people were few. There was no inducement to persons of enterprise to settle in Bray, which was a mere fishing-station; and besides, there was "considerable High Church feeling" in the place.

The services, however, were continued, being chiefly conducted by licentiates, until in 1846 the Rev. John Powell, who had already been labouring there for about a year as licentiate, was ordained as assistant minister in Bray. A local committee had previously been organised to sustain and promote the interests of the congregation. The members of committee were Messrs. Lane, Leckie, Hamilton, Allison, and Lumsden; Mr. Alison being secretary, and Mr. Lumsden, treasurer. The call to Mr. Powell was signed by C. S. Leckie, William Allison, J. Hamilton, Alexander Clark, William Lumsden, and John McIntosh, and offered £35 of stipend. During Mr. Powell's ministry in Bray he taught a school in what is now called Novara House, in which many of the present merchants of Bray received their early education. Mr. Powell did not remain long in Bray, and accepted a call to Carlow in 1848.

After Mr. Powell's removal, the Presbytery seemed still undecided as to whether Bray should still be maintained as a congregation. A special visitation was held at Bray in January, 1849, to report to the Mission Directors concerning its state and prospects. The members of the congregational committee present on that occasion were William Allison, John Grant, Nathaniel Beggs, J. Lumsden, and Alexander Clarke. It was stated that the committee undertook to raise £21 annually, and that the congregation was prepared to give a unanimous call to the Rev. James Patterson, licentiate of the Newry Presbytery.

The Presbytery and the Mission Board seem to have

made up their minds that Bray was worth trying again, for on the 24th of April, 1849, the Rev. James Patterson was ordained as its minister. Mr. Patterson's call was signed by twenty-one persons, of whom scarcely twelve were professed Presbyterians, the remainder being of other denominations. At the first communion at which he presided, there were eight communicants; the average attendance at public worship was twenty-five. The Sabbath collections amounted to £6 per annum, and the missionary collections were about £4.

Under Mr. Patterson's faithful and energetic ministry the congregation steadily grew and prospered. At a visitation Presbytery held in 1854, Mr. Nathaniel Beggs was ordained to the office of the eldership. At this visitation Mr. Patterson reported that he preached once a fortnight at Kilpedder, Co. Wicklow, and that the average attendance there was from fifty to sixty.

Gradually the old place of worship in the Main Street became too small, and in 1858 the present beautiful church on the Quinsboro' Road was dedicated for divine worship, the Rev. Dr. Cooke of Belfast conducting the services on the occasion. By Mr. Patterson's efforts a manse was also built about the same time.

Bray congregation was one of the first in recent years to avail itself of an instrumental accompaniment in the service of praise, and was for several years reported to the Assembly as being guilty of this ecclesiastical offence.

In the year 1881 the Rev. James Patterson obtained leave for his congregation to choose an assistant and successor. He had laboured for nearly thirty-three years as minister of Bray, and advancing years made him feel the necessity of a little rest.[1] The present

---

[1] Mr. Patterson died in February, 1886.

minister, Rev. Clarke H. Irwin, M.A., was ordained there in December, 1881. In 1887 a schoolhouse was erected, where there is at present a flourishing school in connection with the National Board. The foundation stone was laid by the Earl of Meath. A teacher's residence has been added within the present year, 1890.

BRUNSWICK STREET MISSION CHURCH, DUBLIN.

In 1853 the General Assembly resolved to establish a mission in Dublin as part of its Irish Mission, and the Rev. Hamilton Magee was asked to undertake it. Mr. Magee had previously laboured as missionary in Connaught from the year 1848. There his colleagues were the Revs. John Hall, Matthew Kerr, and T. Y. Killen. He came to Dublin in February, 1854. In 1858 a church was built with schools attached for carrying on his work. In 1864 a new church was built in Jervis Street. For a time Dr. Magee was set apart for the work of the press, the training of colporteurs, etc. For sixteen years he edited *Plain Words*, and subsequently the *Key of Truth*, now the *Christian Irishman*. He was also the first editor of the *Presbyterian Churchman*. In all these publications Dr. Magee has had as his motto, "Speaking the truth in love," and has laboured to promote a spirit of inquiry and a spirit of kindliness and charity amongst both Protestants and Roman Catholics. Some years ago he received the degree of D.D. from the Presbyterian Theological Faculty.

For a time the pastorate of Jervis Street was occupied by the Rev. J. G. Philips, B.A., now of Damascus, and the Rev. William Moore, M.A., now of Spain. After Mr. Moore's acceptance of a call to Gloucester Street, Dublin, the congregation of Jervis Street removed to

Brunswick Street, and Dr. Magee resumed the congregational work. In 1886 the Rev. Alexander Hall, B.A., was ordained assistant missionary pastor at Brunswick Street. Mr. Hall removed to Drogheda in 1889.

CARLOW.

In 1655 there was an Independent minister in Carlow under the Commonwealth. His name was Roger Muckle. Later on the congregation became Presbyterian and was connected with the Synod of Munster. Mr. Batty and Mr. Logan succeeded Mr. Muckle, and from 1724 to 1742, at least, the Rev. D. Syms was minister there.[1] About 1750 the congregation became extinct. But about the year 1818 the Presbyterians of Carlow became so numerous that they once more desired to have a minister of their own. The Rev. Henry Cooke, then minister of Duneane, was attending medical classes in Trinity College at that time, and he used to go to Carlow by coach every Saturday, preach there on Sabbath, and return again to his studies on Monday morning. It should be mentioned that here, as in many other cases, the Trustees of the General Fund took an important part in the revival of Presbyterianism, for in 1817 they had requested Mr. Baird, minister of Stratford-on-Slaney, to preach as frequently as he could in Carlow, and report upon the prospect of reviving the congregation in that town. Mr. Cooke received the special thanks of the General Fund trustees for his zealous exertions to form a congregation at Carlow; and both he and the Rev. Robert Stewart of Broughshane were thanked by the Synod of Munster for their labours there.

---

[1] *Report of Chancery Proceedings*, relative to the General Fund. Dublin, 1851.

Their efforts proved to be successful. A church was built, the foundation stone of which was laid by Mr. C. Butler, sovereign of the town of Carlow, on the 18th June, 1818. The church was opened in 1819 by the Rev. James Horner of Dublin.[1] In 1820 the Rev. James Morgan was ordained in the pastorate at Carlow. Mr. Morgan became a most eminent minister of the Irish Presbyterian Church. He was afterwards minister of Fisherwick Place Church, Belfast, and was the first Convener of the General Assembly's Foreign Mission. He also found time for literary work. His best-known works are *The Scripture Testimony to the Holy Spirit*,[2] and a Commentary on the Epistles of St. John. In 1824 Mr. Morgan removed to Lisburn. He was succeeded by Revs. Edward Alexander (1825-1828), William Blood (1830-1835), and Warrand Carlile (1837-1842).

A visitation Presbytery which was held in Carlow in April, 1842, came to the following finding:—"The Presbytery had great pleasure in observing that Mr. Carlile's labours are highly appreciated and his person respected amongst his people. They regret, however, to find that in one respect the difficulties of his position have been increasing since last visitation in consequence of the growing sectarian and exclusive spirit of the clergy of the Established Church, who now prohibit their people from attendance in the Scots' Church, either for public worship or for any religious meeting whatever." On the evening of that visitation a missionary meeting was held, and a collection was taken for the Home Mission, amounting to £3 13s. In October, 1842, Mr. Carlile went to Jamaica as a missionary in connection with the Scottish Missionary Society.

---

[1] Rev. R. T. Bailey, M.A., in *Missionary Herald*, March, 1890.
[2] Edinburgh: T. and T. Clark, 1865.

The next minister was Rev. David McTaggart (1843-1848). He was succeeded by Rev. John Powell (1848-1855), previously of Bray; Rev. John Barnett (1856-1866), now of Katesbridge; Rev. R. S. Coffey (1866-1875), afterwards of Bandon, and now of Bradford, England; Rev. G. W. Neely (1875-1878); Rev. Neil S. Forsythe (1879-1887); and the present minister, Rev. R. T. Bailey, M.A., who was installed there on December 20th, 1887.

CLONTARF.

Previous to 1818 there had been two Secession congregations in Dublin, Mary's Abbey and Mass Lane. But in that year they united, and formed the congregation of Union Chapel. In the year 1836, however, the Secession Synod thought there was room for another congregation, and opened a mission station, which was soon organised into a congregation. Its first minister was the Rev. William Wilson, previously minister of Dunboe (Secession) congregation, now known as 2nd Dunboe. After his installation, the congregation purchased a house for public worship in D'Olier Street, costing £600. The beginning was most encouraging, the attendance varying from a hundred and fifty to two hundred people. The congregation was then known as 2nd Dublin, and in 1838 it was placed along with the Secession congregations of 1st Dublin, Bray, and Drogheda, under the care of the Secession Presbytery of Dublin. In 1846 the place of worship in D'Olier Street was sold, and a new church was erected by the congregation in Lower Gloucester Street.

In 1854 Mr. Wilson retired from the active duties of the ministry, on account of ill-health, and was succeeded by Rev. James Edgar, ordained there as assistant and successor in 1855. In 1850 the members of Gloucester Street congregation who were associated with Mr. Wilson as Trustees of the General Fund, were Dr. James Foulis Duncan, Mr. William Bell Herron, and Mr. John Hamilton Reid.

The Rev. James Edgar died suddenly in 1863, and in August of the same year the Rev. Robert Watts was installed there. In 1866 Dr. Watts resigned, having been appointed Professor of Systematic Theology in the Assembly's College, Belfast. Dr. Watts has taken a prominent place as a theological writer and controversialist. His principal works are : *The Newer Criticism; Faith and Inspiration;* and *The Reign of Causality.* In December, 1866, the Rev. Robert Hanna was ordained in Gloucester Street. Mr. Hanna removed to England in 1880, and was succeeded by the Rev. William Moore, M.A. In 1883 Mr. Moore was appointed by the General Assembly superintendent of a theological training college at Puerto Santa Maria in Spain, in which country he had laboured as a missionary previous to his settlement in Gloucester Street. In 1884 the present minister, Rev. J. L. Morrow, M.A., was ordained. Mr. Morrow was for some years editor of the *Presbyterian Churchman.* Owing to the increasing number of Presbyterian residents in the district of Clontarf, it was decided at a meeting of Gloucester Street congregation in 1888 to request the Presbytery to transfer the congregation to Clontarf. This request was granted by the Presbytery with the sanction of the General Assembly, and on the 26th July, 1889, the foundation-stones of the new church at Clontarf were laid. By Mr. Morrow's energetic efforts, and the assistance of members of his congregation and other friends, a large sum of money was speedily raised for the building, which was opened in May, 1890, by services conducted by Rev. George Davidson of Edinburgh, and Rev. R. J. Lynd, D.D., Belfast.

DONORE, DUBLIN (formerly BELVIEW).

About 1860 a considerable number of Scotch artisans resided in the south-western district of Dublin, a long distance from any of the then existing Presbyterian churches. The Presbytery of Dublin accordingly resolved to establish a mission in that district, and the Rev. John M. Hamilton, A.M., licentiate of the Presbytery of Route, was invited to take charge of it. This was in 1861. Mr. Hamilton's labours were so successful that in a short time a church was erected at Belview and a congregation organised. The church was opened almost free of debt, mainly through the exertions of the Rev. Dr. Kirkpatrick, by whom the opening sermons were preached on the last Sabbath of October, 1862. Mr. Hamilton was ordained as the first minister of the new congregation, March 31st, 1863.

The church became gradually shut in by the rapidly extending buildings of Guinness's Brewery, until at length it might have almost been regarded as an ecclesiastical appendage of that establishment. The church, moreover, required extensive repairs. The congregation therefore resolved to build a new church. A site was obtained at Donore, on the South Circular Road. The foundation-stone of the new church was laid on the 26th October, 1880, by the Rev. Jackson Smyth, D.D., Moderator of the General Assembly. The church, a substantial and attractive building, was formally opened in July, 1881, by the Rev. W. Fleming Stevenson, D.D., Moderator of the General Assembly, and the

Rev. J. L. Porter, D.D., President of Queen's College, Belfast, who preached on successive Sabbaths. A commodious manse and a lecture-hall were soon added, the total cost of all the new buildings being about £4,300. It is now proposed to erect schools in connection with the congregation.

Mr. Hamilton is Chaplain to the Royal Hibernian Military School, where he officiates every Sabbath in addition to his services at Donore. He is also Clerk of the Presbytery of Dublin.

Drogheda.

The congregation of Drogheda was originally formed by the English Independents and Presbyterians who were in the garrison placed there by Oliver Cromwell about 1650. The first regular was Mr. Jenner, who laboured there from 1652 to 1659. The celebrated Dr. Williams was minister there from 1659 till his removal to Strand Street, Dublin, in 1667. Then came Mr. Toy, who continued till about 1688.[1] The turmoil of the Revolution, and especially the excitement in the neighbourhood of the Boyne, when the troops of James occupied the town, had driven the Presbyterians largely from the place, for there was no regular minister settled there for about ten years after this. But the few Presbyterians who remained had occasional services provided for them by ministers from the North.

The history of Presbyterianism in Drogheda in the early part of the eighteenth century is a history of persecution and suffering. In 1708 the Rev. James Fleming, minister of Lurgan, came to preach there for two Sabbaths. On the Monday after he had preached the

---

[1] Kirkpatrick's *Presbyterian Loyalty* (1713), Part III., Chap. 2.

second Sabbath he and three of his hearers were bound over to stand their trial at the next assizes, at the instigation of Dean Cox, the rector of the parish.[1] The charge against them was riot and unlawful assembly! Several of the congregation were obliged to pay a fine to prevent them from being set in the stocks, as they were peaceably going home from the service, on the charge of travelling on the Lord's Day.

But this was not all. Mr. Fleming was thus dealt with in August. While he was looking forward to his trial at the assizes, the Rev. William Biggar, minister of Bangor, preached to the Presbyterians in Drogheda on the 3rd of October. This was too much for the rector. He again interposed, with the result that Mr. Biggar was committed to prison for three months by the Mayor of Drogheda, "without bail or mainprize." At this time there were about two hundred Presbyterians in Drogheda and its neighbourhood. A memorial to the Lords-Justices of Ireland was drawn up setting forth the hardship of the case. The consequence was that, after being imprisoned for six weeks in the common gaol, Mr. Biggar was released. A *noli prosequi* was subsequently entered in Mr. Fleming's case. The particulars of these cases at Drogheda have been more fully given above. The Mayor's order for Mr. Biggar's committal to prison; "remarks on the mittimus given Mr. Biggar at Drogheda"; and the memorial to the Lords-Justices, will be found in the appendix to Reid's *History of the Presbyterian Church in Ireland*, Vol. III. They are well worth reading. Let it be remembered that at this time, when Presbyterian ministers were thus summoned and imprisoned for preaching the gospel, and Presby-

---

[1] See above, Chap. IV., p. 29; Chap. VII., p. 43.

terian people fined for going to hear their own ministers preach, at the instigation of an Episcopalian rector and with the concurrence of an Episcopalian archbishop, two Roman Catholic priests were permitted to conduct their religious services without molestation in this very town of Drogheda. Yet "the Lords spiritual and temporal" of Ireland were so grieved at the *noli prosequi* being entered, that in the year 1711 they drew up an address to Queen Anne, strongly condemning this lenient treatment of "Dissenters."[1]

Notwithstanding all this intolerance and persecution, the Presbyterian cause in Drogheda continued to hold its own. The Rev. Hugh Henry was ordained as minister of Drogheda in 1711, and laboured there till his death in 1744. In 1745 the congregation at its own request was transferred to the Dublin Presbytery. Mr. Henry was succeeded by Mr. Bryan, Mr. Simpson, and Mr. Fulton. Mr. Fulton was minister in 1763.[2]

In Drogheda, however, as elsewhere in the history of Irish Presbyterianism, moderatism and "new light" doctrines succeeded only too well in effecting the injury which persecution failed to inflict. Towards the close of the eighteenth century the Presbyterian congregation of Drogheda became extinct.

But it was only for a short time. In February, 1820, the Secession Synod commenced operations in Drogheda, and soon after in Collon, a village six miles away, and services were regularly held in both places.[3] In 1822 the Rev. Josias Wilson, previously of Tassagh, was installed there by the Secession Presbytery of Market-

---

[1] See above, Chapter VII., p. 43.
[2] Report of Proceedings *re* General Fund (1851), p. 43.
[3] Reports of Home Mission of Seceding Synod. Library of Assembly's College, Belfast.

hill, as minister of the united congregations of Drogheda and Collon.

When Mr. Wilson went to Drogheda the number of Presbyterians in the town was only fifteen. His great work was "moral excavation." By this the missionary congregation of Drogheda was fostered into life. Through his self-denying exertions a church, manse, and schools were erected in Drogheda at a cost of £2,000, and a respectable congregation was formed and continued to flourish under his ministry. The foundation-stone of the new church was laid in 1826 by the Mayor of Drogheda, W. O. Fairclough, Esq. About a hundred years before, another Mayor of Drogheda had sent a Presbyterian minister to gaol for preaching in a private house. Truly the times were changed.[1]

Mr. Wilson was a vigorous advocate of temperance. In a charge at the ordination of Rev. M. McAuley of Cahans, also delivered at ordination of Rev. Samuel Bigham of Lisbellaw,[2] he said: "I feel it nearly a degradation to you and myself to admonish you against all intemperate habits—and ever warn your people against the pestilential atmosphere of the tavern and the public-house. They are generally sinks of sin, hotbeds of profanity, ante-chambers of hell." In 1835 he removed to Townsend Street, Belfast, and was subsequently minister in London, where he died. A monument is there erected to his memory.

Mr. Wilson was succeeded by Rev. Samuel Boyd, who resigned the congregation and the Presbyterian ministry in 1842, as he no longer believed in infant

---

[1] *Memoir of Rev. Josias Wilson*, by H. Hastings, M.D., Oxon. London: 1850. See also *Discourse* on his death, by Rev. John Weir, Townsend Street, Belfast: 1847. Magee College Library.

[2] Printed at Drogheda, 1829. Library of Assembly's College, Belfast.

baptism, and took exception to other matters in the discipline of the Presbyterian Church. In the same year the Rev. Thomas Logan was installed as minister of Drogheda. Owing to infirmity, Mr. Logan obtained leave for the congregation to choose an assistant and successor, and in 1865 the Rev. A. Ross Crawford was ordained there. Mr. Crawford obtained the degree of LL.D., and was called to the Irish Bar in 1889, in consequence of which he demitted the ministry, and the Rev. Alexander Hall, B.A. (previously of Brunswick Street Mission, Dublin), was installed there in June, 1889.

DUNCANNON.

The first minister of Duncannon congregation, near Waterford, was the Rev. James Caldwell, who was ordained there by the Presbytery of Dublin, March 30th, 1858. He was succeeded by the present minister, Rev. John Browne, who was ordained there on the 13th March, 1860.

ENNISCORTHY.

There was a Presbyterian congregation at Enniscorthy at an early date. The first minister of whom we have any record was Rev. Alexander Coldin. He was reported to the General Assembly of Scotland as one of those obliged to leave Ireland in March, 1689, the troublous time of the Revolutionary wars. He was a graduate of Edinburgh University in 1675. After leaving Enniscorthy, he became minister at Dunse, Scotland, and subsequently at Oxam, in the Presbytery of Jedburgh, where he died in 1738. He was invited by the people of Lewistown, in the United States, to become their minister in 1708, the invitation being conveyed to him in a letter from the celebrated Francis Makemie, by order of the Presbytery of Philadelphia.[1] Subsequent ministers of Enniscorthy, during the eighteenth century, were Mr. Cowden and Mr. Starke, but we have no record of them but their names. In 1826 the Rev. Francis William Geddes was ordained there by the Presbytery of Munster, the Rev. W. McCance of Waterford being one of those taking part in the ordination service. Mr. Geddes was a Scotchman who had served under Wellington in the Peninsular War. He was an ecclesiastical warrior as well, as his reputation in Enniscorthy was that of "a powerful controversial preacher." Mr. Geddes died about 1833. He was succeeded by another minister who, however, remained a very short time.

For a time the congregation became extinct. Enniscorthy was visited occasionally, however, by Presbyterian ministers. Among those who preached there about 1840 were the Rev. Jonathan Simpson, now of Portrush, and the late Rev. Robert Knox, afterwards of Belfast. In Mr. Knox's report to the Home Mission of the Synod of Ulster in 1840, he says regarding Enniscorthy: "I preached in the market-house on a Tuesday evening to about one hundred and thirty persons, most of whom had been at one time Presbyterians. Regular services have since been kept up every Friday evening." He adds, however, that recent interference of the clergy of the Established Church had clouded the prospects there. He also mentions that above thirty families had been connected with the congregation, or had at least contributed to the support of the last minister.

But it was nearly twenty years later before any

---

[1] Briggs: *American Presbyterianism*, Chap. IV.

successful effort was made to revive the cause of Presbyterianism in Enniscorthy. A number of Presbyterians from Scotland and from Ulster came to reside in that neighbourhood for some years before and after 1860. Amongst these settlers the Rev. William Burns of Wexford had for a time two preaching stations—one at Ballingall, seven miles from Enniscorthy in a north-westerly direction, the other near the village of Clonrocke, also seven miles from Enniscorthy on the road to New Ross. Both of these were subsequently abandoned, and a central station was formed at Enniscorthy, where for a time Mr. Burns preached regularly every Sabbath evening. In 1865 Enniscorthy was formed into a congregation under the care of the Presbytery of Dublin. The church was built in 1866 by Mr. Patrick Kew, an elder in Union Chapel, Dublin, and cost about £600. On March 26th, 1867, the present minister, Rev. William Arnold, M.A., was ordained at Enniscorthy. By his zealous efforts, the present beautifully-situated manse was built in 1869, and the congregation was free of debt in a year after he had commenced to occupy it.

Greystones and Kilpedder.

A Presbyterian service has been held at Kilpedder, between Delgany and Newtownmountkennedy, Co. Wicklow, since about 1850. At a visitation Presbytery, held at Bray in 1854, the Rev. James Patterson, minister of Bray, reported that he preached at Kilpedder on the afternoon of every alternate Sabbath, the attendance at the service there being usually between fifty and sixty. In 1858, however, the new Presbyterian church at Bray was built, and the members of Mr. Patterson's congregation there felt that service should be held in their church every Sabbath evening instead of on alternate Sabbaths, as was the case when he preached at Kilpedder. Mr. Henry of Trudder and Mr. Clark of Tinna Park were then active members of the little congregation at Kilpedder, and memorialised the Presbytery to continue the supply of Presbyterian services there. After a time it was arranged that the minister of Wicklow should preach at Kilpedder as part of his duty. The Rev. George McCaughey preached there almost every Sabbath during the greater part of his ministry at Wicklow. During his charge of Kilpedder the present neat church was built by the generosity of the late Mr. Clark of Tinna Park, the services having previously been held in a large room. Mrs. Clark, who has since removed to Glasgow, to the great regret of the congregation at Kilpedder, was also a generous supporter of the Presbyterian services there.

Meantime the growing watering-place of Greystones, on the County Wicklow coast, had been attracting the attention of the Dublin Presbytery, as it was known that many Presbyterian visitors frequented it during the summer months. As Greystones is but a short distance from Kilpedder, it was accordingly arranged by the Presbytery and the Board of Missions, that a service should be commenced at Greystones, and that a licentiate should conduct the services at both places, and labour in the surrounding neighbourhood. The first Presbyterian services were held at Greystones in the summer of 1885. Here a kindly manifestation of good feeling and Christian brotherhood took place. The Episcopalian minister of Greystones, Rev. Edward S. Daunt, a man of lovable disposition and earnest spirit, granted the use of the schoolhouse under his management, and it was there that for the first summer the Presbyterian services were held every Lord's Day. Soon after this a site for the erection of a Presbyterian church was granted by W. R. La Touche, Esq., D.L., of Bellevue, and in 1886 the summer services were held in a large tent erected there, pending the building of the church. The foundation-stone of the new church at Greystones was laid on March 3rd, 1887, by Mr. La Touche, and amongst those who took part in the services of the occasion were the Moderator of the General Assembly (Rev. Robert Ross, D.D., of Derry), Rev. J. W. Whigham, D.D., Rev. E. S. Daunt (Episcopalian), and Rev. J. C. Bass (Methodist). It was a pleasant exhibition of Christian unity. The church was opened for public worship in July, 1887, by the Rev. J. W. Whigham and the Rev. J. S. Hamilton, M.A., of Rutland Square. In June, 1889, the General Assembly granted leave to organise into a congregation the mission stations of Greystones and Kilpedder. This has been done, and the Rev. Samuel Lundie, previously of McKelvey's Grove, has just been installed in this promising sphere, May, 1890.

KILKENNY.

The congregation of Kilkenny was organised in 1838. Its first minister was the Rev. Joshua Collins, ordained there in 1841. In 1847 Mr. Collins accepted the pastorate of Berry Street Church, Belfast. He was succeeded by Rev. James Porter, who was ordained at Kilkenny in 1848. In 1877 Mr. Porter resigned, and accepted ordination by the Bishop of Kilmore as a deacon of the Episcopal Church. In the same year the Rev. David Mitchell, previously of Buncrana, was installed as his successor. Mr. Mitchell's pastorate at

Kilkenny was a short one, for in 1879 he removed to Tullamore, and afterwards to Warrenpoint. In 1880 the Rev. W. Cooke, previously of Drumkeen, was installed at Kilkenny. Mr. Cooke died in 1887, and was succeeded by the Rev. J. H. Morton, M.A., installed there in the same year.

KILLUCAN.

In the year 1843 the members of the Presbyterian Church in and around Killucan, having been for some time supplied with preaching by the Presbytery of Bailieborough, memorialised that court to erect them into a congregation. The Presbytery of Bailieborough granted the request, and formed the congregation of Killucan on November 9th, 1843. The first minister was the Rev. Henry Sheil McKee, M.A., who was ordained there August 14th, 1844. On October 3rd, 1844, the foundation-stone of the church was laid by Benjamin Digby, Esq., of Ballinacurra House, Moyvore, on a site granted by the Earl of Longford. The Rev. John Boyd of Moyvore conducted the religious services on the occasion.[1] The church was opened for public worship by the Rev. W. B. Kirkpatrick, D.D., of Dublin, December 10th, 1845. In 1846 the following gentlemen were ordained as the first elders of the congregation : Messrs. George Ronaldson, John N. McCulloch, James Maxwell and Robert Millie. The congregation was transferred from the Presbytery of Bailieborough to the Presbytery of Dublin in the year 1849.[2] In 1850 Messrs. Richard Armstrong Gray, David Moore and William McCulloch, were ordained here to the office of

---

[1] Records of congregation of Killucan.
[2] *Minutes of General Assembly*, 1849.

the eldership. A manse was built in 1850 on a plot of ground adjoining the church. Mission stations were opened and regular services were held by the minister of Killucan in Edenderry, Rathmoyle, and Castlepollard. In 1865 Dr. McKee was appointed to the Professorship of Latin and Greek in Magee College, Derry, and resigned the pastorate of Killucan. He was succeeded by the present minister, Rev. John Rainey, B.A., who was ordained there in March, 1866. The market-house at Castlepollard, in which services had hitherto been held, being found unsuitable, a subscription was raised, and a little church built on a site granted by William Pollard Urquhart, Esq., M.P., in 1867. Services are also conducted at Castlepollard by Rev. James Mitchell of Tully.

KINGSTOWN.

The now flourishing congregation of Kingstown had humble beginnings. From the year 1818 several Scotch engineers, mechanics and others, came over to work at the erection of the new harbour and piers. Messrs. Rennie and Aird were the chief engineers, both Presbyterians. About 1822 services were commenced in a loft in Dunleary, and were conducted by members of the Dublin Presbytery. The services were afterwards held in a loft in the harbour workyard, duly seated, and were well attended.[1] In 1827 the congregation was formally organised by the Presbytery of Dublin, and the first minister, Rev. William Freeland, LL.D., was ordained there on Sabbath, June 1st, 1828.[2] It is not usual now to have ordination services on the Lord's Day; the convenience of ministers being

---

[1] MS. statement of Rev. John Armstrong.
[2] *Minutes of Dublin Presbytery.*

probably the reason for preferring a week-day. Mr. John Reid and Mr. McCulloch were at the same time set apart to the eldership. Dr. Freeland was a man of much ability, and a very instructive expositor of Scripture. He was for a time very popular. His ministry was attended by many members of the then Established Church, including Fellows of Trinity College, naval officers and others. But some disagreements having arisen between him and members of the congregation, his usefulness in Kingstown became impaired, and by the advice of the Synod of Ulster he resigned in 1838. He afterwards became minister of Ballygawley congregation, which, however, he resigned in 1841. In 1838 the congregation of Kingstown called the Rev. James White, licentiate of Bailieborough Presbytery, to be their minister. He accepted the call; but a delay took place owing to some previous financial difficulty in the congregation, and Mr. White accepted a call to 1st Carrickfergus, of which he was sole minister for over fifty years. The congregation was two years without a settled minister, till the ordination of the Rev. John Armstrong, June 30th, 1840.

Under Mr. Armstrong's faithful ministry the congregation grew and flourished. When he began his pastorate there the attendance at public worship was less than thirty people. When he left there were forty-seven families connected with the congregation, after the secession of the Congregationalists, who had previously attended the Presbyterian church, but then formed a separate congregation under the pastorate of Mr. J. Denham Smith. Mr. Armstrong, owing to failing health, resigned the congregation in 1859. Though residing in England, he still continues to be a member of the Dublin Presbytery.

The Rev. S. J. Hanson, previously minister at Conlig, Co. Down, was installed at Kingstown, February 23rd, 1860. He was but a short time in the pastorate there, when, in 1862, the present beautiful church and adjoining manse were built. The erection of the new church was largely owing to the munificence of four members, Messrs. Ferguson, Findlater, Hope, and Weir. Of these four, Mr. Weir alone survives. Mr. Hanson received a call to 1st Newry, in 1867, but declined to accept it. He died on February 1st, 1890, within a few days of completing the thirtieth year of his pastorate at Kingstown. He was an eloquent and impressive preacher, and a man of kindly and gentle disposition. It was his habit for many years to give his people a New Year's motto, and to add to the motto verses of his own composition. His motto for 1890 was "Abide with us" (Luke xxiv. 29), and the closing verses of his New Year's poem were:

> "O solemn thought, to think
> That this year I may die,
> And all my cherished earthly hopes
> In the cold grave with me lie.
>
> "So be it, Lord; Thy will be done—
> But, Lord, abide with me,
> To cheer me through the Jordan flood,
> And bring me home to Thee."

LUCAN.

For some years prior to 1876 the Presbytery of Dublin carried on a mission at Lucan, principally under the care of the Rev. Dr. Black, then of Ormond Quay. After Dr. Black's removal to Inverness, the Rev. W. F. White was appointed itinerant missionary by the Board of Missions, and was installed at Lucan by the Dublin Presbytery, March 3rd, 1876. In December of the same year the congregation was formally organised. Through Mr. White's energetic efforts a neat church was erected, and a manse was purchased in a fine situation and with several acres of land attached. Mr. White died on June 29th, 1887, and was succeeded by the present minister, Rev. George McCaughey, B.A., previously minister of Wicklow, who was installed at Lucan, November 11th, 1887.

Besides the services at Lucan, service is held by the minister every Sabbath at Chapelizod, between Lucan and Dublin. The congregational committee at Lucan at present consists of Messrs. Patrick W. Barr, John Barr, William Harrison, and William Ronaldson. The treasurer is Mr. Henry Jack.

MOUNTMELLICK.

During the last century the Presbyterians of Mountmellick were occasionally supplied with services by the ministers of the now extinct congregations of Aughmacart and Ballybrittas. The Secession Synod was the first to establish a regular congregation in Mountmellick. From 1820 to 1829 it maintained a constant supply of licentiates, and finally the Rev. Thomas Clarke was ordained as minister there by a Commission of Synod, September 25th, 1829. Mr. Clarke, however, only remained for two years, when he removed to Magheramlet, Co. Down. For some time after his removal in 1831 the congregation continued to be supplied by licentiates, but after a time even these temporary supplies were discontinued. In 1843, however, an influx of Scotch Presbyterians caused the congregation to be revived again. For a while a fortnightly service was regularly held by the Rev. John Edmonds, itinerant missionary of the General Assembly, and in

1846 the Rev. David Greer was ordained there by the Presbytery of Athlone. Mr. Greer removed to the Mariners' Church, Belfast, in 1849, and afterwards was for some years a minister in America, whence he returned to Ireland, and became minister of Cavanaleck, where he died in 1884. In 1850 the congregation of Mountmellick was transferred to the Presbytery of Dublin, and was placed under the care of the Rev. Henry McManus. Mr. McManus was installed on September 6th, 1853, and on the same day the foundation-stone of the new church was laid by William Todd, Esq., of Dublin. The church was opened by the Rev. Dr. Morgan of Belfast, August 27th, 1854. Mr. McManus was author of *Sketches of the Irish Highlands* (London: 1863). He resigned the pastorate of Mountmellick in 1858, and died in Dublin in 1864. The present minister, Rev. Robert H. Harshaw, was installed there on March 22nd, 1859.[1]

NAAS.

About the close of 1856 or beginning of 1857 the Rev. James Shannon was appointed as itinerant missionary in County Kildare, and was received under the care of the Dublin Presbytery. Services had previously been held at Naas by Rev. John Hall of Athy (now of Waterford) and the Rev. R. McMorris, now of Manorcunningham, Co. Donegal. A staunch supporter of Presbyterianism in Naas at that time was Mr. Alex. Maxwell. Mr. Maxwell's nephew, Mr. George Maxwell, was afterwards for many years elder and treasurer of the congregation. In August, 1857, the Presbyterians residing in Naas and its neighbourhood were formally

---

[1] MS. records of congregation. See also Killen's *History of Congregations*.

organised into a congregation, and on January 1st, 1858, Mr. Shannon was installed in Naas as their first pastor. Mr. Shannon died suddenly of heart disease while crossing in the steamer between Dublin and Holyhead, May 20th, 1879. He was succeeded by the Rev. William Elliott, M.A., the present minister, who was ordained at Naas, October 21st, 1879. Mr. Elliott has faithfully carried on and extended the pioneer work so successfully done by Mr. Shannon. His district covers a large area of country, and he holds regular services not only in the town of Naas, but at the mission stations of Straffan, Coolcarrigan, Newbridge, etc. The neat church, in the centre of the town, and the manse, situated on a considerable piece of ground outside the town, were built during the ministry of Mr. Shannon. The foundation-stone of the church was laid by John La Touche, Esq., D.L., and the church was opened in 1867 by the Rev. Dr. Wilson of Limerick.

During Mr. Elliott's ministry two schools have been opened in connection with the congregation, one at Naas and the other at Newbridge.

Nenagh and Cloughjordan.

The mission stations of Nenagh and Cloughjordan were first ministered to by the Rev. Matthew Kerr (now of Cork). After labouring for several years in Connaught, Mr. Kerr was appointed by the Board of Missions in 1862 to the office of missionary in Tipperary. Residing at Templemore, Mr. Kerr carried on his missionary labours over a widely-extended district, conducting services every Sabbath at stations many miles apart. Among these stations were Nenagh and Cloughjordan. Mr. Kerr removed to Queen Street,

Cork, in 1874. He was succeeded by the Rev. Robert R. Drysdale, who was ordained in October, 1877. Mr. Drysdale removed to Creggan in 1882, and was succeeded by the Rev. James Douglas, licentiate of the Free Church of Scotland, who was ordained at Nenagh, February 8th, 1883. Residing at Nenagh, Mr. Douglas has services at Nenagh, Cloughjordan and Roscrea.

ORMOND QUAY, DUBLIN (formerly USHER'S QUAY).

The congregation of Ormond Quay is the oldest Presbyterian congregation in Dublin. Before the present church on Ormond Quay was built, the congregation worshipped in a church on Usher's Quay. This congregation was made up of two branches, Usher's Quay and Plunket Street, of which Plunket Street was the oldest. Let us then, first of all, trace the history of Plunket Street.

Shortly after the Restoration, about 1660 or 1661, a Presbyterian congregation was formed at Bull Alley. The Rev. William Jacque, who was probably its first minister, was loosed from its charge about 1667. Taking some of his people with him, he then formed the congregation of Capel Street (afterwards Mary's Abbey and now Rutland Square). Soon after this the Rev. William Keys became minister at Bull Alley. The Rev. Patrick Adair, the oldest historian of the Irish Presbyterian Church, preached at Bull Alley on a communion Sabbath in 1672.[1] Mr. Keys was succeeded by Rev. Alexander Sinclair. Mr. Sinclair was a native of Belfast, and was licensed by the Presbytery of Antrim in 1680. After being minister at Waterford and spending some time at Bristol, he was called in

---

[1] Witherow : *Presbyterian Memorials*, I., 41.

1692 to become minister of the new church at Plunket Street, which was built in that year by the congregation of Bull Alley. He was Moderator of the Synod of Ulster in 1704. For a time Mr. Sinclair seems to have had as colleague Rev. James Arbuckle, but Mr. Arbuckle, with a portion of the congregation, joined Usher's Quay in 1713. In 1717 the Rev. Thomas Maquay was ordained as colleague of Mr. Sinclair. Mr. Maquay was a native of the city of Dublin. Mr. Sinclair died in 1722, and Mr. Maquay in 1729.[1]

The next minister of Plunket Street was the Rev. Matthew Chalmers. He only lived for a year after becoming minister of Plunket Street. He was succeeded by the Rev. John Alexander. Mr. Alexander, who was born and educated in Ulster, was for a time minister of the Presbyterian congregation at Stratford-on-Avon in England, whence he removed to Dublin. He was the lineal descendant of a noble family in Scotland. His grandson, Mr. Humphrys of Worcester, established his right to the peerage, and was recognised by the Supreme Courts of Scotland as Earl of Stirling.[2] Mr. Alexander was installed at Plunket Street, November 15th, 1730. In 1734 he was Moderator of the Synod of Ulster. He died in 1743. Relatives of this Mr. Alexander still reside at Fivemiletown, Co. Tyrone.

After Mr. Alexander came the Rev. William Patten, who was minister at Plunket Street from 1745 to 1749. He was succeeded by the Rev. Ebenezer Kelburn. Of Mr. Kelburn himself I have not been able to trace any particulars. His son, Rev. Sinclair Kelburn, A.B., was the celebrated minister of the 3rd Congregation of Belfast, who became a leader of the United Irishmen,

---

[1] Dr. William Frazer's MS. *History of General Fund.*
[2] Armstrong's *History of the Dublin Churches.*

and was imprisoned in Kilmainham in 1798.[1] The Rev. Ebenezer Kelburn died in 1773, having been minister of Plunket Street for twenty-four years.

After Mr. Kelburn's death the congregation of Plunket Street united with that of Usher's Quay. The church was disposed of to Lady Huntingdon in 1773, and service was held in it as in her other chapels. The people worshipping there were known as Calvinistic Independents. Rev. Mr. Cooper, one of the Secretaries of the Irish Evangelical Society, was their minister in 1814. Independent ministers continued to officiate till the time of Rev. S. G. Morrison, who was installed there as an Independent minister in 1843. Mr. Morrison then removed to Union Chapel, Lower Abbey Street, and became Presbyterian minister of that church.

Let us now trace the history of the Usher's Quay branch, with which the old Presbyterian congregation of Plunket Street united in 1773.

In 1684 a section of the Capel Street congregation became discontented with the ministry of Mr. Jacque, and founded another congregation at Newmarket in the Coombe. The first minister was one who at the time of the Revolution played an important part in Irish history. This was the Rev. Alexander Osborne Walker, whom Professor Witherow has justly called "the *soi-disant* governor of Derry," said in his *True Account of the Siege of Londonderry*, that Mr. Osborne, was "a spy upon the whole North, employed by Lord Tyrconnel," the Lord-Deputy of King James. The very reverse, however, was the case.[2]

---

[1] Witherow: *Presbyterian Memorials*, II., 243-246. See above p. 80.

Witherow: *Presbyterian Memorials*, I., 81 ; Witherow: *Derry and Enniskillen*, 61-67, 303-323 : Reid : *History*, II., 364-366.

Mr. Osborne had been previously minister at Brigh, Co. Tyrone. After he removed to Dublin his Northern brethren looked to him to keep them informed as to the designs of Tyrconnel. Curiously enough, Tyrconnel, acting on behalf of King James, and wanting to put down the opposition of Ulster, sent for Mr. Osborne. Knowing that he was well acquainted with the North, he proposed to him that he should go to the Protestant leaders of Ulster, who had taken up arms on behalf of the Prince of Orange, and assure them that the Government would grant them a free pardon in case they laid down their arms, but in case of resistance would visit them with utter destruction. Mr. Osborne did so; but so far from trusting Tyrconnel, he in the most earnest manner advised the Ulster leaders "as they valued their lives and interests not to put confidence in the Lord Tyrconnel, or any of his promises, but if they possibly could, to defend themselves to the utmost." The result of this advice was that the Ulster leaders rejected the proposals of Tyrconnel. They were put upon their guard. They were awakened to their danger, and, largely through the timely and prudent action of this Presbyterian minister from Dublin, Ulster was saved.

In 1707 the congregation built a new church on a plot of ground called "Usher's Garden," at the rear of Usher's Quay, and for more than a century the congregation bore the name of Usher's Quay. At this time the Rev. Henry Hook was their minister. The congregation, like that of Capel Street, was largely composed of Presbyterians from the North of Ireland. Mr. Hook was succeeded by the Rev. James Arbuckle who, with a portion of his previous congregation at Plunket Street, joined Usher's Quay in 1713. Mr. Arbuckle died in

1721, and was succeeded by the Rev. William Gray, previously of Taboyn (now Monreagh, near Derry). Mr. Gray was not installed in Usher's Quay till 1724. He returned to the North in 1728, and settling again in the neighbourhood of his old charge, founded the congregation of St. Johnston. He was succeeded by the Rev. Robert MacMaster (previously minister at Connor, County Antrim), who was installed in Usher's Quay in 1729.

Mr. MacMaster was an able preacher and a zealous pastor. He was Moderator of the Synod of Ulster in 1739. He published at least three of his sermons. One of these, *Liberty without Licentiousness*, which he preached as Moderator of the Synod when resigning office in 1740, has been pronounced by Professor Witherow the best reply to Abernethy's sermon on *Personal Persuasion*, preached before the Belfast Society in 1719.

In 1745 the Rev. William McBeath, previously of Urney, near Strabane, was installed as colleague to Mr. MacMaster. In 1750 we find Mr. MacMaster and Dr. George Machonchy, an elder of Usher's Quay congregation, appointed among the first trustees of the Synod of Ulster Widows' Fund, just then originated by Mr. William Bruce, of Wood Street congregation. Mr. MacMaster died in 1754, and Mr. McBeath in 1755.

The next minister was the Rev. Thomas Vance, previously of Ramelton, who was installed in Usher's Quay in 1755. A sermon of his, published in 1760, bears the title "*A Thanksgiving Sermon* for the late Successes of His Majesty's Arms. Preached in Dublin, November 29th, 1759." It is dedicated to the Right Hon. William Pitt.[1] Mr. Vance's first colleague was

---

[1] Witherow: *Presbyterian Memorials*, II., 325.

the Rev. Robert Nichol, who was ordained in Usher's Quay, September 11th, 1760. He died in 1762. He was succeeded by the Rev. James Caldwell, who was ordained on the 16th June, 1763, the sermon on that occasion being preached by the Rev. Charles McCollum, minister of Capel Street.[1] Mr. Vance died in 1772. Mr. Caldwell then became sole minister.

In 1773 the congregation of Plunket Street, as we have seen, united with Usher's Quay. In 1780 the Rev. Hugh Moore, previously of Billy (now Bushmills), was installed as colleague of Mr. Caldwell. Mr. Caldwell died in 1783. Mr. Moore was minister of Usher's Quay for the long period of forty-four years.

His first colleague was the Rev. William Wilson, previously, for twenty years, minister of Magherafelt. Mr. Wilson was installed in Usher's Quay in 1785. He had been Moderator of the Synod of Ulster in 1783. His son, Rev. James Wilson, D.D., became a Fellow of Trinity College, Dublin, and Professor of Mathematics there, and was afterwards Rector of Clonfeacle, Co. Tyrone. In 1799 the amount of stipend paid to the two ministers of Usher's Quay, Mr. Moore and Mr. Wilson, was £234.[2] The stipend paid at the same time to the two ministers of Mary's Abbey was £250, and, even allowing for the fact that there were two ministers in each, the amount paid by each of these congregations was among the five or six largest stipends in the Synod of Ulster. The rebellion of 1798 helped to scatter many of the smaller congregations in the South and West, but it does not seem to have had

---

[1] *Miscellaneous Sermons by Ministers of the Synod of Ulster*, 1735, 1797.

[2] Reid: *History*, III., 539.

any perceptible effect on the numbers or prosperity of the Presbyterian churches of Dublin.

Mr. Wilson died in 1807, and was succeeded as colleague by Rev. W. D. H. McEwen, who was ordained in Usher's Quay, March 16th, 1808. Mr. McEwen's father was Presbyterian minister of Killinchy, Co. Down. Mr. McEwen resigned in 1813. He was succeeded by Rev. Samuel Simpson, M.A., who was ordained as colleague to Mr. Moore, May 23rd, 1815.

Mr. Simpson was a graduate of the University of Glasgow, and a licentiate of the Presbytery of Belfast. He has left on record some interesting reminiscences of the state of religious life in Dublin when he came to the metropolis.[1]

"Genuine vital religion," he says, "was at that time at a very low ebb in England, Scotland, and Ulster. A cold orthodoxy pervaded many pulpits, whilst in others, if the Friend of Sinners was adverted to, it was generally in the way of cold reserve or indirect allusion. So far as I could learn, there was not a parish church in Dublin in 1815, and for some time afterwards, where the fundamentals of the gospel, as ruin by the fall, redemption by Christ, and regeneration by the Spirit, were statedly proclaimed, except by the Rev. Benjamin Mathias of Bethesda Chapel, Rev. Robert Nixon, Chaplain of Stevens' Hospital, and Rev. Messrs. Barker and White of Little George's, who sounded the gospel trumpet distinctly and courageously. Since that time many faithful heralds of the cross have been sent to the parish churches and free churches of this city, where souls have been converted and believers edified."

---

[1] MS. *Reminiscences of Presbyterianism in Dublin forty-five years ago.* By Rev. S. Simpson, A.M. This was written in 1860, and is preserved in the minute-book of the Presbytery of Dublin.

In Plunket Street Independent Church, he says, the Rev. Timothy Priestley preached, and was succeeded by the Rev. William Cooper, "who preached the truth as it is in Jesus faithfully and successfully for many years; but that house of worship has been for a considerable time closed; so also is Ebenezer Chapel in D'Olier Street; Zion Chapel in King's Inn Street is without a stated pastor; and the only remaining Independent chapel in Dublin [1860] is that of York Street, under the faithful ministry of Dr. Urwick."

The Rev. Hugh Moore died in 1824, but for many years previous he had been unable to officiate, in consequence of a paralytic affection. Mr. Simpson then became sole minister of Usher's Quay.

The Rev. Richard Dill, previously of Tandragee, was installed as his colleague on August 26th, 1835. On that occasion Mr. Dill made a "statement of his belief," which was entered on the minutes of Presbytery. It was in 1836 that the Synod of Ulster passed the resolution requiring all licentiates and ministers, at ordination or installation, to subscribe to the Confession of Faith. Mr. Dill was a member of a family which bulked largely, both in numbers and in ability, in the ministry of the Irish Presbyterian Church. The Dills were of Dutch extraction. Their ancestor was a soldier of William III., who settled at Fannet, Co. Donegal. At one time there were ten Dills in the Irish Presbyterian ministry. Richard Dill of Dublin, says Professor Croskery,[1] "was the most graceful orator of the family." He took a prominent part in the Magee College controversy (see above, Chap. XXV.), and has recorded his

---

[1] Croskery, and Witherow: *Life of Dr. A. P. Goudy*, p. 42.

views of that conflict in his book entitled *Prelatico-Presbyterianism*.

One of the most important services which Mr. Dill rendered to Irish Presbyterianism, and indeed to the Presbyterianism of the United Kingdom, was his masterly exposure of the treatment of Presbyterian soldiers in the army. When minister in Dublin in 1847 or 1848 he found that should a Presbyterian soldier be taken ill he was not allowed to speak with a minister of his own Church, except he could first obtain the permission of the Episcopalian chaplain. Mr. Dill's spirit was stirred within him at this instance of the religious inequality of the times. He resolved to do all in his power to remove this injustice, and by his indomitable energy and perseverance he at last succeeded. The result of his efforts, which were supported by the General Assembly, and specially by Dr. Goudy, Rev. John Macnaughtan, and Rev. John Rogers, was, that for the first time Presbyterian chaplains were attached to the army, and subsequently it was arranged that their number should be in proportion to the number of Presbyterian soldiers, and that their salary should be the same as that of the Episcopalian chaplains.

It was during Mr. Dill's ministry that Mrs. Magee, a widow lady of Usher's Quay congregation, died, leaving £60,000 to Presbyterian objects, of which £20,000 were bequeathed for Magee College. Mrs. Magee also left an endowment to the congregation of Usher's Quay.

In 1842 the Rev. Samuel Simpson, and Dr. William Madden and William Wilson Jameson, elders of Usher's Quay congregation, though themselves Trinitarians, were removed by the Lord Chancellor from the Trusteeship of the General Fund, for having joined the Unitarians in their pleading and defence.

In 1847 the congregation of Usher's Quay was transferred from the care of the Dublin Presbytery to that of the Presbytery of Bailieborough. It became re-connected with the Dublin Presbytery after Mr. Dill's death.

The new church at Ormond Quay was now built, and the congregation removed there in January, 1848, the old church on Usher's Quay being since used as a store.

In the appointment of new Trustees of the General Fund made by decree of the Lord Chancellor in 1851, the following were the representatives of Ormond Quay congregation: Rev. Richard Dill, Mr. James Henry, Dr. William Frazer, and Mr. James Bryce.

Mr. Dill died on the 8th of December, 1858. His funeral sermon was preached in Ormond Quay by the Rev. S. G. Morrison of Union Chapel, Lower Abbey Street. A funeral sermon was also preached by Dr. Brown of Aghadowey.

The next minister was the Rev. John James Black (now LL.D.), previously of Westport, who was installed on May 31st, 1859. Dr. Black accepted a call to the Free High Church at Inverness in 1871, and was succeeded in Ormond Quay by the Rev. James Cargin, M.A., who was installed on January 14th, 1873. Mr. Cargin removed to the pastorate of 1st Derry in 1880.

He was succeeded by the present minister, Rev. Samuel Prenter, M.A. (previously minister at Bolton, England), who was installed in Ormond Quay, July 13th, 1881.

Ormond Quay church is the most richly endowed of all the Presbyterian congregations in the city of Dublin. It maintains schools in Dominick Street, and a Female Orphanage in Upper Dorset Street, besides providing for the maintenance of poor widows.

Rathgar.

The early history of Rathgar congregation is associated with two great and honoured names, John Hall and Fleming Stevenson. The story of its origin has been well told by the biographer of Dr. Stevenson.[1] "In the autumn of 1859 a movement was set on foot for the erection of a new church in Rathgar, a pleasant and rapidly increasing suburb of Dublin. It had its origin in a prayer-meeting which had been held for some months previously in the adjoining district of Rathmines. Dr. Hall, now of New York, at that time the junior minister of Mary's Abbey, took a deep interest in the meeting, conducting it for some months during the summer, and urging the members to form themselves into a congregation. At first the feeling that there did not exist material out of which it could be formed was so strong that there was no response. But Dr. Hall persevered, and on making a canvass of the neighbourhood, the two friends who had undertaken the work reported to the Presbytery of Dublin that twenty-one families were prepared to join. In November the little meeting was raised into the status of a congregation, and with constant prayer for guidance step by step, and a deep sense of the responsibility and far-reaching issues involved in their choice, they began to look out for a pastor. Dr. Hall directed their attention to the young minister whose earnest thoughtful preaching was drawing men of all classes round him in Belfast."

This was William Fleming Stevenson, then the probationer-minister of the humble mission church of

---

[1] *Life and Letters of William Fleming Stevenson, D.D.* By his Wife. London: T. Nelson and Sons.

Alfred Street, Belfast. The unanimous call, signed by only twenty-seven persons, was accepted by Mr. Stevenson after careful consideration, and he was ordained in Rathgar on March 1st, 1860. The first services were held in the "old schoolhouse," in Upper Rathmines, now used as a mission hall in connection with the congregation.

In July, 1860, the foundation-stone of Christ Church, Rathgar, was laid by the Rev. Dr. Cooke of Belfast, and the beautiful new building was opened in February, 1862, by the Rev. Norman Macleod, D.D. Since then the church, originally seated for four hundred and fifty, has been twice enlarged. For twenty-seven years Fleming Stevenson was the faithful and laborious minister of Rathgar. Succeeding Dr. Morgan as Convener of the Foreign Mission of the Irish Presbyterian Church, he inspired not only his own congregation but the entire Church with something of his own missionary enthusiasm. He was Moderator of the General Assembly in 1881, when the Assembly met in Dublin. In the same year he received the degree of D.D. from the University of Edinburgh. He was a man of broad sympathies and of gentle and loving spirit. His literary powers were of the highest order, but his overmastering sense of duty in other departments compelled him to repress his love for literary work. He was a frequent contributor to *Good Words*, under the editorship of Dr. Norman Macleod, and has left an abiding memorial in his book entitled "*Praying and Working*, being some account of what men can do when in earnest." Dr. Stevenson died suddenly on September 16th, 1886, shortly after retiring to rest. The hymn he had chosen to sing at family worship that evening was "Let me be with Thee where Thou art." This, too, was amongst the hymns which were sung at his funeral service by the people whom he loved and who loved him so well, in Christ Church, Rathgar.

Dr. Stevenson was succeeded by the present minister, Rev. George Hanson, M.A., previously of 1st Ballymena, who was installed in Rathgar in December, 1886.

Rathgar is one of the foremost congregations in the Irish Presbyterian Church. Its congregational organisation is very complete.

RUTLAND SQUARE, DUBLIN (formerly CAPEL STREET and MARY'S ABBEY).

The present congregation of Rutland Square had its origin in Capel Street about 1667. Its first minister was the Rev. William Jacque, who had previously been minister at Bull Alley.[1] He was succeeded by Rev. Alexander Hutcheson, who, however, on account of ill-health, resigned Capel Street after about a year's ministry, and returned to his previous charge in Saintfield in 1692. The congregation then called to be their minister the Rev. Robert Henry of Carrickfergus, who was also at that time Clerk of the Synod of Ulster. He was installed in Capel Street about the close of the year 1692. His eldest son, Hugh Henry, became a banker in Dublin, and in 1715 was M.P. for the borough of Antrim.[2] He was one of the founders of the General Fund. The second son of Rev. Robert Henry, Mr. Joseph Henry of Straffan, Co. Kildare, married the eldest daughter of the Earl of Moira.

Mr. Henry died in 1699. The congregation chose as his successor the Rev. Francis Iredell, minister of

---

[1] See above, p. 251.   [2] Reid: II., 405 n.

Donegore, Co. Antrim. Of him Professor Witherow says:[1] "It shows the estimation in which he was held by his brethren that, although so recently ordained [1688], he was appointed along with the Rev. William Adair of Ballyeaston, to present the address of the Northern Presbyterians to Duke Schomberg, when he came to Ireland at the head of King William's army, in August, 1689. His gifts as a preacher were such as to secure him very popular acceptance. In 1696 the Synod of Ulster decided he should accept a call presented to him by the congregation of Armagh; but notwithstanding their decision, he determined to stay at Donegore—a piece of ecclesiastical contumacy for which he was afterwards rebuked. Ministers at that time were held under more control than now, and were expected to go to any sphere for which their ecclesiastical superiors judged that they were best fitted. In 1699 the Synod compelled him to accept a call to the congregation of Capel Street, afterwards better known as Mary's Abbey, Dublin; the people promising to bear the expenses of his removal, and to pay him a salary of £100 per annum." This kindly compulsion, however, seems to have suited Mr. Iredell very well. He was installed in Dublin in June, 1699, and remained there till his death in 1739.

Mr. Iredell took a very prominent part in public affairs during his ministry in Dublin. In 1701 he preached the annual sermon before the Societies for the Reformation of Manners in that city. The same year he was elected Moderator of the Synod of Ulster. In September of the same year he and Rev. Alexander Sinclair, minister of Plunket Street, were chosen by the

---

[1] *Presbyterian Memorials:* 149, seq.

general committee of the Synod of Ulster to present to the new Lord Lieutenant, the Earl of Rochester, a congratulatory address from the Presbyterian ministers and people in the North of Ireland. But Mr. Iredell had other duties than that of making smooth speeches. In 1711 he was chosen by the committee of the Synod to go to London and lay before the Queen their vindication against the malignant representations of the Irish House of Lords regarding the Presbyterians of Ireland.[1]

Mr. Iredell was a "Subscriber" and a staunch upholder of the Confession of Faith. He dissented from the resolution of the Synod of Ulster in 1721, by which all the members of Synod who were willing to do so were permitted, but not enjoined, to subscribe the Westminster Confession.

Mr. Iredell's influence as a public man may also be estimated by the fact that, alarmed by the excessive emigration from Ulster in 1728, the Lords-Justices of Ireland consulted him and his colleague, Mr. Craghead, as to its cause.

Before Mr. Iredell's death he had three colleagues. The first of these was the Rev. John Milling. He had been previously minister at Leyden, and when the growth of Capel Street congregation necessitated the appointment of a second minister, he was installed there in June, 1702. But his ministry was brief. He died in 1705, and his funeral sermon was preached by Mr. Iredell. The next colleague was Rev. Laughlin Campbell, previously minister at Campbelltown, Kintyre. His ministry was also brief, as he was installed in September, 1707, and died in October, 1708.

Mr. Iredell's third and last colleague was the Rev.

---

[1] See above, p. 46.

Robert Craghead, A.M. Mr. Craghead was son of the Rev. Robert Craghead of Derry, and had been educated at the Universities of Glasgow, Edinburgh, and Leyden. He was ordained in Capel Street, October 11th, 1709. In 1714 he published a funeral sermon which he had preached on the death of the Countess of Granard, who had long been a regular member of Capel Street congregation. The sermon was dedicated to the Countess of Donegall, daughter of the deceased lady. In 1719 Mr. Craghead was chosen Moderator of the Synod of Ulster. In his retiring sermon, preached in 1820, he made special reference to the Subscription Controversy then agitating the Church. He himself was a decided believer in the doctrine of the Trinity, but, unlike his colleague Mr. Iredell, he favoured the attitude of non-subscription. His sermon was afterwards published under the title of "*A Plea for Peace;* or the Nature, Causes, Mischief, and Remedy of Church Divisions." In the years 1729 and 1731 Mr. Craghead was sent to London to negotiate with the Government on important matters affecting the interests of Irish Presbyterians. On the first occasion, favoured with a note of introduction from the Primate of Ireland, Archbishop Boulter, to Sir Robert Walpole, the Prime Minister, he succeeded in obtaining the payment of some years' arrears of the Regium Donum. On the second occasion his commission was to urge upon the English Government the repeal of the Test Act. In this, however, he was not so successful. Stronger measures were necessary, and the tyrannous enactment was not repealed for fifty years. Mr. Craghead died on July 30th, 1738.

At Mr. Craghead's death a small section of the congregation of Capel Street seceded, and formed the congregation of Stafford Street, which had an independent existence for twenty-four years, and then united with that of Wood Street.

Mr. Iredell died in 1739. The next minister was Rev. James Smith, formerly minister at Newtownards, who was installed in Capel Street, February 15th, 1740. Before his death in 1745, a colleague had been chosen in the pastorate of the congregation. This was the Rev. Charles McCollum, previously minister at Loughbrickland. He was installed in Capel Street in 1745. He was Moderator of the Synod of Ulster in 1760. Mr. McCollum was author of a *New Version of the Psalms*, which was published in Dublin in 1765. In that year he demitted the pastorate of Capel Street.

Mr. McCollum's colleague was the Rev. William Wight, who was ordained in Capel Street, August 9th, 1753. He became Professor of Church History in Glasgow in 1762, and afterwards Professor of Divinity in the same university.[1]

In the year 1750 we find Dr. George Martin, an elder of Capel Street congregation, one of the first trustees of the Widows' Fund then formed in connection with the Synod of Ulster, the founder of which was Mr. William Bruce, an elder of Wood Street congregation, also in the city of Dublin.

Mr. McCollum was succeeded by the Rev. William Knox, who was ordained May 21st, 1765. His pastorate was the briefest in the history of this congregation, for he accepted a call to Dunboe (now 1st Dunboe), near Coleraine, and was installed there on August 18th, 1765. At Dunboe Mr. Knox had a long pastorate. His death took place there in 1801.

The Rev. John Beard, installed in Capel Street,

---

[1] Killen: *History of Congregations.*

January, 1767, was the next minister. He was deposed by the Presbytery for misconduct in 1777. He then joined the Established Church, and obtained the benefice of Cloughran.

About 1777 the church, hitherto known as Capel Street, was rebuilt. The entrance from Capel Street was closed up, and the congregation adopted the name of Mary's Abbey.

The Rev. Benjamin McDowell, who was the next minister, was installed in Mary's Abbey in 1778. He was minister of Mary's Abbey for forty-six years. He had previously been minister of Ballykelly, Co. Derry, for a period of twelve years. He was born at Elizabethtown, New Jersey, where his father, an emigrant from Connor, Co. Antrim, had settled about 1739. He was educated at Princeton and afterwards at the University of Glasgow. When at Ballykelly he chiefly distinguished himself as a controversialist, though at the same time he was a faithful and successful pastor. In opposition to the "New Light" doctrines, and specially in reply to the Rev. John Cameron of Dunluce, he published four successive pamphlets in vindication of subscription to creeds and in defence of the Confession of Faith.[1] After he came to Dublin he was less of a controversialist, but not less determined in his attachment to orthodox doctrine and Presbyterian government. One of his best writings was a treatise on *The Nature of the Presbyterian Form of Church Government*, published in Dublin in 1808. In 1786 Mr. McDowell was Moderator of the Synod of Ulster. Soon after this he received the degree of D.D.

---

[1] Witherow : *Presbyterian Memorials*, 146-150.

When Mr. McDowell came to Mary's Abbey in 1778 he found that under the ministry of his predecessor it had dwindled away to six families and a few individuals. But his able preaching and faithful week-day labours were soon instrumental in reviving the decaying cause. Once more a colleague in the pastorate was required, and in 1791 the Rev. James Horner (afterwards D.D.) was ordained as co-pastor.

We have some interesting glimpses of the condition and life of the congregation about this time. In the summer of 1796 the Rev. Samuel Pearce of Birmingham visited Dublin. Writing to Lady Huntingdon of the Dublin Presbyterian churches,[1] he says of Mary's Abbey: the congregation "is large and flourishing; the place of worship ninety feet by seventy, and in the morning well filled. Dr. McDowell is the senior pastor of this church—a very affectionate spiritual man. The Doctor is a warm friend to the Society at whose request I went to Ireland [the General Evangelical Society]. . . . I am at the house of a Mr. Hutton, late high sheriff of the city, a gentleman of opulence, respectability, and evangelical piety, a Calvinistic Presbyterian, and elder of Dr. McDowell's Church."

This Mr. Hutton was Lord Mayor of Dublin in 1802. At the expiration of his term of office he was voted a gold box and a valuable piece of plate, and his great attention to the observance of the Sabbath was mentioned in three public addresses from the citizens. About the same time he opened a school at the rear of his house for the education of poor children, in which lectures were delivered every Sunday evening to overflowing congregations.

---

[1] *Life and Times of Selina, Countess of Huntingdon.* London: 1841. II., 21.

It is sometimes thought that to hold a service on Christmas Day, or even to refer to Christmas at a Sabbath service, is an innovation in the Presbyterian Church. We find, however, from the old records of Mary's Abbey congregation, that a service was regularly held there on Christmas Day for many years at the close of the last and at the beginning of the present century. The earliest note we have been able to trace was in 1798, when the collection on Christmas Day is given as £1 6s. 6½d. This was about the amount of the usual Sabbath morning collection at that time. We traced the Christmas service as far as the year 1818, after which date some collection books are missing.

In 1799 the total stipend paid to the two ministers was £250.[1] This was the largest total of stipend paid by any Presbyterian congregation in Ireland at that time.

Like his colleague Dr. McDowell, Dr. Horner had a long pastorate. Ordained at Mary's Abbey in 1791, he remained there till his death in 1843. He, too, was an able and faithful minister. He was specially noted for his wisdom and common-sense. Along with the Rev. Henry Cooke (then of Donegore) and the Rev. Robert Stewart of Broughshane, he was one of the first missionary agents of the Synod of Ulster, and did much to extend the operations of the Presbyterian Church throughout the South and West. He was the originator of what we now commonly speak of as the Code of Discipline. At the annual meeting of the Synod of Ulster in 1808 he first brought forward the necessity of appointing a committee "to draw up a code of

---

[1] Reid: *History*, III., 539.

disciplinary laws for the government of the body." This was done after a considerable delay, and in 1825 the first " Constitution and discipline of the Presbyterian Church " in Ireland appeared in print.

In 1813, owing to the increasing infirmity of Dr. McDowell, the Rev. James Carlile was ordained as his assistant. Mr. Carlile was born at Paisley, Scotland. His family came originally from Dumfriesshire, and he was distantly related to the celebrated Thomas Carlyle.[1] He was asked to preach in Dublin soon after being licensed, on the recommendation of Mr. James Ferrier, a Paisley man, and head of the well-known firm of Ferrier, Pollock & Co. It was Mr. Carlile who, in 1817, only four years after his ordination, delivered the fearless and powerful speech in the Synod of Ulster, in which he denounced the interference of Lord Castlereagh with the proceedings of the Synod and its relation to the Belfast Institution.[2] He was appointed one of the first Commissioners of National Education in 1831, and afterwards Resident Commissioner. He went through an almost incredible amount of labour in the four or five years commencing with 1832. He travelled through a great part of Ireland for the purpose of fixing the sites of the new schools, and had a large share in the compilation of the lesson-books which were issued by the Commissioners. Dr. Carlile was himself a clear and vigorous writer. Several of his works were published. Among these are: *Two Sermons preached in Mary's Abbey, Dublin*, by James Carlile, D.D., on " The Duties of Protestants and Roman Catholics mutually toward

---

[1] *Irish Worthies*, by Rev. Thomas Hamilton, M.A. Belfast: 1875. Sketch of Rev. James Carlile, D.D., by his nephew, Rev. Gavin Carlyle, M.A., of London.

[2] See above, p. 92.

each other" (Dublin : 1824) ; *A Series of Sermons on the Nature and Effects of Repentance and Faith* (Dublin : 1821) ; *Old Doctrines of the Bible* (Dublin : 1823); *The Deity of Christ* (Dublin : 1828); *Letters on the Divine Origin and Authority of the Holy Scriptures* (Dublin : 1833); and a volume, published after his death, on *Saints in their Final Glory* (Dublin : 1854). Some of these works are of great value and well worthy of perusal.

The congregation of Mary's Abbey, thus equipped with three ministers (1813-1824, when McDowell, Horner, and Carlile were colleagues), was at this time in a most flourishing condition. In a history of Dublin published in 1818,[1] the number of members of Mary's Abbey congregation is stated to be two thousand. This, of course, includes all the persons connected with the congregation.

In 1824 Dr. McDowell, the venerable senior pastor, died. A marble tablet to his memory was placed in the interior of the church. This tablet is now to be seen in the porch of the new church at Rutland Square.

At a congregational meeting held on February 2nd, 1826, it was resolved that the service should commence in the forenoon at 11.30, and in the afternoon at 3. Evening services are a modern innovation.

In 1828, Dr. Horner becoming infirm, the congregation began to look out for an assistant to him. Their thoughts turned to the Rev. Henry Cooke, then minister of Killyleagh, who had already distinguished himself as the champion of orthodoxy in the Arian controversy. Mr. Cooke, however, declined the call, and in the

---

[1] *History of Dublin.* By J. Warburton, Esq., Deputy-Keeper of Records in the Birmingham Tower, Rev. J. Whitelaw, Vicar of St. Catherine's, and Rev. Robert Walsh, M.R.I.A.

following year became minister of the new church of May Street, Belfast, now imperishably associated with his illustrious memory. Just ten years afterwards he received from the Dublin Corporation, the freedom of the City of Dublin, " in consideration of the zeal which he has so long manifested in support of pure religion."

In the beginning of 1829 the Rev. W. B. Kirkpatrick, licentiate of the Presbytery of Armagh, having preached two Sabbaths in Mary's Abbey, was then at a congregational meeting invited to preach *four Sabbaths on trial*. People did not in those days believe in the possibility of testing a man's power of preaching by the two sermons of a single Lord's Day. Travelling, besides, was more tedious, and it was hardly worth a preacher's while to travel the long journey in those days by road for only a single Sabbath. Anyhow, Mr. Kirkpatrick came safely through the "trial," was unanimously called in April, and ordained as assistant and successor to Dr. Horner. Once more there were three ministers in Mary's Abbey. Mr. Kirkpatrick, like his colleagues and most of his predecessors, took a prominent place in the city of Dublin and in the work of the Presbyterian Church throughout the South and West. He was Convener of the Committee on the State of Religion, and Convener of the Church Extension Mission. In 1850 he was elected Moderator of the General Assembly. He was appointed by the Government a Commissioner of Charitable Bequests and also a Commissioner of Endowed Schools. The temperance cause found in him one of its most devoted advocates. He was a man of considerable literary power, but his pastoral and public labours left him little time for literary work. One little book of his remains to show what manner of man he was and by what spirit he was animated. It is entitled *Chapters in Irish History*. As I have said elsewhere,[1] "it is at once loyal and liberal, well-informed, and ably written. The spirit is that of a true historian, anxious to know and to state the truth, and of a true Christian, anxious to heal the wounds of the past and to unite Irishmen in a common brotherhood of peace and industry." In his preaching his great aim was to preach the gospel in its simplicity; and in private conversation he ever sought to guide the thoughts of his people to eternal things.

In 1832 the congregation of Mary's Abbey consisted of two hundred and twenty families, and a hundred and forty individual subscribers. The strength of the congregation, and the Presbyterian population of the city, had so much increased, that the elders of Mary's Abbey and Usher's Quay consulted together about the necessity for forming an additional congregation in the city of Dublin. In 1838 the united Sessions of these congregations issued a printed statement on this subject. The result was that in 1840 the foundation-stone of a new church was laid at Adelaide Road. These elders were men of public spirit, far-seeing, and prudent. They were not actuated by that short-sighted and selfish policy which so often opposes Church extension on the ground that existing congregations will be injured. As a rule churches do not die by expansion, but by contraction. The old congregation of Mary's Abbey, which has been the parent hive from which so many of our more modern Dublin congregations have come, is healthy and hopeful still.

In 1840 public baptism was for the first time introduced into this congregation.

---

[1] *Famous Irish Preachers.* Dublin: Mecredy and Kyle, 1889.

The Rev. Dr. Carlile, who had long taken an interest in the mission work at Birr, obtained the sanction of the Session and congregation to a proposal that he made that, while still retaining his position as one of the ministers of Mary's Abbey, he should devote the remaining years of his life to the service of that mission. He went to Birr in 1840 and remained there till his death in 1854. Dr. Horner died in 1843.

On the death of Dr. Carlile, Mr. Kirkpatrick was left in sole charge of the congregation, and for the first time in more than sixty years, Mary's Abbey had only one minister. But it was only for a short time.

In September, 1858, the Rev. John Hall (now D.D.), previously minister of 1st Armagh, was installed as colleague to Dr. Kirkpatrick. Dr. Hall was the first editor of the *Children's Missionary Herald;* and was, for many years of his ministry in Dublin, editor of the *Evangelical Witness.* This was a monthly magazine, begun in 1862 by Dr. Hall, and, after his removal to America, continued by Rev. Thomas Croskery and afterwards by Rev. T. Y. Killen. It then became a weekly paper under the title of the *Witness*, and after some time the *Presbyterian Churchman* succeeded it as the monthly magazine of the Irish Presbyterian Church. Some of the best talent in the Church contributed to the *Evangelical Witness* under Dr. Hall's editorship, and that magazine soon became a power in shaping and leading Presbyterian opinion. Dr. Hall had a high repute in Dublin as an impressive and evangelical preacher. His influence was very great not only in the Presbyterian Church, but amongst other denominations also. Now, however, as minister of the Fifth Avenue Presbyterian Church, New York, he wields an influence not second to that of any other religious teacher in the United States.

The congregation of Mary's Abbey had for some time been considering the propriety of building a new church, or enlarging and improving the old one, when the generous offer was made by Alexander Findlater, Esq., J.P., a member of Kingstown congregation, to build for them a church at his own expense. A commanding site was purchased by the congregation in Rutland Square, at a cost of £2,600. Here the new and beautiful church was built, at an expenditure of about £14,000. A memorial window was erected by the congregation to "commemorate the munificence and perpetuate the name of Alexander Findlater, the founder and donor of this church." The church was seated to accommodate eight hundred and fifty persons, and has schoolroom or lecture-hall beneath. The foundation-stone was laid in November, 1862, and the building was completed in October, 1864.

On November 13th, 1864, being a communion Sabbath, the closing services were held in the old church of Mary's Abbey, in which the congregation had worshipped since 1777, and on the same spot where their former church of Capel Street had been since 1667.

On two days of the same week, 18th and 19th of November, the opening services were held in Rutland Square Church. Sermons were preached on these days by the Rev. Dr. Cooke of Belfast, and the Rev. Dr. Horatius Bonar of Edinburgh. In the evening of each day public meetings were held, at which addresses were given by Rev. Hamilton Magee, Rev. Thomas Lyttle, Rev. John Hall, Rev. W. Fleming Stevenson, Rev. W. B. Kirkpatrick, D.D., and Rev. Robert Watts, D.D.

The first Sabbath on which the congregation met for worship in Rutland Square Church was November 20th, 1864. On that day the sermons were preached by Dr. Kirkpatrick and Mr. Hall.[1]

In 1867 Dr. Hall accepted a call to New York. He was succeeded by Rev. David McKee (previously of Ballywalter), who was installed in Rutland Square, February 8th, 1869. Mr. McKee removed to New Zealand, where he has since died, in the year 1879. He was a man of independent mind, of sweet and gentle spirit, and of much originality and power as a preacher. The next colleague-minister was the Rev. Andrew Charles Murphy, D.Lit. (previously of 1st Derry), who was installed in Rutland Square, January 20th, 1880.

Dr. Kirkpatrick died in 1882, after an active ministry of more than fifty years in Dublin. In 1883 Dr. Murphy accepted a call to the congregation of Crouch Hill, London, whence he has since returned to Ireland and is now minister of Elmwood Church, Belfast.

The next minister was the Rev. John Sinclair Hamilton, M.A. (previously of 1st Banbridge), who was installed in Rutland Square, March 20th, 1884. In November, 1888, Mr. Hamilton resigned the pastorate on account of ill-health, and removed to the United States, where he afterwards resumed work as minister of the Presbyterian Church, but died in New York, April, 1890. He was succeeded by the present minister, Rev. James Denham Osborne, M.A. (previously of 1st Ballymoney), who was installed in Rutland Square, June, 1889.

---

[1] All these sermons and addresses, containing much interesting matter, have been preserved in a volume entitled "*Memorial Services* in connection with the removal of the congregation of Mary's Abbey to Rutland Square, Dublin." Dublin: 1865.

SANDYMOUNT.

Like the congregations of Adelaide Road, Donore, and Rathgar, the congregation of Sandymount is one of the fruits of the modern growth of Presbyterianism in Dublin and its suburbs. Its first minister was the Rev. Thomas Lyttle, who was ordained there on February 4th, 1857. Mr. Lyttle was a faithful pastor and a man of much ability and public spirit. He was for some years Clerk of the Dublin Presbytery, and also editor of the *Presbyterian Churchman*. He took an active part in promoting the welfare of the Presbyterian Association of the city of Dublin in its old quarters in Westmoreland Street, and was one of the chief originators of the purchase of the capacious building at 16, Upper Sackville Street, which, with its fine suite of reading-rooms, library, lecture-hall, etc., is now the headquarters of Presbyterianism in the metropolis. Even a man of Mr. Lyttle's genial and kindly spirit did not escape the rude repulse of bigotry and intolerance. In 1867 he reported to the Presbytery of Dublin that he had asked the Rev. Dr. Ryder, Rector of Donnybrook, to permit him to conduct a service in the graveyard at Donnybrook, on the occasion of the interment there of the child of a member of his (Mr. Lyttle's) congregation. Dr. Ryder declined to give the permission, on the ground "that it would be quite unprecedented that any clergyman who does not belong to the parish church should officiate in the parish graveyard." Mr. Lyttle further reported that Dr. Ryder's predecessor had also refused him under similar circumstances. A committee of Presbytery was appointed to inquire into the law on the subject. This committee reported to the Presbytery in 1868 that they had acted in connection with the Assembly's Committee in correspondence with Government, and had waited on the Lord Lieutenant, who admitted the grievance. On the recommendation of the committee, the Presbytery agreed to petition Parliament to amend the existing law. During Mr. Lyttle's ministry, the present beautiful church, lecture-hall, and the adjoining manse were built. Mr. Lyttle died on November 21st, 1880. He was succeeded by the Rev. Alexander Rentoul, M.A., previously minister at Liverpool and at Longford, who was installed in Sandymount, April 21st, 1881. Mr. Rentoul was a son of the Rev. James B. Rentoul, D.D., of Garvagh, Co. Derry, one of the fathers of the Secession Synod. One of his brothers is the Rev. Professor Rentoul, D.D., of Ormond College, Melbourne; another is the Rev. R. W. Rentoul, B.A., of Darlington, England, and the third is the Rev. Alfred H. Rentoul, M.A., of Longford. Here were four sons, all ministers—all following the profession of their honoured father. Mr. Alexander Rentoul was a man of eminent ability and piety, an eloquent preacher and a zealous pastor. After years of weak health, he died on August 29th, 1889. The present minister, Rev. James A. Campbell, previously of 2nd Omagh, was installed in Sandymount, May 2nd, 1890.

Tullamore.

The congregation of Tullamore was organised by the Athlone Presbytery in 1856. The first minister was the Rev. Samuel Kelly, licentiate of the Presbytery of Bailieborough, who was ordained there December 3rd, 1857. Mr. Kelly received an appointment to Australia on the Colonial Mission, and was designated to that work, April 22nd, 1858. He was succeeded by the

Rev. James Duff Cuffey, who was ordained there June 30th, 1859. In the following week the congregation was transferred by the General Assembly from the Presbytery of Athlone to that of Dublin. Mr. Cuffey died on May 5th, 1863. He was succeeded by Rev. Andrew Burrowes, who was ordained at Tullamore, June 29th, 1864. The congregation, which had hitherto worshipped in a house rented and fitted up for the purpose, increased so much under the ministry of Mr. Burrowes that they resolved to build a church. The church was opened in 1866 by the Rev. Dr. Edgar of Belfast. Mr. Burrowes removed to Waterford in 1868. He was succeeded by the Rev. Robert H. Smythe, who was ordained at Tullamore, December 17th, 1868. During Mr. Smythe's ministry the church was enlarged, and mission stations were opened in neighbouring towns. Mr. Smythe removed to Carrowdore, Co. Down, in 1879, and was succeeded by the Rev. David Mitchel, previously of Kilkenny. Mr. Mitchel's pastorate at Tullamore was a brief one. He was ordained there August 21st, 1879, and left it for Warrenpoint, June 21st, 1880. He was succeeded by Rev. W. S. Frackelton, previously a minister in the United States, who was installed at Tullamore, November 19th, 1880. Mr. Frackelton was appointed in 1884 to engage in the Colonial Mission in New South Wales. He was succeeded by the present minister, Rev. Henry Patterson Glenn, A.B., who was ordained at Tullamore, December 10th, 1884. Under Mr. Glenn's ministry a school has been established, and flourishing mission stations are maintained by him at Clara and elsewhere in his extensive district.[1]

---

[1] See also Killen's *History of Congregations*.

WEXFORD.

The first minister of the Presbyterian congregation at Wexford appears to have been the Rev. Gideon Jacque. He was ordained there in 1681.[1] Like Mr. Coldin of Enniscorthy, Mr. Jacque removed to Scotland about the beginning of 1689, after the outbreak of the Revolutionary war. He remained in Scotland, where he was minister of the parish of Liberton,[2] till 1695, when he returned to Wexford. He remained at Wexford till 1706.

We have no further trace of Presbyterianism in Wexford till the visit of the Rev. Robert Knox to that town in 1840. He found about fifteen Presbyterian families in or about Wexford, who professed their willingness to assist in the maintenance of a Presbyterian Church there.[3] On November 25th the Presbytery of Dublin formally organised the congregation of Wexford, the people there promising a stipend of £23 a year (to be supplemented, of course, by Regium Donum and a grant from the mission funds). The Rev. R. Dickson was ordained as minister there, September 22nd, 1841. Mr. Dickson resigned in 1844, having accepted a call to Ballysillan, near Belfast. He was succeeded by the Rev. John P. Bond, who was ordained there on March 24th, 1846. In 1844 Mr. Bond, then a licentiate, published a pamphlet bearing this title: *A Convert's Plea against Prelacy*, by John P. Bond, Ramelton, formerly an Episcopalian, now a licentiate of the Presbyterian Church in Ireland (Belfast: 1844). Mr. Bond's pastorate at Wexford and his belief in

---

[1] Appendix to *Account of Emlyn's Trial*.
[2] Reid: *History*, II., 417.
[3] Reports of Home Mission of Synod of Ulster.

Presbyterianism were, however, of short duration. About 1850 he resigned Wexford and returned to the Episcopal Church. He then wrote another pamphlet in defence of his conduct in making this second change. One of his hearers at Wexford bound the two pamphlets together and labelled them "Consistency."[1] Mr. Bond's successor was the Rev. William Burns, who was ordained in Wexford, March 26th, 1850. The present manse, which is one of the best and most beautifully situated ministers' residences in the Dublin Presbytery, was built during the ministry of Mr. Burns. He remained at Wexford till his death on May 9th, 1881. The next minister was the Rev. Samuel McCune, B.A., who was installed on October 25th, 1881. Mr. McCune removed to Magherafelt, and was succeeded by the present minister, Rev. James Steen. Mr. Steen, who had been previously minister at Drum and at Castlebar, was installed in Wexford, May 29th, 1888.

WICKLOW.

There appears to have been a Presbyterian congregation in Wicklow soon after the passing of the Act of Uniformity. The first Presbyterian minister of Wicklow of whom we have any record was the Rev. Robert Kelso. He had been ordained at Raloo, near Larne, in 1673, but after a ministry there of one year, he came to Wicklow in 1674, and remained there till 1685. He then removed to Enniskillen, where, as Presbyterian minister, he took a foremost part in the gallant defence of that town in 1688-89.[2] There he laboured, says

---

[1] Related by the late Professor Witherow to the Author, September 15th, 1885.

[2] Witherow : *Derry and Enniskillen*, p. 215.

McCormick in his *Account of the Inniskilling Men,* " both publicly and privately in animating his hearers to take up arms and stand upon their own defence, showing example himself by wearing arms and marching in the head of them when together."

After Mr. Kelso's removal, we have no further trace of Presbyterianism in the town of Wicklow for more than a century. Doubtless soon after that time most of the Presbyterian residents there took refuge in Scotland or Ulster when the war of the Revolution commenced in Ireland.

A singular circumstance led to the revival of Presbyterianism in Wicklow. About 1855, on the death of Archdeacon Magee, the three parishes of which he was incumbent were made independent charges. One of these was Killiskey, about five miles from the town of Wicklow. The parish church was known by the name of Nunscross. The curate of this parish was the Rev. William Vickars, a pious man, laborious pastor, and earnest preacher. He had been in sole charge of the parish for seventeen years. It was naturally supposed that he would succeed to the living on the death of Archdeacon Magee. To the surprise of the parishioners, it was said that Archbishop Whately intended to remove him from his charge without giving him any other appointment, and to put over them an inexperienced young man, fresh from college. Accordingly they drew up a memorial expressing their prayer that Mr. Vickars should be continued in Nunscross. But it was of no avail. The young minister referred to was appointed. The result was that a portion of the congregation ceased to worship at the parish church, and met on Sabbaths at a school-room in the neighbourhood called Kilfee, near the Devil's Glen. A requisition was got up to the Rev.

Dr. Kirkpatrick of Dublin, who was then on a visit to his brother-in-law in that neighbourhood, to conduct Divine service in the schoolhouse. Dr. Kirkpatrick complied, and preached there for several Sabbaths. Afterwards ministers were sent from the North of Ireland, and amongst them the Rev. John M. Bleckley, B.A., who was at that time assistant to the Rev. Richard Dill of Knowhead near Derry. Mr. Bleckley was so much liked by the people that they sent a memorial to the Board of Missions, asking that Mr. Bleckley should be appointed as their minister, and to act as missionary in the surrounding district. Mr. Bleckley came to Wicklow in 1856. His first services were held at Kilfee, and in 1857 a place for services was secured in Wicklow, where service was held first on Wednesday evenings and afterwards on Sabbath evenings. In 1860 the congregation was formally organised, and a new church was subsequently built in the town of Wicklow. This church was opened in 1863 by the Rev. Dr. Kirkpatrick and the Rev. Dr. John Hall of Dublin.

Mr. Bleckley was a minister of much ability and power. He was son of the Rev. John Bleckley of Monaghan. Before he was twelve years old he had read a very large course of classics, with French, and a considerable portion of the Psalms in Hebrew. He was educated at Trinity College, Dublin, where he graduated with a high place in first class, and then at the New College, Edinburgh. He was much beloved in Wicklow and the extensive district round about it in which he laboured. In 1866 he accepted a call to the congregation of Queen Street, Cork. He came to Cork very ill, but preached his first sermon as minister of Queen Street on Sabbath, February 10th, 1867. On that day week at the evening service it was announced to his sorrowing people that he had just gone to his everlasting rest.[1]

The next minister at Wicklow was the Rev. George McCaughey, B.A., who was ordained there September 24th, 1867. Few ministers have a pastorate so laborious as his was. For many years, in addition to his services in the town of Wicklow, he preached every Sabbath at the mission stations of either Kilpedder or Roundwood, neither of them less than ten miles distant. During the week he travelled long distances to minister to the mission stations of Shillelagh (forty miles distant by rail), Ballycullen, Arklow, Clorah, and Kilcarra. Mr. McCaughey removed to Lucan in 1887, and was succeeded at Wicklow by the present minister, the Rev. Samuel Matthews, B.A., who was installed there on March 26th, 1888. The labours of the minister of Wicklow are such as ought to command the sympathy and interest of the whole Irish Presbyterian Church.

---

[1] *Sermons on the Christian Armour and other Subjects.* By the late Rev. J. M. Bleckley, A.B., Wicklow. With Memoir. Edited by Rev. I. N. Harkness. Dublin : 1868.

VI.

PRESBYTERY OF MUNSTER.

CLONMEL.

IN 1673 Mr. William Cock was ordained here,[1] but whether or not he was the first minister we cannot definitely ascertain. The next minister of whom we have any other record than the name, is Rev. William Jackson, who was minister in 1726, but there were before him Mr. Shaw, Mr. Palmer, and Mr. Card. Mr. Jackson was Moderator of the Presbytery of Munster when the Trinitarian resolutions were passed by that body in favour of the Presbytery of Antrim, 1726.

After Mr. Jackson came the Rev. John Mears, previously minister of Newtownards. Mr. Mears, too, was a Trinitarian. When minister of Newtownards he repeatedly expressed in the Synod of Ulster his assent to the Westminster Confession and his belief in the doctrine of the Trinity, but declined subscription.[2] In 1722, when still in Newtownards, Mr. Mears had made overtures to the Bishop of Down for joining the Established Church. "When the Presbytery called him to account for this proceeding, he professed hearty repentance, and asked forgiveness, first of God, and then of his Presbytery and congregation, for what he called 'his

---

[1] Killen's *History of Congregations.*
[2] Appendix to *Account of Emlyn's Trial*

temptation of Satan.'"[1] Mr. Mears was the author of a *Catechism*, or an Instruction in the Christian Religion for the use of Adults, and also *A Short Explanation of the Lord's Supper*. He removed to Stafford Street, Dublin, in 1740, and afterwards became minister of Wood Street. He was succeeded in Clonmel by Rev. J. Mackay.

After Mr. Mackay, Clonmel enjoyed for a season the services of one of the most eminent Presbyterian ministers of Ireland, the celebrated Dr. William Campbell. Dr. Campbell had an early connection with Clonmel, for, after leaving college and receiving licence to preach, he had acted for seven years as tutor to young Mr. Bagwell of that town. He was minister at Antrim from 1759 to 1764, and then was minister of 1st Armagh from 1764 to 1789. Dr. Campbell was the author of the famous reply to Dr. Woodward, Bishop of Cloyne, entitled: *A Vindication of the Principles and Character of the Presbyterians in Ireland;* addressed to the Bishop of Cloyne, in answer to his book entitled, *The Present State of the Church of Ireland* (Dublin: 1787). This work ran through four editions.[2] Dr. Campbell also distinguished himself by his negotiations with the Government of the day, by which he succeeded in obtaining an increase of £1,000 in the Regium Donum paid to Irish Presbyterian ministers. He was minister of Clonmel from 1789 till his death in 1805. Dr. Campbell was succeeded by Mr. Worrall,[3]

---

[1] Witherow: *Memorials*, II., 27.   [2] Ibid: *Memorials*, II., 173.

[3] Rev. James Worrall was minister from 1807 till his death in 1824. Rev. William Crozier, M.A., was ordained at Clonmel in 1825. He removed in 1832 to Rademon, Co. Down, where he died in 1873. He was a non-subscriber, and the subscription controversy divided the congregation of Clonmel during his ministry there. His son, Rev. John A. Crozier, is the Unitarian minister at Newry.—Rev. James Orr suc-

Mr. Crozier, and Mr. Orr, who was there in 1839. Mr. Orr and the few people who were with him were then stated to be Arians. Meantime those who adhered to the Trinitarian faith had in 1832 applied to the Synod of Ulster for supply of preaching. At a meeting of the Dublin Presbytery in 1830, the Moderator, Rev. S. Simpson, reported that in his visit to the South of Ireland as a Deputation from the Scottish Missionary Society, he had found both in Cork and Clonmel a number of families and individuals who desired to be supplied with worship according to the Presbyterian discipline.[1] In 1836 the Rev. John Dill was ordained their minister. At this time Clonmel was under the care of the Presbytery of Dublin.[2] In 1843 Clonmel was transferred to the newly-formed Presbytery of Cork. Mr. Dill died in 1868, and was succeeded by the Rev. H. H. Beattie, now LL.D., and Chaplain to the Forces. Dr. Beattie resigned in 1878, and after his resignation the Presbyteries of Cork and Munster agreed to unite the two congregations of Fethard and Clonmel. The General Assembly sanctioned the union, and transferred Clonmel to the care of the Munster Presbytery. The congregation of Clonmel having previously agreed to give a call to Rev. James Wilson of Fethard, he was installed by the Presbytery of Munster in Clonmel as a joint charge, June 27th, 1878.[3]

FETHARD.

Fethard, Co. Tipperary, is one of the most ancient congregations in the South of Ireland. Its earliest

---

ceeded Mr. Crozier at Clonmel, and died only a few years ago. *Letter of Rev. John A. Crozier to Rev. D. D. Jeremy, May,* 1890.

[1] *Minutes of Presbytery of Dublin.*
[2] *Minutes of Synod of Ulster.*
[3] *Minutes of Presbytery of Munster.*

ministers, whose names we can find, were Mr. Hemphill, Mr. Bryson, and Mr. R. Rodgers. In 1769 the Rev. James Rodgers, then minister of Fethard, was present at the annual meeting of the Synod of Ulster. As a member of the Southern Association, he was invited to sit and vote as a member of the Synod.[1] Mr. Rodgers was succeeded by Rev. James Allen. Mr. Allen appears to have had a long pastorate. He was minister there in the year 1804.[2] He was succeeded by Rev. Mr. Ferris. Mr. Ferris was minister in the year 1840. In 1848 there were in Fethard congregation fourteen families and thirty-four communicants. The Rev. Isaiah Breakey, son of Rev. Andrew Breakey of Killyleagh, was ordained as minister there in 1851. At the same meeting of the Presbytery of Munster, the congregation of Fethard was recommended " to substitute the Psalms of David in the stead of the hymns at present in use."[3] Mr. Breakey's ministry was a short one. He died in 1854, and was succeeded by Rev. W. F. White, licentiate of Monaghan Presbytery, who was ordained there May 30th, 1854. Mr. White accepted a call of the Missionary Directors to go as missionary to New Brunswick, and resigned his pastorate in 1857. The Rev. William Johnston was ordained at Fethard, August 10th, 1857. In 1860 the congregation consisted of twenty families and thirty-six communicants. In 1873 Mr. Johnston was loosed from Fethard, having accepted a call to be missionary at Courtrai, Belgium. The Rev. James Wilson was ordained as his successor, September 30th, 1873. In 1878, as we have seen, this

---

[1] Reid : III., 331.
[2] MS. *Minutes of General Fund.*
[3] *Minutes of Munster Presbytery.*

congregation was united with that of Clonmel, and Mr. Wilson became minister of the joint charge.

KILRUSH.

In the year 1860 the Presbytery of Munster agreed to grant the prayer of residents at Kilrush, Co. Clare, to be organised into a congregation, and in December, 1860, the Rev. William Sorsby, the present minister, was installed in the pastorate. In 1865 the congregation consisted of sixteen families and twenty-one communicants, with an average attendance of twenty-five at public worship.

LIMERICK.

The ancient city of Limerick, famous for the brave exploits of Sarsfield, the Irish general, during its siege by the army of William III., famous also as being "the City of the Violated Treaty," has for more than two centuries been one of the centres of the Presbyterian Church in the South of Ireland. There was a Presbyterian congregation there in Cromwell's time, which met for worship in an old Augustinian nunnery, termed St. Peter's Cell, at the end of Pump Lane or Peter Street, near the town wall.[1] The first minister was Mr. Squire. He was succeeded by the celebrated Rev. William Biggar. Mr. Biggar, while minister at Limerick, was invited by some Presbyterians of Galway to preach to them. For doing so he was imprisoned in Galway for the crime "of dividing the Protestant interest."[2] This was in 1698. Mr. Biggar afterwards became minister of Bangor, Co. Down.[3] While there he was

---

[1] MS. *History of the General Fund*, by Dr. William Frazer, M.R.I.A., etc.

[2] See above, p. 16; History of Galway congregation, above, p. 172.

[3] Wodrow MSS., Folio XXXV., No. 73; History of Drogheda congregation, above, p. 236.

invited to preach to the Presbyterians at Drogheda. Here again he was imprisoned for preaching the gospel. This was in 1708. Mr. Biggar's successor at Limerick was Rev. S. Smith. After him came Dr. Laban and Mr. Wallace. It was probably during the ministry of one of these that in 1763 a meeting-house and house for the minister was "decently furnished" at a cost of above £500.[1] Mr. Wallace was succeeded by Rev. Abraham Seawright, who was minister in 1804. At that time the income of the congregation was:—Interest on £300=£18; house valued at £22 15s., and the subscriptions of 10 subscribers £25 5s. 10½d., besides an allowance of £75 from Regium Donum and a grant from the General Fund.[2] Mr. Seawright was succeeded by Rev. John Pinkerton. During Mr. Pinkerton's ministry, in 1817, a new "meeting-house" was erected at a cost of £520. Mr. Pinkerton died on December 21st, 1840, and was succeeded by Rev. Mr. McCorkle, who had been his assistant since 1837. (Mr. Dickie and Mr. Nelson had previously been assistants to Mr. Pinkerton.) Mr. McCorkle, who was a Scotchman, resigned the charge of Limerick in March, 1844, and returned to Scotland. On December 31st, 1844, the present pastor, Rev. David Wilson, D.D., was installed. He had previously been, for a few months, minister at Carnmoney, near Belfast.

When Dr. Wilson came to Limerick, the congregation consisted of nineteen families. The elders of Limerick congregation in 1845 were Messrs. William Glover (jeweller), William Fraser (manager of the Bank of Ireland), and Robert Stuart. In 1846 Dr. Wilson's ministry had proved so successful that a new church

---

[1] MS, *History of General Fund.*   [2] *Minutes of General Fund.*

was built, capable of holding four times the number of people that the old one contained. It is situated in Glentworth Street, and is on the property of the Earl of Limerick. In 1852 there were sixty-one families, thirty-one individuals, and a hundred and one communicants connected with the congregation, the average attendance at public worship being in the morning two hundred and fifty and in the evening over fifty.[1] It is now the second largest Presbyterian congregation in the South of Ireland outside the city and suburbs of Dublin, numbering eighty-eight families, and contributing with great liberality to missions and other religious objects.

Dr. Wilson is much respected by all denominations in Limerick. It is in striking and pleasant contrast to the days when his predecessor, Rev. William Biggar, was imprisoned for preaching, to note that Dr. Wilson has been President, and is now Vice-President of the Limerick Protestant Young Men's Association, of which the Protestant Episcopalian Bishops of Limerick and Cashel are patrons, and which combines on its roll members of all Protestant denominations. For a considerable time Dr. Wilson ministered to persons from Nenagh, in the County Tipperary, to Loop Head, in Clare, near which he several times preached—his whole district being then about eighty miles in length and upwards of forty miles in breadth. For years he conducted five services every Sabbath, often journeying long distances to preach to soldiers and others. Dr. Wilson has been twice Moderator of the General Assembly, and is Convener of the Colonial Mission. In 1868 he was appointed member of the Royal Commission of Inquiry into Primary Education (Ireland), and

---

[1] *Minutes of Munster Presbytery.*

took an active part in its proceedings. He has been a devoted minister of Christ, a faithful pastor, a zealous advocate of every good cause, and a wise and prudent counsellor in Church courts.

PORTLAW.

The first minister of Portlaw was the Rev. James Cleland, who was ordained there by the Presbytery of Munster, May 9th, 1843. At that time, and for many years after, there was a considerable Presbyterian population at Portlaw, many being Scotchmen employed in the works of Messrs. Malcolmson. In 1848 there were connected with the congregation thirty families and thirty-two communicants, the average attendance at public worship being sixty-five in the morning and forty-five in the evening. Mr. Cleland resigned in 1854, and was succeeded by the Rev. David Ferguson, licentiate of Connaught Presbytery, who was ordained there May 31st, 1854. In 1867 there were forty families connected with the congregation. But the cessation of the factory sadly reduced its numbers, and after the death of Mr. Ferguson, February 8th, 1887, the Presbytery recommended the General Assembly to unite Portlaw with the congregation of Waterford, under the care of the Rev. John Hall, which was accordingly done.

SUMMERHILL.

The congregation of Summerhill, Co. Meath, has an ancient and interesting history. It owes its origin to the patronage and fostering care of the Langford family, whose mansion still adorns the neighbourhood of Summerhill. At first the ministers were chaplains of the Langford family. The services were held in the private chapel of the castle, and were attended not only by the members of the family, who were staunch and consistent Presbyterians, but by several families who had settled in this district from the Langford estates in Ulster.[1] At last, however, the attendance at the Presbyterian service so much increased that Sir Arthur Langford erected a church for the Presbyterian congregation. It was the doors and windows of this church that Dean Swift, then rector of Laracor (the parish in which Summerhill is situated), caused to be nailed up.[2] Then, in the year 1714, Sir Arthur Langford, not to be outdone, erected a dwelling-house for the minister, which may still be seen by the traveller who enters Summerhill on the road from Dublin. One door of this dwelling-house leads to the minister's private apartments; the other leads to the place of worship where the Presbyterian congregation still assembles. The old pulpit is still there, and from that pulpit, in that unpretentious sanctuary, the gospel message was delivered by such men as John Owen, Philip Henry, Doddridge, and other Puritan divines. It was with no common interest that I made a pilgrimage several months ago to this lasting memorial of the persecutions of other days, this shrine of Presbyterian loyalty. Sir Arthur Langford not only erected this unique place of worship and of residence, but also bequeathed a rent charge of £30 per annum for ever, for the support of the Presbyterian interest in this place. The house, garden, and several acres of land, are also the property of the church, the generous gift of this true-hearted Presbyterian gentleman.

The first minister of Summerhill of whom we have

---

[1] Armstrong's *Account of the Presbyterian Congregations of Dublin.*
[2] See above Chapter VII., p. 49; *Report of Proceedings*, p. 39; Armstrong's *Account*, etc.

any record is the Rev. A. Wood. He was pastor from 1710 to 1747. On his tombstone in Agher churchyard, Co. Meath, it is stated that he was thirty-seven years pastor at Summerhill and that he died February 8th, 1747, in his 64th year. He was succeeded by the Rev. Andrew Millar, who was minister from 1748 to 1778. His tombstone may also be seen in Agher churchyard. The Rev. Patrick Vance was minister of Summerhill from 1779 to 1791. He was succeeded by the Rev. David Trotter. Mr. Trotter's pastorate lasted over fifty years. In his old age he had as assistant and successor, for a short time, Rev. Mr. McDowell. Mr. Trotter's son, Dr. Trotter, was for many years the popular medical officer of Summerhill and an elder in the Presbyterian Church. The name is still perpetuated by a grandson of the old minister, Mr. David Trotter, J.P., of Summerhill. A granddaughter of Mr. Trotter, Miss Higgins, afterwards became the wife of the present minister, Mr. Craig.

The Rev. Samuel Craig, son of the Rev. Mr. Craig of Crossroads, near Derry (one of the fathers of the Secession Synod), came to Summerhill in the year 1843. After labouring for some time as a probationer, he was ordained there by the Presbytery of Munster, February 4th, 1845. In the year 1849 there were fourteen families, four single individuals, and twenty communicants connected with the congregation. In 1879 there were thirteen families and twenty-two communicants.[1]

The early years of Mr. Craig's ministry were years that might have tried the stoutest heart. Seeing the ignorance of the people, he rented a house, engaged an efficient teacher, and had soon a large mixed attendance

---

[1] *Minutes of Presbytery of Munster.*

of all denominations, but after a year or so opposition arose and the school was broken up. About that time the country was agitated by the Repeal movement. For three days before the great meeting at Tara (only a few miles from Summerhill) Mr. Craig, to use his own words[1] "saw the rich and poor, the lame and blind, male and female" passing his door in a continuous stream to the Hill of Tara. During the Young Ireland movement, too, the signal fires were lit night after night; alarming rumours kept every one in terror; and it was dangerous to venture out at night unless well armed.

But the years of the famine and its consequences were the most terrible of all. In 1846 the dire calamity of the potato failure took place. The labouring class had no provision made against the evil day. The cry of the hungry was loud. Public works were established, but the famished men were unable to work. A Government loan at last brought some relief. A Relief Committee was appointed. For once denominational distinctions and sectarian bitterness were forgotten. The Dispensary doctor was appointed chairman, a kind-hearted Roman Catholic gentleman was appointed treasurer, and Mr. Craig was secretary. The court-house where they had to meet had to be guarded by a strong force of police, to keep in check the ferocious mob outside, who threatened the lives of those within, while candidates were examined for receipt of food. The whole arrangements for the distribution of food devolved upon the young Presbyterian minister. He soon had a stirabout kitchen in full play, with a staff of obedient men, a boiler of a

---

[1] MS. statement in possession of the Author.

hundred and fifty gallon capacity, a clerk to check tickets of applicants, and carters to draw meal and coal. For about twelve months Mr. Craig discharged this onerous duty of feeding daily an average of about a thousand persons. No doubt he was sustained by the sense of duty, and inspired by pity for the famishing creatures who confronted him day after day, with tattered garments, haggard look, and emaciated frames, as they stood waiting their turn to be served. Surely "the blessing of him that was ready to perish" came upon him, for "he delivered the poor that cried."

Scarcely was one trial fairly grappled with and almost overcome when another still more terrible arose. The privations of the famine year told heavily on the health of the inhabitants, and a virulent fever set in. Strangely enough, upon Mr. Craig there fell once more the necessity of dealing with this new and dreaded enemy. Many who might have been expected to help were panic-stricken with fear. The Dispensary doctor was an aged man, in delicate health, and not equal to the task of meeting the heavy strain upon him. Mr. Craig who, during the famine time, had been in frequent correspondence with the Government authorities, received a communication from Dublin, requesting him to make arrangements for the erection of a temporary fever hospital. With the concurrence of the doctor and the local clergy he undertook the responsibility. Unused lofts in the farmyard of a neighbouring nobleman were kindly placed at his disposal. Soon he had separate wards arranged, with thirty beds for males, and thirty for females. In a short time all the beds were filled. Day and night Mr. Craig passed through the wards. Note-book in hand, he examined every patient, and reported to the doctor, who made out prescriptions accordingly. In cases of death, which occurred every day, he went personally to the dead-house, pronounced death, and ordered the coffins. Some of the sights he witnessed in the houses of fever-stricken families at that time are too horrible to mention. Fathers and husbands hopelessly drunk while wives or children were lying dead, no friend to perform the necessary offices to the sick and dying—and all the while this young minister, of a different religion from most of them, was labouring day and night to alleviate their sufferings, stay the ravages of disease, and perform the most menial offices in his errand of mercy. Many acts of heroism were performed in the famine-time and in the years of the fever and the cholera, but none more heroic than those of the Presbyterian minister of Summerhill.

All the while he did not neglect the spiritual duties of his ministry. He travelled long distances in troublous times to visit and preach to scattered families of the Presbyterian faith. Time has made ravages in the little congregation, never very large. There is not much to cheer the heart of the aged minister, who has spent nearly fifty years of his life in that isolated portion of the Church. Every Irish Presbyterian ought to take an interest in him for his work's sake, and in the historic little congregation of Summerhill.

The neighbourhood of Summerhill would well repay a visit. Within a few miles are to be seen the Hill of Tara; Dangan Castle, where the Duke of Wellington is said to have been born;[1] the old castle and graveyard of Trim; and Laracor, associated with the life of Dean Swift.

---

[1] Sir Bernard Burke, however, has lately shown that the great Duke was born in the city of Dublin.

Tipperary.

In the town of Tipperary there is one of the oldest Presbyterian congregations in the South of Ireland. Yet it is difficult to get much information, beyond the names of the ministers, prior to the present century. Its first minister was Mr. Shaw, who would seem to have been settled there about the time of the Act of Uniformity. He was succeeded by Mr. Cocks, ordained there in 1673. The ministers during the greater part of the eighteenth century were Mr. Edgar, Mr. Smyth, and Mr. Seawright. Mr. Smyth was a leading man. He left his valuable library to the Synod of Munster, and it was deposited in the Strand Street vestry-room. He also bequeathed to the Synod £200, the interest of which was to be expended in buying new books.[1] In 1804 the Rev. John Lister was minister. The congregation, like many others in the South, appears to have had but a feeble existence at the beginning of the present century. In 1804 there were ten subscribers, who contributed £15, and the minister had a grant from the General Fund, besides £58 from the Regium Donum. But Mr. Lister's death probably scattered the little flock. In 1824 we find it reported to the Synod of Ulster that the congregation of Tipperary had been re-erected. It was some time, however, before a regular minister was appointed.

At a special meeting of the Synod of Ulster held in Mary's Abbey Church, Dublin, in 1833, the Rev. James Wilson (Magherafelt) gave an account of a visit he had paid to Tipperary by appointment of the Synod's Mission.[2]

---

[1] Appendix to *Account of Emlyn's Trial*.
[2] *Missionary Sermons and Speeches*, delivered at a Special Meeting of the Synod of Ulster, September, 1833. Belfast: W. McComb, 1834.

"My visit to Tipperary," he says, "was made under circumstances somewhat peculiar. There are a few Presbyterians in that town, the remains of a congregation that existed there between twenty and thirty years ago. Either by the direct preaching of Arianism, or rather, I believe, by the absence of all doctrinal teaching whatever, the people became indifferent to religion, lapsed into error, and the Presbyterian congregation of Tipperary and its minister departed this life together. The place had been visited, from time to time, by ministers of this body, and the congregation was likely to be reorganised; but those visits being discontinued for some time, they applied to the Synod of Munster, at its last meeting, for preaching; and having represented that none but an orthodox minister would be acceptable in Tipperary, they were placed under the care of a committee, who are styled the orthodox members of that body. A supplication, however, being afterwards forwarded from certain persons in that town to the Presbytery of Dublin, for a minister of the Synod of Ulster to be sent to preach to them, the brethren of Dublin instructed me to go thither and examine into the matter. There I met the committee of the Munster Synod. The people were unanimous in their aversion to Arianism, though some of them could not be reconciled to certain of the articles of our Westminster Confession. The committee did here publicly declare, that to that Confession they had subscribed, and never yet recanted; that its doctrines were those which they believed and preached, and were determined to maintain. They denied holding any spiritual communion with the heterodox of their own body; that the only communion they maintained with them was in money matters; and that their earnest desire was, to get orthodox and zealous ministers settled in all their vacancies. . . . It appeared that there were about £80 per annum in their grant for a minister, so soon as he should be ordained. The resolution, therefore, to which the Presbyterians of Tipperary finally came, was that they should continue their connexion with the committee appointed by the Synod of Munster, who should take care to procure them an evangelical minister from some orthodox body of Presbyterians, as the Church of Scotland, the Synod of Ulster, etc.

"A very interesting station which I visited is Dundrum, six miles from Tipperary, where a few Scotch families reside. The minister of Fethard, fifteen miles distant, opened this station some time ago, and preaches occasionally in a spacious schoolhouse, erected by Lord Heywarden for the tenantry of his estate. . . . Nor should I omit to state here, the perfect personal security which a Presbyterian missionary may feel, although he has about him few of his own denomination. The district around the last-mentioned place, Dundrum, has been one of the most turbulent in that turbulent country. It is but a few miles, on the one hand, from where the Rev. Mr. Going was shot, and, on the other, from where the Rev. Mr. Whitty was stoned to death. The minister of the parish, whose life has been frequently attempted, is obliged, at this moment, to keep a party of police constantly in his house, for the protection of his person and property; and so apprehensive is he of danger, that, even on the Sabbath, he feels it necessary to walk between two of them with loaded firelocks, to and from the church where he officiates. And yet, at this place, I had a large assembly of peaceful and attentive hearers, comprehending persons of the different denominations, to whom I preached three times, concluding each time with candle-light, and afterwards walked half a mile to the village, without molestation, and without apprehension."[1]

In 1841 the Rev. Mr. Alexander, then missionary at Tipperary, was present at meetings of the Presbytery of Munster. The work of re-organising the congregation was so successful, that on the 7th December, 1842, the Rev. Archibald Heron, licentiate of the Tyrone Presbytery, was ordained as minister there, the congregation having promised a stipend of £30 per annum. Mr. Heron resigned the pastorate of Tipperary in 1845, and the Rev. Joseph Crawford McCullagh was ordained there, June 25th, 1845. In 1847 there were connected with the congregation ten families, three single individuals, and fourteen communicants, the attendance at public worship varying from thirty to fifty. Mr. McCullagh left Tipperary for the congregation of 1st Bangor in 1857, and was succeeded by the Rev. John Holmes, the present minister, who was

---

[1] See above, pp. 108, 109.

ordained at Tipperary, June 23rd, 1857. Mr. Holmes was a licentiate of the Comber Presbytery. Under his faithful pastorate the congregation has flourished. In 1883 there were twenty-one families, thirty-two communicants, and an average attendance of forty at public worship.

WATERFORD.

The first minister of the Presbyterian Church in Waterford was Rev. W. Liston, ordained there in 1673. The next minister was the Rev. Alexander Sinclair. Mr. Sinclair was born at Belfast about 1658, and licensed by the Presbytery of Antrim in 1680. After being some time in Dublin as private chaplain, he was sent as a supply to Waterford. He was persecuted by the authorities, but appealed to Lord Clarendon and was protected.[1] He was ordained as minister at Waterford in 1686. During the revolutionary war he fled to Bristol. He afterwards became minister of Plunket Street, Dublin, and remained there till his death in 1723. Mr. Sinclair was Moderator of the Synod of Ulster in 1704, and during all his ministry took an active part in public affairs.

Mr. Sinclair was succeeded at Waterford by Mr. Batty, Mr. Brett, Mr. Cocks, Mr. Dennistoun, Mr. Brown, and Mr. Hamilton. These were the ministers during the eighteenth century. The minister in 1804 was the Rev. James Marshall. At that time the congregational income was very large, when we consider how much greater was then the purchasing power of money. Thirty-two subscribers contributed the sum of £108; the permanent endowment yielded £30;

---

[1] Boyse: *Works*, II., 148; Witherow: *Memorials*, I., 239; Briggs: *American Presbyterianism*, Chap. IV.

the house was valued at £40; besides which the minister got £100 from the Royal Bounty, and a grant from the General Fund. The Rev. William McCance became minister there about 1826. In 1845 the elders of Waterford congregation were Mr. Robert McCall, Mr. John Milling, and Dr. James Cavet.[1] In 1850 the congregation consisted of twenty-three families, with thirty-six communicants, and an average attendance at public worship of sixty in the morning and forty in the evening. In 1862 there were fifty families, sixty communicants, and an average morning attendance of eighty-five. Mr. McCance resigned the active duties of the ministry in October, 1864, after a pastorate at Waterford of more than thirty-eight years. He died on June 26th, 1882.

A second congregation had been formed at Waterford in 1847, and was taken under the care of the Dublin Presbytery. The first minister of this congregation was the Rev. J. W. Kertland (afterwards LL.D.), ordained there June 21st, 1849. Mr. Kertland became government chaplain to the convicts at Spike Island, and died in Dublin in 1885. He resigned Waterford in 1855, and was succeeded by Rev. John Mackeown, who was ordained there December 20th, 1855.

After the resignation of 1st Waterford by Mr. McCance, the Presbyteries of Dublin and Munster, with the co-operation of a Commission of the Mission Board, united the two congregations, the Rev. John Mackeown having resigned 2nd Waterford in order to facilitate the amalgamation. This was in 1865. Mr. Mackeown accepted a call to Lismore, where he still labours.

---

[1] *Minutes of Presbytery of Munster.*

The first minister of the united charge was Rev. James Carson, previously a member of Monaghan Presbytery, who was installed in Waterford, March 29th, 1866. In February, 1868, Mr. Carson resigned, and was designated as missionary to Brisbane. He was succeeded in Waterford by the Rev. Andrew Burrowes, previously minister of Tullamore, who was installed here August 12th, 1869. In 1870 the congregation consisted of fifty-two families, and fifty-four communicants, with an average attendance of a hundred to a hundred and twenty at public worship. In 1876 Mr. Burrowes resigned, having accepted a call to labour as colonial missionary in Canada. The present minister, Rev. John Hall, previously of Magherafelt, was installed in Waterford on July 27th, 1876.

VII.

PRESBYTERY OF NEWRY.[1]

CARLINGFORD.

THE first Presbyterian service in Carlingford of which we have any record was conducted from the windows of a prison. In 1663 several Presbyterian ministers were imprisoned in the Castle of Carlingford for the crime of preaching the Gospel without being episcopally ordained. Among them was the minister of Mourne, on the other side of Carlingford Lough. His congregation, not wishing to be deprived of his services, are said to have frequently come over on the Sabbath-day, when he and his brethren had an opportunity of preaching to them through the grated windows of their prison.

Towards the close of the seventeenth century several Scotch families settled in the neighbourhood of Carlingford. For some years they were connected with the Presbyterian Church at Dundalk, until in 1700 a separate congregation was organised at Carlingford.

The first Presbyterian minister of Carlingford was the Rev. John Wilson, ordained to the joint charge of Dundalk and Carlingford in 1700. Mr. Wilson had a good knowledge of Irish, and was one of the

---

[1] This Presbytery contains twenty-three congregations, but only three of them, Carlingford, Castlebellingham, and Dundalk, are outside the province of Ulster.

eight ministers chosen by the Synod of Ulster to preach the Gospel in Irish. He emigrated to America in 1729. Dundalk had previously been separated from Carlingford, and the Rev. Patrick Simpson ordained there. The next minister was the Rev. Alexander Reid, who was ordained to the joint charge of Carlingford and Narrowwater in 1731, and died in 1737. He was succeeded by the Rev. George Henry, who was ordained there in 1743, and resigned in 1764. The next minister was the Rev. Robert Dickson, who laboured there for nearly forty years. He was ordained there in November, 1765, and died in October, 1804. He was succeeded by the Rev. Samuel Arnold. Mr. Arnold was ordained there in 1805, and continued to minister to the united congregations till the year 1820, when, by order of the Presbytery, he confined his pastoral labours entirely to Narrowwater. The Rev. James Lunn was ordained to the separate charge of Carlingford in July, 1820. Mr. Lunn was one of the ministers who, with their congregations, withdrew from the Synod of Ulster in 1827, after the assertion by that body of the doctrine of the Trinity, and formed the Remonstrant Synod of Ulster.

After this time occasional services were held at Carlingford until 1861, when the Rev. Robert Meares was ordained at Jonesboro, with the understanding that he should have an afternoon service at Carlingford. This arrangement was carried on till 1869, when the Rev. W. J. McCully was ordained minister of Carlingford. Under his ministry, the present church, manse, and schools have been erected.[1]

---

[1] The particulars of this sketch have been taken from a paper on "Presbyterianism in Carlingford," by the Rev. John Elliott (now of Armagh), in the *Evangelical Witness*, February, 1871.

CASTLEBELLINGHAM.

The congregation of Castlebellingham, Co. Louth, was organised in 1840. The Rev. Abraham Irvine was ordained its first minister in 1842. The church was opened for public worship in 1843 by the Rev. Josias Wilson, of Drogheda. Mr. Irvine resigned in 1858, and afterwards removed to America, where he died. He was succeeded by the Rev. John W. Ellison, who was ordained in 1858. In 1877 Mr. Ellison accepted a call to Sunderland, England. He was succeeded by Rev. Isaac Patterson, who was minister from 1878 to 1882. In the latter year the congregation of Jonesboro—which had been formed in 1861 and whose first minister, Rev. Robert Meares, resigned in 1882—was united with that of Castlebellingham. The Rev. Samuel Lyle Harrison, who had previously been minister at Dromore West, was installed as minister of the united congregations of Jonesboro and Castlebellingham in 1882. Mr. Harrison resides at Castlebellingham, and conducts services every Sabbath in both churches, driving a distance of several miles between them. His work is largely of a missionary character, and in visiting and ministering to scattered Presbyterian families he travels over a wide district, including parts of Counties Meath, Louth, and Armagh.

DUNDALK.[1]

The congregation of Dundalk was formed in the year 1650. It is thus one of the oldest Presbyterian congregations in Ireland. Its first minister was the Rev. Joseph Bowersfield. We find his name on the

---
[1] Reid : *History;* Killen : *History of Congregations;* MS. notes of Rev. J. MacMillan.

list of the "Civil Establishment of the Commonwealth for Ireland for the year 1655," as receiving £110 per annum from the public treasury. The congregation was at first Independent, but assumed the Presbyterian form on the arrival of William III., his soldiers, and the colonists that followed in their train.

The next minister was the Rev. John Wilson, who was ordained to the joint charge of Dundalk and Carlingford in the year 1700. After a few years of this arrangement, Dundalk became again a separate congregation, and the Rev. Patrick Simpson was ordained there in 1713. Mr. Wilson remained minister of Carlingford, but emigrated to America in 1729. Like Dr. Neilson, his successor in Dundalk, Mr. Wilson was a good Irish scholar.

Mr. Simpson was minister of Dundalk for nearly fifty years. He died in 1761, and was succeeded by the Rev. Robert Drummond. The next minister was the Rev. Colin Lindsay, who was ordained there in August, 1779. He was succeeded by Rev. Andrew Bryson, ordained there in August, 1786.

Mr. Bryson resigned in 1796, and was succeeded by the Rev. William Neilson, who was ordained there in December, 1796. Mr. Neilson afterwards became D.D. and M.R.I.A. He was a distinguished linguist, and his Irish grammar is still an authority. In 1818 he resigned the pastorate of Dundalk, and became Professor of Greek, Latin and Hebrew, in the Belfast Academical Institution, which was then the theological college of Irish Presbyterianism. On his deathbed he heard the tidings that he had been appointed to the chair of Greek in the University of Glasgow, April 26th, 1821.

After Dr. Neilson, the Rev. David Davidson was

ordained in Dundalk, March 2nd, 1819. He removed to the pastorate of Old Jewry congregation, London, in 1825. He was succeeded by the Rev. William Cunningham, who was ordained as minister of Dundalk, June 23rd, 1825. Mr. Cunningham was described by the late Professor Croskery as being like McCheyne. He was a man of great piety, and was much beloved by his people. But his health failed, and he died, after a brief ministry of less than four years, on May 15th, 1829. The Rev. James Beattie had been ordained as his assistant and successor in 1828. Mr. Beattie died on December 28th, 1851, of fever, caught in the discharge of pastoral duty. He was succeeded by the Rev. William McHinch, who was installed there June 15th, 1852. Mr. McHinch died in 1860, of fever, caught, as in the case of his predecessor, while engaged in ministering to the sick.

Mr. McHinch was succeeded by the Rev. Robert Black, who was installed in Dundalk, June 26th, 1860. For many years Mr. Black took a prominent part in the public work of the Irish Presbyterian Church. He was Convener of the Soldiers' and Sailors' Mission, and was also chosen to fill the Moderatorial chair of the General Assembly. He was wise in council, and able in debate. He died on September 15th, 1885.

The present minister of Dundalk is the Rev. John MacMillan, M.A., formerly of Sion Mills, who was installed as assistant and successor to Mr. Black, May 19th, 1880. Mr. MacMillan is known as an eloquent preacher, and has also taken a prominent place as a speaker in the General Assembly.

The congregation of Dundalk has always been fortunate in having not merely able ministers, but active and energetic members. Amongst its earlier members were

Archibald and Malcolm McNeill, ancestors of Sir John McNeill, the engineer. They came over from Scotland about the close of the seventeenth century. Archibald McNeill was mainly instrumental in building what is now called the Old Presbyterian Church in Dundalk. It was the second church erected for the Presbyterian congregation—the present church being the third building.

Malcolm McNeill built a Presbyterian church at Ballymascanlon, three and a half miles from Dundalk. Under the ivy-covered ruins of this church, which is now in the hands of Episcopalians, rest the remains of six Presbyterian ministers.

Sir John McNeill built his fine residence on the site of what once was the old manse occupied by Rev. Patrick Simpson, his kinsman.

In later years the eldership of Dundalk has included many well-known names. Among these was James Dickie, who was commissioned to go to the Presbytery of Armagh, meeting at Market-hill, October 13th, 1829, and to vote in favour of adhering as a congregation to the Synod of Ulster. This was at the time of the separation of those holding Arian views from the Synod of Ulster, and when the neighbouring congregations of Narrowwater and Carlingford, with their ministers, Mr. Arnold and Mr. Lunn, joined the Remonstrant Synod.

Other well-known members of this congregation have been the Messrs. Patteson, Thomas Coulter, M.D., M.R.I.A., and Thomas Cowan.

In the matter of church worship, the congregation of Dundalk has long taken what in Irish Presbyterian circles would be regarded as an "advanced" position. In the old church a large organ was used for many years. There are many persons living who saw it, and some who heard it, about fifty-five years ago. It was used in the Sabbath worship until it became useless.

Hymns, as well as psalms, have been used in public worship in this congregation since, at least, the beginning of the present century. I have before me a volume of Psalms and Hymns, the preface to which is dated "Newry, 1811," which was in use in Dundalk for many years. A later volume of Psalms and Hymns, published by William Leckie, 59, Bolton Street, Dublin, 1846, was afterwards used. The hymn-book at present in use in Dundalk congregation is one which is largely availed of in the Presbyterian churches of Dublin and the South and West, viz.—" Church Praise," the hymn-book of the Presbyterian Church of England.

It has for some time been the custom in Dundalk for one of the elders to read, in public worship, the portions of Scripture which are chosen as the lessons for the day.

In loyalty to Presbyterian principles, and in generous giving for support of Church and mission work, the congregation of Dundalk stands in the front rank of Irish Presbyterianism.

THE UNITED PRESBYTERIAN CHURCH, LOWER ABBEY STREET, DUBLIN.

This Church had its origin in a mission of the United Presbyterian Church of Scotland, which was commenced in Dublin in the year 1861. In that year David Paton, Esq., of Alloa, gave £1,000 as the nucleus of a fund for a mission in Ireland. Services were first held in Aungier Street, and afterwards in Whitefriars Street. It was felt, however, that if the mission was to succeed, a regular congregation would have to be formed, which would be the centre of evangelistic and other work. Accordingly a number of friends interested in the work rented the Pillar Room of the Rotunda, and opened it for public worship on May 17th, 1863. After some unsuccessful efforts to secure a permanent minister, a call was given to the Rev. James Stevenson, M.A., of Dennyloanhead, Scotland, who accepted it, and was installed in Dublin, July 18th, 1866. The congregation thus formed continued to worship in the Rotunda till February, 1867, when it removed to the old Metropolitan Hall. Services were held there for the next two years. The foundation stone of the United Presbyterian Church, Lower Abbey Street, was laid on May 6th, 1868, by the late D. Anderson, Esq., of Glasgow. The church, a handsome and commodious building, was erected at a cost of nearly £6,000, and was opened by the late Rev. Professor Eadie, D.D., on April 4th, 1869.

The Rev. James Stevenson removed to Leith, and was succeeded by the present minister, Rev. William Proctor, formerly of Penang and Oban. The congregation is entirely self-supporting, and its members carry on vigorous educational and mission work, both in Whitefriars Street and the North Strand, for which they have hitherto received pecuniary aid from the Mission Board of the United Presbyterian Church of Scotland. During Mr. Proctor's ministry a lecture-hall has been added to the church in Lower Abbey Street, and all departments of congregational work are in a high state of efficiency. The liberality of the members of the United Presbyterian Church, and their activity in Christian work, are worthy of all praise. The congregation is largely composed of Scotch families. While it has abundantly justified its existence, and has been an important factor in the Christian life and work of the city of Dublin, yet there would seem no longer any necessity for maintaining it aloof from the Presbyterian Church of Ireland. It might continue to preserve its distinctive features and carry on its special work, while at the same time incorporated with the other Presbyterian congregations of Dublin.

DUBLIN CONGREGATIONS WHICH HAVE BECOME UNITARIAN.

STRAND STREET (now STEPHEN'S GREEN; formerly WOOD STREET and COOK STREET).

The oldest branch of what subsequently became the congregation of Strand Street, was the congregation of Wood Street. This congregation was in existence in the time of Oliver Cromwell. In 1647 its pastor was the great Puritan divine, Rev. John Owen, D.D. He was succeeded by another great Puritan, Rev. Stephen Charnock. In 1652 Charnock was Senior Proctor of the University of Oxford, having previously been made Fellow of New College, Oxford. In 1653 he was called to constant public employment in Ireland. He resided in the family of Sir Harry Cromwell, then Lord Lieutenant, and preached in Wood Street on the Lord's Day, having persons of the greatest distinction in Dublin for his auditors.[1] He returned to England in 1661, and died in 1680. He was succeeded in Wood Street by the Rev. Daniel Williams. Mr. Williams came to Ireland as chaplain to the Countess of Meath. Having preached for a while to the Presbyterian congregation at Drogheda, he accepted a call to the pastorate of Wood Street in 1667. He removed to

---

[1] Calamy: *Nonconformist Memorials*, I., 208 *et seq.*

London in 1687, and was minister of Hand Alley congregation, Bishopsgate Street, till his death. He was the friend of Richard Baxter, and after the Revolution was sometimes consulted by King William on Irish affairs.[1] In 1709 he received the degree of D.D. from both the Universities of Edinburgh and Glasgow. His theological works occupy four volumes quarto. He died in 1716 and was buried in the cemetery of Bunhill Fields. Dr. Williams, through his marriage with a Dublin lady, became possessed of considerable wealth. Partly in his lifetime, and partly by bequest, he devoted all his means to religious and charitable objects. He founded charity schools in Wales and bursaries in Glasgow University. He left money to support two missionaries to the American Indians, money for the poor of Wood Street congregation, and the interest of £1,000 to be devoted to preaching the Gospel in Irish. His famous library of 30,000 volumes was bequeathed for the use of Dissenters, and is now situated in Grafton Street, London, near University College. Dr. Williams was a Calvinistic Trinitarian Presbyterian. Such were some of the great English founders of Presbyterianism in Dublin.

The next minister of Wood Street was also a great Englishman, but, unlike his predecessors, he spent the greater part of his ministry in Ireland. This was the Rev. Joseph Boyse. He came to Ireland first as chaplain to the Countess of Donegall, and in 1683 was chosen as colleague to Dr. Williams in Wood Street, where he remained for forty-five years. Mr. Boyse was a voluminous writer. His first controversial work was *Vindiciæ Calvinisticæ*, a criticism of the reasons

---

[1] Calamy : III., 518.

given by Dr. Manly, Dean of Derry, for joining the Church of Rome, and of an answer to these by Dr. King (afterwards Archbishop), in which the latter made a bitter attack on the Presbyterians. One of his works achieved a unique notoriety. This was his sermon on *The Office of a Scriptural Bishop*, published in a two-volume edition of his sermons, 1708. In 1711 the following resolution was passed by the Irish House of Lords : [1] " Resolved, on the Question that a book entitled ' Sermons preached on various subjects, Vol. I., by J. B.' . . . is false and scandalous and contains matter highly reflecting on the Legislature, and on the Episcopal order : Ordered, on Motion, that the Sheriffs of the City of Dublin do cause the said book to be burnt by the hands of the common Hangman Tomorrow at Twelve of the Clock, before the Tholsel." Mr. Boyse was an advocate of non-subscription, but he was himself an orthodox Presbyterian. He supported the resolution passed by the Synod of Ulster in 1721 (to which Mr. Iredell of Capel Street took exception), permitting all the members of Synod, who were willing to do so, to subscribe the Westminster Confession of Faith. So far he went in favour of subscription. But at the same meeting of Synod he proposed the " charitable declaration," which the Synod also passed, declaring that they did not insinuate any reflection on the brethren who did not sign the Confession as if they were unsound in the faith, and recommending members of congregations not to entertain suspicions of non-subscribing ministers, but to " look upon this as a matter wherein Christians and ministers are to exercise mutual forbearance." Mr. Boyse gave plain proof of

---

[1] *Journals of Irish House of Lords*, November 9th, 1711. See above, pp. 45, 46.

his belief in the doctrine of the Trinity and the Divinity of Christ in his reply to his own colleague, Mr. Emlyn, entitled *A Vindication of the true Deity of our Blessed Saviour.* After a laborious ministry and a studious and active life, Mr. Boyse died on November 22nd, 1728.[1]

Mr. Boyse's leaning toward non-subscription had a significant commentary in the Arianism of the Rev. Thomas Emlyn. Mr. Emlyn was colleague to Mr. Boyse from 1691 till his deposition for Arianism in 1703. The story of Mr. Emlyn is narrated above, Chapter III. He became minister in London, where he died in 1743. Mr. Emlyn was the first minister who introduced Unitarian principles into Ireland. His deposition shows at any rate that neither the Dublin ministers of that time, nor the congregation of Wood Street, however much some of them might be opposed to subscription, had any sympathy with those Arian doctrines now professed by the successors of the ministers and congregation of Wood Street.

After the deposition of Mr. Emlyn, the Rev. Joseph Boyse had as his colleague the Rev. Richard Choppin. Mr. Choppin was himself a native of Dublin, and was ordained in Wood Street in 1704. He died in 1741.

During Mr. Choppin's ministry, and with his active co-operation, the General Fund was formed in 1710 (see above, Chapter V.). Besides Mr. Choppin, two members of his congregation, Sir Arthur Langford and Dr. Duncan Cuming, were the principal promoters of the fund. Sir Arthur Langford gave a contribution of £500 at its origination, and afterwards a legacy of

---

[1] Witherow: *Presbyterian Memorials*, I., 79-87.

£3,000. The members of Wood Street congregation altogether contributed the bulk of the money originally raised. Many wealthy and influential people were associated with the congregation at this time and for a considerable part of the eighteenth century, when Parliament met in Dublin. Among them were Sir Arthur Langford, already referred to, the liberal patron of the Presbyterian congregation of Summerhill. Besides his contributions to the General Fund, he bequeathed £1,500 for the use of the ministers of Wood Street and their successors. Another was Lady Loftus, one of the Ely family. She died in 1702. She bequeathed £500 in trust for the ministers of Wood Street, the interest of which was to be partly devoted to the support of the ministers of Wood Street, and partly to charitable purposes. This sum was afterwards, by desire of Mr. Boyse, transferred to the care of the General Fund Trustees. Another wealthy member of Wood Street and benefactor of the General Fund was Mrs. Susanna Langford, sister of Sir Arthur Langford. She died in 1726.

Another prominent member of Wood Street congregation and benefactor of Irish Presbyterianism was Mr. William Bruce. Mr. Bruce's brother, the Rev. Patrick Bruce, minister at Drumbo and afterwards at Killyleagh, was great-grandfather of the present baronet of that name, Sir Hervey Bruce, of Downhill, near Coleraine. Mr. William Bruce was the originator of the Widows' Fund of the Synod of Ulster, and brought forward his proposal of that benevolent arrangement for the widows of ministers at the meeting of Synod in 1750. He died in 1755. He was an elder of Wood Street congregation. Another elder of Wood Street, and one of the first trustees of the Widows' Fund, was Mr.

Alexander Stewart. This Mr. Stewart was son of Lieutenant-Colonel Stewart of Ballylawn, near Lough Swilly, Co. Donegal. He inherited his father's estate there in 1731. By marriage with his cousin, Miss Mary Cowan, he obtained a fortune of £100,000. He was member for the city of Derry in 1760. In 1743 he purchased the estate of Newtownards and subsequently other estates in the counties of Down and Derry. His son Robert became Marquis of Londonderry, and thus Mr. Alexander Stewart, Presbyterian elder of Wood Street, was grandfather of the celebrated Lord Castlereagh.[1]

After Mr. Boyse's death, the Rev. John Abernethy of Antrim was called to the congregation of Wood Street as colleague to Mr. Choppin in 1730. Abernethy had already distinguished himself by his defence of non-subscription. He was founder of the Belfast Society,[2] and his sermon on *Religious Obedience founded on Personal Persuasion* was practically the beginning of the non-subscription controversy. Professor Witherow has said of him, "There can be no doubt that John Abernethy of Antrim is the true founder of the freethinking school of Irish Presbyterians."[3] Mr. Abernethy was an able man and a practical preacher. His greatest work was a series of sermons entitled *Discourses on the Being and Attributes of God*, which the celebrated Dr. Johnson is said to have read with great admiration, until he heard that it was written by a Presbyterian, when he closed the book and never opened it again. Mr. Abernethy died in 1740. Though a non-subscriber, Mr. Abernethy was a Trinitarian.

---

[1] Reid: *History*, III., 286, 287, n. See above, Chapter XII.
[2] See above, Chapter IX.
[3] *Presbyterian Memorials*, I., 196.

The same may be said of his successor, Rev. James Duchal, D.D., who in his *Presumptive Arguments for the Truth and Divine Authority of the Christian Religion*, strongly asserts the Deity of the Lord Jesus Christ. Dr. Duchal was previously minister at Antrim, and was minister of Wood Street from 1741 till his death in 1761. The Rev. Archibald Maclaine, D.D., afterwards known as the translator of Mosheim's *Ecclesiastical History*, and son of Rev. Thomas Maclaine of Monaghan, was assistant to Dr. Duchal from 1745 to 1747.

In 1747 the Rev. Samuel Bruce, son of the Rev. Michael Bruce of Holywood and great-grandson of the Rev. Michael Bruce of Killinchy, succeeded Mr. Maclaine as colleague to Dr. Duchal. After the death of Dr. Duchal, the Rev. John Mears, then minister of the small congregation of Stafford Street,[1] united with his people in joining the congregation of Wood Street. He then became colleague to Mr. Bruce. Mr. Mears was an advocate of non-subscription, but like his predecessors was a firm believer in the Divinity of Christ and the doctrine of the Trinity.

In 1764 the congregation of Wood Street removed to a new church which they had built at Strand Street. Henceforth, for upwards of a century, the congregation bore the latter name. Mr. Mears preached the opening sermon on that occasion. He died in 1767.

In 1766 the Rev. John Moody (afterwards D.D.) became minister at Strand Street, probably succeeding Rev. Samuel Bruce. Dr. Moody was minister there for nearly fifty years. Robert Stewart, Esq., M.P. for Co. Down, and afterwards Marquis of Londonderry, was a member of Strand Street during Dr. Moody's

---

[1] See on CLONMEL, above, p. 287.

ministry, and it was Dr. Moody who baptized his son, afterwards Lord Castlereagh.

In January, 1769, the Rev. Thomas Plunket became colleague to Dr. Moody. Mr. Plunket had previously been for twenty years minister at Enniskillen. He had been licensed and ordained by the Presbytery of Monaghan, a "subscribing" Presbytery, and, as he also received calls from Corboy and Capel Street, Dublin (now Rutland Square)—both of which were orthodox congregations—there is every reason to believe that Mr. Plunket was not only a Trinitarian but a subscriber. Mr. Plunket's father was the Rev. Patrick Plunket, minister of Glennan, Co. Monaghan. The eldest son of Rev. Thomas Plunket, Patrick Plunket, M.D., was one of the most eminent physicians in Ireland.[1] The youngest son became the illustrious Lord Plunket, Lord Chancellor of Ireland, and grandfather of Lord Plunket, the present Protestant Archbishop of Dublin. Mr. Plunket died in 1778.

His successor as colleague to Dr. Moody was the Rev. William Bruce, D.D., who was previously minister at Lisburn, and came to Strand Street in 1782. He was son of the Rev. Samuel Bruce, a former minister of this congregation, and therefore one of a family of Presbyterian ministers reaching back to the Reformation. He removed to Belfast in 1790, where he became minister of the 1st Congregation, and presided over the Belfast Academy for upwards of thirty years. He died in 1841 in the eighty-fourth year of his age.[2]

In 1787 Strand Street congregation was increased by the union with it of Cook Street, another ancient

---

[1] Armstrong's *History of the Dublin Churches.*
[2] Reid: *History*, III., 389, n.

Presbyterian congregation in Dublin. We must now look back a little to trace the history of Cook Street.

In 1665 or 1666, after the passing of the Irish Act of Uniformity, the Rev. Edward Baynes, minister of St. John's parish, Dublin, seceded from the Established Church, taking many of his congregation with him. They first met for worship in a place in Winetavern Street, called the Magazine. This place contained five other houses, one of which was the Court of King's Bench.[1] Mr. Baynes died in 1670, and was succeeded by the Rev. Thomas Harrison, D.D. Dr. Harrison was another ejected minister, previously parish minister of Christ Church, Dublin. He, like Stephen Charnock, had been for a time chaplain in the family of Sir Harry Cromwell. He returned to England, and it was while exercising his ministry at Chester that he was silenced by the Act of Uniformity.[2] He then came over to Dublin, and became minister of the congregation at Winetavern Street in 1670. Dr. Harrison wrote several religious works, and was so ready in the Scriptures that he was called by many "the walking Bible." Lord Thomond (who had no great respect for ecclesiastics of any sort) had a high opinion of his abilities. He often used to say that he had rather hear Dr. Harrison say grace over an egg than hear the bishops pray and preach. He was a Congregationalist in his view of Church government, and though his people were all Presbyterians, the utmost harmony prevailed between them.

In 1673 the congregation removed to a new church which they had erected in Cook Street, and here a Presbyterian Church existed for more than a century.

---
[1] Gilbert: *History of Dublin* (1845), I., 157.
[2] Calamy: *Nonconformist Memorials.*

At this time many persons of rank and fortune were connected with Cook Street congregation; among them were Sir John Clotworthy, afterwards Lord Massereene, Lady Chichester, afterwards Countess of Donegall, and Lady Cole, of the Enniskillen family.

Dr. Harrison died in 1682.[1] The whole city of Dublin seemed to lament his death, and there was a general mourning. His funeral sermon was preached by the Rev. Daniel Williams, D.D., of Wood Street. In the next few years several ministers preached at Cook Street, some of them evidently for a very short time. Among them was the celebrated John Howe, another great English Puritan divine, who was for some years minister at Antrim.

From 1690 to 1705 the minister of Cook Street was the Rev. Elias Travers, nephew of the Earl of Radnor. Mr. Travers died in 1705, and was succeeded by the Rev. Thomas Steward (afterwards D.D.). Mr. Steward's income from his congregation was £80 a year.[2] Though he sympathised with the non-subscribers, Mr. Steward was himself orthodox. In 1724 he removed to the Presbyterian congregation of Bury St. Edmunds, England, and died about 1750.

Shortly before Mr. Steward's removal to England he had as colleague Rev. James Strong. Mr. Strong was minister from 1721 to 1767. During many years of his ministry (1739 to 1765) he had as colleague the Rev. William McCay, who then removed to Aughmacart. Mr. McCay was succeeded by Rev. Dr. William Dunne.

In 1787 Dr. Dunne and his congregation joined the congregation of Strand Street.

The Rev. James Armstrong, M.A., became minister

---

[1] See below, p. 324.   [2] Witherow : *Presbyterian Memorials*, I., 175.

of Strand Street in 1806. About that time the congregation seems to have become Arian. In the year 1818 it had five hundred and sixty members,[1] which term no doubt includes all persons connected with the congregation. Dr. Moody, who had been in the pastorate of the congregation since 1766, died about 1814. After his death his sermons were published in two volumes (Dublin: 1814). Among the list of subscribers given in the first volume appear such names as Rev. Sir H. H. H. Bruce, Bart.; Rt. Hon. W. C. Plunket (10 sets); Daniel O'Connell, Esq., Merrion Square; Nat. Callwell, Esq.; Peter Digges La Touche Esq.; Messrs. Allman, Bandon; Richard Dowden Esq., Cork; William and Christopher Dowden Esqrs., Bandon; Richard Wheeler, Esq., Bandon, etc.

The Rev. W. H. Drummond, D.D., became colleague to Mr. Armstrong in 1815. He was a man of great ability. Among his published works were a poem on the Giant's Causeway, and a spirited translation of Lucretius.

Mr. Armstrong, too, was an able writer. His taste seems to have been specially for historical study. In 1815 he wrote a *Short Account of the General Fund*, and in 1829 he published an interesting book containing the addresses delivered at the ordination of the Rev. James Martineau in the co-pastorate of Eustace Street congregation. But the specially interesting part of the book, from a historical point of view, is the *Appendix, Containing Some Account of the Presbyterian Congregations in Dublin*, by Rev. James Armstrong, M.A. Mr. Armstrong died in 1840.

Mr. Armstrong was succeeded by his son, the Rev.

---

[1] Warburton, Whitelaw, and Walsh: *History of Dublin*.

George Allman Armstrong, ordained July 18th, 1841. In 1842 Dr. Drummond and Mr. Armstrong, then ministers of Strand Street, being Unitarians, were removed by the judgment of the Lord Chancellor from the Trusteeship of the General Fund. The following lay members of Strand Street Church were also removed from the Trusteeship: Thomas Wilson, John Barton, John Strong Armstrong, Brindley Hone. In an advertisement of a sermon to be preached in Strand Street (*Saunder's Newsletter*, February 1st, 1844) it is stated that benefactions will be received by the ministers, Rev. Dr. Drummond and Rev. Geo. A. Armstrong, by the Treasurer, Thomas Wilson, Esq., Temple Street, or by Robert Andrews, John S. Armstrong, John Barton, H. Bruce, Andrew Carmichael, John Classon, Edward Gaskin, James Haughton, Brindley Hone, Thomas Hutton, James Moody. Rev. G. A. Armstrong died March 9th, 1889, after a ministry of almost forty-eight years.

In 1854 the old communion cups bequeathed in 1682 by Dr. Thomas Harrison to the congregation of Cook Street were still in use in Strand Street.

The congregation of Strand Street removed in 1863 to the present Unitarian church of St. Stephen's Green.

The old communion cups of Cook Street congregation are still in use in St. Stephen's Green church, and bear the following inscription: "The legacy of Dr. Thomas Harrison, Dec[d] September y[e] 18th, Anno Dom: 1682, for the service of the Lord's Supper, bequeathed to y[e] use of his church at y[e] Meeting House in Cook Streete, Dublin."

The present minister of Stephen's Green church is the Rev. D. D. Jeremy, M.A., who was for some years colleague to the Rev. G. A. Armstrong.

Whatever may be thought of the theological opinions of the Unitarians, it must be recognised that they have included amongst their numbers, in Dublin and elsewhere, some of the most intellectual, cultured, and philanthropic of our citizens.

EUSTACE STREET (formerly NEW ROW).

The first ministers of New Row congregation were the Revs. Samuel Winter, D.D., and Samuel Mather, who established the congregation there after the passing of the Act of Uniformity, when they left the Established Church. Dr. Winter had been Provost of Trinity College. Mr. Mather was a Senior Fellow of Trinity, and before 1665 had preached every Lord's Day morning in the parish church of St. Nicholas, where he had been ordained on December 5th, 1656, according to the Presbyterian form, by Dr. Winter, Rev. Mr. Taylor of Carrickfergus, and Rev. Mr. Jenner of Drogheda.[1] After having suffered various persecutions for his Nonconformist principles, Mather died on October 29th, 1671, and was interred in his former church of St. Nicholas.[2] He was succeeded by his brother, Rev. Nathaniel Mather. Mr. Mather went to England in 1689, and died there in 1697. He was for a time minister at Rotterdam. His remains lie in Bunhill Fields.

The Rev. Timothy Taylor was ordained as colleague of Rev. Samuel Mather in 1668, and continued with Rev. Nathaniel Mather till 1682. After Mr. Taylor came the Rev. Nathaniel Weld, who was minister from 1682 till his death in 1730.

In 1728 the congregation of New Row removed to

---

[1] Calamy: *Nonconformist Memorials.*
[2] Gilbert: *History of Dublin.*

the new church which they had erected in Eustace Street. "It must have been at that time considered an imposing structure; for a Quaker, looking up at the stately front, is reported to have said, 'Where there is so much vanity without, there cannot be much religion within!'"[1] Mr. Weld was succeeded by his son, Rev. Isaac Weld (afterwards D.D.), who was ordained in Eustace Street in 1732. Dr. Isaac Weld died in 1778.

The most eminent minister of this congregation, perhaps the most eminent minister in the history of Dublin Presbyterianism, was the Rev. John Leland, D.D. Professor Witherow says he was "the ablest theologian who occupied a pulpit in the Presbyterian Church of Ireland throughout the whole of the eighteenth century." He was ordained in New Row in 1716 as colleague to the Rev. Nathaniel Weld. Dr. Leland wrote and published many important works. In a century of doubt he stood forth as one of the most learned and successful defenders of the Christian faith. His principal works were: *Reflections on the late Lord Bolingbroke's Letters on the Study and Use of History; A View of the Principal Deistical Writers* (fourth edition, 2 vols., London: 1764); *The Divine Authority of the Old and New Testament;* and *The Advantage and Necessity of the Christian Revelation.* Bishop Hare said of the last-named book: "This work is the best and most useful English book I ever read."[2] Dr. Leland was a firm believer in the Deity of Christ, a truth which he unfolds in his published sermons with much fervour and power. He died in 1766.

Dr. Leland was succeeded by Rev. Samuel Thomas, who was colleague of Dr. Isaac Weld from 1767 to

---

[1] Witherow: *Presbyterian Memorials*, I., 127, 128.
[2] *Ibid.*, I., 334.

1777. In that year the Rev. Philip Taylor, son-in-law of Dr. Isaac Weld, became minister at Eustace Street. The Rev. Joseph Hutton was ordained as colleague to Mr. Taylor on March 21st, 1788. It was not till considerably after the beginning of the present century that the congregation of Eustace Street became Unitarian. In the Report of the case of the Attorney-General (for George Matthews and others) against the Revs. Joseph Hutton and J. C. Ledlie, D.D., and others, in 1844, Mr. Sergeant Warren said of Eustace Street, "I admit that in 1828 or 1830 the main bulk of the congregation became Unitarians; and from that time they have been exclusively and avowedly an Unitarian congregation. There is a strong contrast in what took place before and after 1830. In 1830 they had attained such boldness in uttering their opinions that a society was formed, called the Irish Unitarian Christian Society, which had for its object the spread of Unitarian doctrine."

In 1828 the Rev. James Martineau was ordained as co-pastor of the Rev. Philip Taylor and Rev. Joseph Hutton in Eustace Street. The Rev. Joseph Hutton preached the sermon on that occasion; the Rev. James Armstrong of Strand Street gave a discourse on Presbyterian ordination; an address was given by the Rev. James Martineau, with a statement of his own belief; the ordination prayer was offered by the Rev. Philip Taylor; and the charge to Mr. Martineau and the congregation was given by the Rev. W. H. Drummond, D.D., of Strand Street. Mr. Martineau resigned in 1852, and was succeeded by the Rev. J. C. Ledlie, D.D. Mr. Martineau is a brother of the late well-known writer, Harriet Martineau. He was born and educated in England. After leaving Dublin he was for some time Unitarian minister at Liverpool. In 1841 he was appointed Professor of Mental and Moral Philosophy in Manchester New College, of which institution he afterwards became Principal. During his professoriate he was for some years minister of Little Portland Street Chapel, where such men as Darwin and Lyell were occasional worshippers. He has written many important books, such as *Studies of Christianity; Modern Materialism; Types of Ethical Theory;* and *Study of Religion.* He has obtained honorary degrees from Harvard, Leyden, and Edinburgh, and is a D.C.L. of Oxford. In 1842 the Rev. Joseph Hutton, the Rev. James Crawford Ledlie, ministers of Eustace Street, and the following members of that congregation were removed by the Lord Chancellor from the Trusteeship of the General Fund: William Drennan, Nathaniel Hone, Robert Moore Peile, and William Biggar.

Dr. Ledlie died in 1852, and Mr. Hutton in 1856. Mr. Hutton's ministry extended over the remarkable period of sixty-eight years. In 1867 the congregation of Eustace Street united with that of Stephen's Green.

SOME EXTINCT CONGREGATIONS.

AUGHMACART.

Aughmacart, in Queen's County, between Mountmellick and Kilkenny, was the site of a Presbyterian congregation during the greater part of the eighteenth century. The first minister appears to have been the Rev. Robert Rutherford, who was ordained there by the Presbytery of Monaghan in 1713. Mr. Rutherford removed to America in 1730. He was succeeded by the Rev. Stephen Magachin. After Mr. Magachin came Rev. James Dobbyn. Mr. Dobbyn was succeeded by the Rev. Wm. McCay (or Magachin), previously minister at Cook Street, Dublin, who was installed at Aughmacart in 1765. Mr. McCay remained there till his death in 1796, after which the congregation became extinct.[1]

There was valuable property at Aughmacart connected with the Presbyterian Church.[2] In 1719 Henry Lewis (who held these lands from the Dawson family under a lease of lives renewable for ever) granted no less than *sixty acres* at Aughmacart to Duncan Comyng and John Curtis, then acting trustees of the General Fund, at a yearly rent of one peppercorn, in trust for the use of the Presbyterian minister of Aughmacart, *and a reversion to the use of the General Fund, should the congregation cease to exist.*

These acting trustees leased twenty acres (for lives renewable for ever) to John Moffit, at a yearly rent of 5s. 3d. per acre, and a quarter's rent on the fall of each life.

John Curtis, survivor of these acting trustees, leased the residue of forty acres (for lives renewable for ever) to William Minchin, at a yearly rent of £14, and 20s. payable on the fall of each life.

The rents of both farms were to be applied to support the minister at Aughmacart. Such payment was regularly made to Mr. Rutherford, Mr. Magachin, Mr. Dobbyn, and Mr. McCay. When the congregation became extinct, the interest reverted to the General Fund, but no rents were received by them.

Armstrong, in his *Short Account of the General Fund*, states that the difficulty of enforcing payment arose from the neglect of the trustees in reviving the trust.

---

[1] Appendix to Account of Emlyn's Trial.
[2] MS. *History of the General Fund*, by Dr. William Frazer, M.R.I.A. 1862.

Thomas Litton and John Hutchinson revived it, and succeeded John Curtis in the management of this property. At their decease it was neglected to be revived, and in 1815 rested in Edward Litton, heir-at-law of Thomas Litton.

Here is valuable property of the Presbyterian Church alienated through carelessness. The "New Light" doctrines of the close of the eighteenth and the beginning of the nineteenth centuries do not seem to have been favourable to earnestness in anything. General indifference was the order of the day.

But this is not all. Henry Lewis further granted *sixty acres*, as a glebe for the minister, to Rev. R. Rutherford during his lifetime and to his successors, and in case the congregation became extinct, the land was to revert to the representatives of Henry Lewis, *upon condition of their paying £10 per annum to the Trustees of the General Fund.* In 1724 Mr. Rutherford mortgaged his interest to the acting trustees, Thomas Corker and John Marriott, for £50, and on his removal to America in 1730, he sold the entire of his interest for £100 additional. After 1796 these sixty acres reverted to the family of Mr. Lewis, *but the £10 yearly has never been paid.*

BALLYBRITTAS.

There was a Presbyterian congregation at Ballybrittas[1] during the greater part of the eighteenth and part of the nineteenth century. The first minister whose name is recorded was the Rev. Mr. Hemphill. In 1728, probably during his ministry, the church was built.

---

[1] Ballybrittas is in Queen's County, about four miles from Monastarevan station on the G. S. and W. R.

In that year Henry Porter granted a site for a meeting-house, the site consisting of less than an acre, with right of turbary and water. Mr. Hemphill's successors were Rev. J. Magachin, Mr. Robinson, and another Mr. Magachin. It is possible that some of these at least were the ministers of Aughmacart referred to above, but this I cannot definitely ascertain. In 1770 it was agreed by the Trustees of the General Fund: "As Edenderry has ceased to be a congregation, and Mr. McGachin is no longer capable of preaching at Ballybrittas, and Mr. Harpur is agreeable to the people there, it is the resolution of the Fund to allow the Rev. Mr. Harpur £35 per ann. for supplying Rahue and Ballybrittas alternately." The Rev. Ephraim Harpur was at that time minister of Rahue. After Mr. Harpur's death, about 1810, the congregation of Ballybrittas became extinct. It fared better with the property here than at Aughmacart. In 1821 the Dean of Killaloe purchased the interest of the Trustees of the General Fund in the Ballybrittas property for £115 5s. 4d., which was agreed upon by arbitration. This money was vested in stock for the use of the Fund.

Edenderry.

A Presbyterian congregation was in existence at Edenderry, King's County, in the beginning of the eighteenth century, if not sooner. About 1710 the congregation of Edenderry was annexed to the Presbytery of Armagh. In 1711 the Rev. Thomas Anderson was ordained there by that Presbytery. He was minister there for several years, and was succeeded by Rev. Mr. Robinson, and Rev. Mr. Futt. About 1770 the congregation ceased to exist.

Leap.

The congregation of Leap (or Horse Leap), near Birr, in King's County, was in existence early in the eighteenth century. Its ministers were Rev. Mr. Squire, Rev. Mr. Tate, Rev. Mr. Atkinson, and Rev. A. Blair. In 1786 Mr. Blair removed to Lisburn, where he died in 1790. Shortly after his departure from Leap, Rev. Messrs. Taylor and Moody of Dublin visited that place at the desire of the Trustees of the General Fund. They found "the meeting-house" very much out of repair and unfit for public worship. They also were of opinion that, in consequence of deaths, removals, and intermarriages, the congregation was almost entirely dissolved, and that there was no reasonable hope of reviving it. Here also a considerable endowment seems to have been lost to the Presbyterian Church. After Mr. Blair's removal the Trustees of the General Fund, understanding that a certain sum was lodged with Mr. Darby of the Leap, for the support of the Presbyterian interest, and conceiving themselves entitled, from the nature of their trust, and from the support so long afforded by them to the congregation of Leap, to the management of this sum, applied to Mr. Darby to have it transferred to them, offering at the same time to indemnify him. In reply Mr. Darby stated that the sum was £170, the interest of which would be paid to Mr. Blair for his life, and at his death the representatives of the original donors would consider how the principal should be applied, and then communicate with the General Fund. In 1790 Mr. Blair died, and the money has since remained in the hands of the Darby family. In 1815 this endowment amounted with interest to £420.

RAHUE.

Rahue or Rahew is in the County Westmeath, about five miles from Tyrrell's Pass, between Mullingar and Tullamore. There was a Presbyterian congregation there for many years. Its ministers whose names are on record were Mr. Walker, Mr. Johnston, and Rev. Ephraim Harpur. Mr. Harpur was minister there for at least thirty-five years. He was minister in 1770, when he was requested to undertake an additional service at Ballybrittas, and he was minister as late as 1804. Soon after this he died, and the congregation became extinct.

The Rev. Dr. Horner, of Mary's Abbey, Dublin, gave a report to the Presbytery of Dublin in 1821 of a visit he had made to various places in Westmeath. At Tyrrell's Pass he was informed by an elderly lady who resided there, that she remembered a considerable number of Presbyterians living in Tyrrell's Pass who attended at Rahue; but that since Mr. Harpur's death, the church and congregation at Rahue being left in a deserted state, these Presbyterians had become Methodists. She mentioned some, however, who still professed an attachment to the religion of their fathers.

Proceeding thence to Rahue, there also he learned much from an old Presbyterian lady concerning the fate of the congregation. She said she remembered it a good congregation, and had often seen a number of carriages at the place of worship on the Sabbath; but that it had declined greatly before Mr. Harpur's death, in consequence, she thought, of his neglecting it. She also stated that a gentleman had left a legacy of £10 annually and a piece of ground for the support of the congregation, but that his son had pulled down the meeting-house and refused to give either the land or the annuity left by his father, and that after his mother's death the property was sold to pay his debts. This lady also informed him that the Baptists had established several schools in the neighbourhood, and that one of them was built upon the site of the meeting-house. In this building Baptist ministers sometimes preached on the Lord's Day, and when there was no minister, a few assembled to read the Scriptures and join in prayer. These people, she believed, were the descendants of the Presbyterians who formerly lived in that neighbourhood.

Such was the fate of the Presbyterian congregation of Rahue.

STRATFORD.

Stratford-on-Slaney, in the County Wicklow, had a Presbyterian congregation as early as 1799,[1] but we have no trace of its history before that. The Rev. Andrew McCaldin was installed there as minister by the Dublin Presbytery in December, 1804. He was succeeded by the Rev. Mr. Baird. Mr. Baird died in July, 1817. The next minister was the Rev. Joseph Scott, who came there in 1818. In 1831, Mr. Scott being then the minister, the congregation seems to have been in a flourishing condition. There were three elders, about twenty-five families, forty communicants, and an attendance varying from sixty to a hundred on the Lord's Day.[2] Mr. Scott died on December 25th, 1835. The Rev. Robert Arnold was ordained there on August 31st, 1836. Mr. Arnold resigned the pastorate of Stratford in 1839. At that

---
[1] Reid: *History*, III., 540.
[2] *Minutes of Dublin Presbytery*.

time the works at Stratford formerly owned by Mr. James Orr came into possession of Mr. Greenham. Mr. Greenham employed a large number of Scotchmen, and was anxious for the appointment of a Presbyterian minister there. There were also Presbyterians at Baltinglass. The Rev. Robert Dunlop was ordained at Stratford, November 19th, 1839. At a visitation held there in 1842 it was stated that the church was held on a lease for nine hundred and ninety-nine years. Mr. Dunlop resigned the pastoral charge of Stratford in 1846, and the Dublin Presbytery committed the congregation to the care of the Mission Board as a centre of missionary work. In 1848 the Mission Board decided to withdraw a regular supply from Stratford, but agreed to pay the travelling expenses of the minister of Carlow, who might statedly preach there. Mr. Powell, then minister of Carlow, was accordingly instructed by the Presbytery to make arrangements for supplying Stratford as a preaching-station. This arrangement, if carried out, does not appear to have been very successful, for the congregation appeared no more after this year on the roll of the Dublin Presbytery. Its communion service was in 1849 ordered by the Presbytery to be forwarded to Dublin and deposited with Rev. W. B. Kirkpatrick (then Moderator of Presbytery) as the property of the Presbytery of Dublin.

Yet the Presbytery did not altogether lose sight of Stratford. In 1854 the Rev. John Hall, of Athy (now of Waterford), reported that he had visited Stratford as directed by the Presbytery. He found the church getting out of repair, and occupied partly as a store; few Protestants in the place; and but little encouragement to resume preaching in Stratford. A committee consisting of Rev. John Hall, with Messrs. Todd and

Drury, elders, was appointed to visit Stratford and make further inquiries. There is no record of any report from this committee, and thus abruptly the story of Stratford comes to an end.

INDEX.

	PAGE
ABBEY Street congregation (*see also* Union Chapel)	215-19
Abernethy, Rev. John	54-6, 65, 318
Act of Uniformity	1, 8, 9, 128
Adair, Rev. David	187, 191, 197
—— Rev. Patrick	251
—— Rev. William	172
Adelaide Road congregation	112, 127, 132, 219-21, 274
Aghada	204
Agreement and Resolution of Ministers at Cork (1657)	5
Agreement and Resolution of Ministers at Dublin (1658)	6, 7
Agreement between Synod of Ulster and Presbytery of Dublin (1710)	38, 39
Alexander, Rev. Edward	231
—— Rev. John	252
Allen, Rev. E. H.	166
—— Rev. James	98, 289
—— Rev. Robert	182
Allman, Francis	203
American Presbyterianism and the Presbytery of Dublin	40, 41
Anderson, Rev. Thomas	331
—— Rev. Walter	174
Andrews, Rev. Samuel	198
Anne, Queen, and the Presbyterians	26, 30
Arbuckle, Rev. James	252, 254
Arianism 18-23, 67, 95, 115-17, 131, 139, 203, 213, 287, 316, 323, 327	
Armstrong, Rev. G. A.	124, 324
—— Rev. James	322, 323
—— Rev. John	246
—— Rev. Thomas	179-82
Arnold, Rev. Robert	334

	PAGE
Arnold, Rev. Samuel	306
——— Rev. William	241
Arrest of a whole Presbytery	46, 47
Ash, Rev. Luke	192
Ashmore, Rev. John	186
Ashwood, Rev. John	209
Athenry congregation	165
Athlone congregation	111, 165
——— Presbytery	133
Athy congregation	132, 221, 222
Attempts to suppress Presbyterianism in Dublin, Galway, and Drogheda	10, 16
Aughmacart congregation	248, 328-30
BAILEY, Rev. R. T.	232
Bailieborough Presbytery	177
Baird, Rev. John (Mallow)	210
——— Rev. Mr. (Stratford-on-Slaney)	100, 334
Balbriggan	132
Ballacolla congregation	223
Ballina congregation	179-82
Ballinasloe congregation	166-68
Ballinglen congregation	182, 183
Ballybrittas congregation	248, 330
Ballymahon	112
Ballymote congregation	183
Bandon congregation	97, 111, 115-17, 198-204
Baptist Church	162
Barber, Rev. Samuel	81
Barnett, Rev. John	185, 232
Barr, Rev. Isaac	189
Batty, Rev. M.	302
Baynes, Rev. Edward	9, 321
Beard, Rev. John	267, 268
Beattie, Rev. H. H.	288
——— Rev. James	309
Belfast Institution	92-4, 139, 140, 143
——— party, The	141
——— Society	54
Bellis, Rev. George	107
Belturbet Presbyterian Church	47
Bi-centenary Fund	131
Biggar, Rev. William	16, 29, 236, 290

INDEX. 339

	PAGE
Bigger, Rev. Professor	147
Billy Bluff and Squire Firebrand	81, 82
Bingham, Rev. James	204
Birr congregation	117, 118, 223
Bishop of Derry and Dr. Cooke	121
Bishops and Presbyterian marriages	75
—— and the petition to Queen Anne	42-5
—— joining in Presbyterian ordination	5
—— silencing Presbyterian ministers	5
Black, Rev. Dr. J. J.	198, 247, 260
—— Rev. Robert	309
Blair, Rev. A.	332
Bleckley, Rev. John M.	284
Bolton, Duke of	52
Bond, Captain Willoughby	175
—— Rev. James	169
—— Rev. John P.	281, 282
Bonfire argument	45, 46
Booth, Sir Robert Gore	184
Boulter, Archbishop, and the Presbyterians	64, 65
Bowersfield, Rev. Joseph	307
Boyd, Rev. John (Moyvore)	173
—— Rev. M. (Drogheda)	131
—— Rev. Samuel	238
Boyle, Archbishop	10
—— congregation	184, 185
Boyse, Rev. Joseph	19, 56, 314-18
—— sermons publicly burned	45, 46
Bramhall, Bishop	5
Brannigan, Rev. Michael	182, 183, 186
Bray congregation	99, 100, 113, 225-29
Breakey, Rev. Isaiah	289
Briggs, Rev. Dr. (quoted)	40
Brinkley, Rev. M.	212
Brown, Rev. Andrew	188, 195
—— Rev. John, D.D.	141, 260
—— Rev. N. M., D.D.	141
—— Rev. S. E.	166
—— Rev. Thomas	204
Browne, Rev. John	239
Bruce, Mr. William	68, 317
—— Rev. Dr. William	77, 320
—— Rev. Samuel	319

	PAGE
Bruce, Sir Hervey	317
Brunswick Street congregation	229
Bryson, Rev. Andrew	308
—— Rev. M. (Fethard)	289
Bull-Alley congregation	9, 251, 252
Burghers and anti-burghers	67, 215, 216
Burke, Rev. William	169, 175
Burkitt, Rev. T. H.	165
Burns, Rev. William	241, 282
Burrowes, Rev. Andrew	280, 304
CAIRNS, Rev. John	182, 195, 196
—— Rev. T. R.	182
Calamy, Rev. Dr.	28
Caldwell, Rev. Booth	183, 192
—— Rev. James (Duncannon)	239
—— Rev. James (Usher's Quay)	256
—— Rev. R. A.	185
—— Rev. Samuel E.	188
Campbell, Mr. James	167, 172
—— Rev. James A.	279
—— Rev. Dr. William	97, 287
—— Rev. Laughlin	265
—— vindication of the Presbyterians	76, 77
Capel Street congregation	9, 251
Carden, Rev. Dr.	220, 221
Cargin, Rev. James	260
Carlile, Rev. James, D.D.	92-4, 99, 117, 118, 125, 126, 271-75
—— Rev. Warrand	231
Carlingford congregation	306
Carlow congregation	100, 101, 106, 111, 230-32, 335
Carnew	106
Carson, Rev. James	304
Cartwright, Thomas	4, 5
Castlebar congregation	195, 196
Castlebellingham congregation	307
Castlemartyr	204
Castlepollard	176
Castlereagh, Lord	68, 91-4, 318, 320
Catholic Emancipation	134
Chalmers, Rev. Matthew	252
Chambers, Rev. John	224
—— Rev. Robert	9

	PAGE
Chancery proceedings regarding General Fund	123-127
Charlemont, Earl of	76
Charles II. and the Presbyterians	11, 12
Charlton, Rev. J. H.	206
Charnock, Rev. Stephen	9, 313
Choppin, Rev. Richard	35, 37, 56, 316
Christian Irishman	229
Christmas, Observance of	270
Clanbrassil, Lady	11
Clancarty, Earl of	166
Clarendon, Earl of	12, 13
Clarke, James, Esq.	99, 216
—— Rev. J. G. (Athy)	222
—— Rev. J. King (Fermoy)	208
—— Rev. John C. (Galway)	172
—— Rev. Thomas	248
Clayton, Bishop, an Arian	67
Cleland, Rev. James	293
Clogher congregation	185, 186
Clonakilty congregation	205, 206
Clonmel congregation	97, 106, 107, 111, 286-88
Clontarf congregation (*see also* Gloucester Street)	127, 232-34
Clotworthy, Sir John	322
Cock, Rev. William	200, 286, 299
Coffey, Rev. R. S.	204, 232
Coldin, Rev. Alexander	40, 239
Cole, Lady	322
Collins, Rev. Joshua	243
Colville, Rev. M.	59, 60
Commutation Fund	156
Confession of Faith	6, 7, 18, 55-8
Congregational Church	99, 162
Connaught Presbytery	179
Convention of 1660 and the Presbyterians	8
Cook Street congregation	9, 320-24
Cooke, Rev. Henry, D.D.	101, 105, 107, 119-21, 136, 138, 171, 180, 183, 196, 228, 230, 262, 272, 276
—— Rev. William	244
Cooper, Rev. M.	99, 258
Corboy congregation	169
Cork, Congregations of	97, 107
—— Ministers at (1657)	5
—— Presbytery	133, 198

INDEX.

	PAGE
Corry, Sir James P., M.P.	137
Coulter, Dr. Thomas	310
—— Rev. D. S. K.	187
Cowan, Rev. Robert	206
—— Thomas	310
Cox, Dean, and the Presbyterians	29
—— Rev. Samuel	8
Craghead, Rev. Robert	55, 64, 65, 266
Craig, Rev. Samuel	295-98
Crawford, Rev. Dr. A. Ross	239
—— Rev. S. G.	198
Creeds	6, 7, 54-61
Creevelea congregation	186
Creggs congregation	168
Creighton, Rev. D. H.	226
—— Rev. Robert	103, 196, 197
Croskery, Rev. Professor, D.D.	146, 205, 206
Crotty, Rev. William	117, 223
Crowbar Brigade, The	181
Crozier, Rev. William	287 *n.*
Cuffey, Rev. J. D.	280
Cumyng, Dr. Duncan	19, 35, 37
Cunningham, Rev. William	309
DALKEY	132
D'Aubigné, Dr. Merle	145
Daunt, Rev. Edward S.	242
Damer, Joseph	34
Davidson, Rev. David	308, 309
Declaration of liberty of conscience (1687)	13
De Foe and Irish Presbyterians	27
Dewart, Rev. John	184
Dickie, James	310
Dickson, Rev. Dr. W. S.	80, 81
—— Rev. R. (Carlingford)	306
—— Rev. R. (Wexford)	281
—— Thomas A., M.P.	137
Digby, M. Benjamin	173, 244
Dill, Rev. E. M.	205, 214
—— Rev. John	288
—— Rev. Richard	126, 139-45, 258-60
—— Rev. S. M.	141
Disestablishment of the Irish Church	155-57

INDEX. 343

	PAGE
"Dissenter"	119, 120
Dobbyn, Rev. James	328
Donegall, Countess of	266, 314, 322
Donore congregation	234, 235
Donaldson, Rev. Joseph	208
Douglas, Rev. James	251
Dougherty, Rev. Professor	147
Dowden, Richard	203
—— William	203
Downpatrick Missionary Herald	201 *n.*
Drogheda congregation	100, 113, 235-39
—— Persecution at	28, 29, 43
Dromore West congregation	186, 187
Drummond, Rev. Robert	308
—— Rev. W. H.	124, 323, 324
Drysdale, Rev. R. R.	251
Dublin and Dr. Cooke	118
—— elders	68, 69
—— ministers reprimanded	70
—— Presbytery	38-41, 59-61, 69, 70, 104-12, 215
Duchal, Rev. James, D.D.	319
Duff, Rev. Robert	182
Duncan, Dr. J. F.	233
Duncannon congregation	239
Dundalk congregation	307-11
Dunlop, Rev. Robert	334
—— Rev. Samuel	166
Dunn, Rev. Dr. William	77, 322
Dunne, Colonel	69
Dysart, Rev. Thomas	210
ECHLIN, Bishop	5
Edenderry congregation	331
Edgar, Rev. James	232, 233
—— Rev. John, D.D.	181, 195, 280
—— Rev. R. McCheyne	210, 221
Edmonds, Rev. John	166, 174, 248
Edwards, Rev. Thomas	191
Elders and the Presbytery	105
Elliott, Rev. John	306 *n.*
Ellison, Rev. J. W.	307
Emigration to America and its causes	41, 62-4
Emlyn, Rev. Thomas	19-23, 124, 316

	PAGE
Endowments lost	328-30, 332, 333, 334
Ennis congregation	169
Enniscorthy congregation	113, 114, 239-41
Enniskillen family	322
Episcopal Church and Arianism	67
—— Present condition of	160, 161
Episcopalian friendliness	118-20, 133, 161, 242
—— intolerance	120-22, 130, 231, 278, 306
Eustace Street congregation	98, 111
—— Fund (*see* General Fund)	
Evangelical Society, Irish	99
Evictions	181
Eyre, Robert Hedges, Esq.	108
FAMINE	135, 296, 297
Fearon, Rev. William	178, 183
Fenian movement, The	151-54
Ferguson, Rev. A.	168, 169
—— Rev. David	293
Fermoy congregation	103, 104, 124, 206-8
Ferrier, Mr. James	105, 124
Ferris, Rev. M.	289
Fethard congregation	98, 288, 289
"Fighting Friday"	145
Findlater, Alexander	276
—— A. S.	147
First Irish Presbytery	4
Fisher, Rev. John	173
—— Rev. Joseph	172
Fitzwilliam, Earl of	77, 78
Fleming, Rev. James	28, 29, 184, 236
—— Rev. R. W.	169
—— Rev. William	169
Forbes, Mr.	105
—— Sir Arthur	11
Forsythe, Rev. Neil S.	232
Frackelton, Rev. W. S.	280
Frazer, Dr. William	260
—— History of General Fund	290
Freedom of Dublin city conferred on Dr. Cooke	119
Freeland, Rev. Dr.	246
Froude (quoted)	9 *n.*, 135 *n.*
Fullerton	3

	PAGE
GAILEY, Rev. Albert	... 211
—— Rev. James	... 211
Galway congregation	107, 111, 171
—— Persecution at	... 16
Gault, Rev. Robert	115, 201
Geddes, Rev. F. W.	... 240
General Assembly and the Land Question	... 136
—— Fund	32-6, 37, 97, 123-27, 230
George I. and the Presbyterians	... 50
Gibson, Rev. Alexander	... 174
—— Rev. C. B.	... 209
—— James, Q.C.	... 143
Gill, Rev. W. J.	... 209
Given, Rev. Professor, D.D.	... 146
Gladstone, Right Hon. W. E.	155, 157, 158
Glendinning, George	... 103
Glendy, Rev. John	82, 83
Glenn, Rev. H. P.	... 280
Gloucester Street congregation (*see also* Clontarf) ...	127, 232, 233
Gore, Sir Arthur	... 189
—— Sir Arthur Knox	... 180
Goudy, Rev. Dr.	137, 141
Graham, Rev. Professor	... 147
Granard, Countess of	... 266
——- Earl of	11, 173
Grattan and the Presbyterians	... 76
—— Henry	... 86
Greer, Samuel McCurdy	136, 137
—— Rev. David	... 249
Grey, Rev. J. B.	... 226
Greystones and Kilpedder	241-43
HALL, Rev. Alexander	230-39
—— Rev. James	... 195
—— Rev. John, D.D.	185, 261, 275-77
—— Rev. John (Waterford)	222-49, 293, 304, 335
Hamilton (Lord Claneboy)	... 3
—— Rev. Alexander (Galway)	... 172
—— Rev. Dr. Thomas	ix, 147 *n.*, 271 *n.*
—— Rev. Dr. W. Ross	... 172
—— Rev. John (Turlough)	187, 195
—— Rev. John M. (Donore)	234, 235
—— Rev. John S. (Rutland Square)	... 277

	PAGE
Handock, Major	165
Hanna, Rev. Robert	233
—·— Rev. S., D.D.	169
Hanson, Rev. George	263
—— Rev. S. J.	247
Harding, Rev. M.	200
Hare, Rev. William	169
Harpur, Rev. Ephraim	330-32
Harrison, Rev. Dr. Thomas	9, 321, 322, 324
—— Rev. S. L.	168, 186-87, 307
Harshaw, Rev. R. H.	174, 249
Hazlitt, Rev. Mr.	201
Hemphill, Rev. M.	289, 330
Henderson, Rev. Archibald	165
Henry, Mr. Hugh	263
—— Rev. George	306
—— Rev. Henry	194
—— Rev. Hugh	237
—— Rev. John	169
—— Rev. Robert	263
—— Rev. Samuel	188, 192
Heron, Rev. Archibald	301
—— Rev. James	193
—— Rev. Professor	146
Hincks, Rev. Thomas Dix	97, 206, 212, 213
Hogg, Rev. William	204
Hollymount congregation	187, 188
Holmes, Miss Elizabeth	186
—— Rev. John	301, 302
Home Rule Bill	158
Hook, Rev. Henry	254
—— Rev. Thomas	172
Horner, Rev. James, D.D.	70, 105, 106, 166, 173, 196, 231, 269-75, 333
—— Rev. W. H.	224
Howe, Rev. John	322
Hoyle, Rev. Nathaniel	9
Hunter, Rev. Hugh	204, 210
—— Rev. J. W. (Adelaide Road)	220
—— Rev. Mr. (Bandon)	200, 203
Huntingdon, Lady	96 n., 99, 253
Huston, Rev. Clarke, D.D.	137, 141
Hutcheson, Rev. Alexander	263
—— Rev. Thomas	216

	PAGE
Hutton, Henry, Lord Mayor of Dublin	96, 269
—— Rev. Joseph	326-28
Hymns	208, 311
INSTRUMENTAL music	228, 310
Iredell, Rev. Francis	46, 47, 50, 60, 263-67
Irish Church Act	155, 156
—— Evangelical Society	99
—— Land Acts	157
—— language, Preaching in	51, 52
—— Parliament (1792) and the Presbyterians	76
—— Presbyterian Representation Society	137
—— Tenant League	137
Irvine, Rev. Abraham	307
Irwin, Rev. C. H.	229
—— Rev. J. M.	224
—— Rev. William, D.D.	204, 205
JACKSON, Rev. William	286
—— Rev. Moffatt	193
Jacque, Rev. Gideon	281
—— Rev. William	251, 253, 263
Jeffrey, Rev. Robert	210
Johnston, Rev. Samuel	186
—— Rev. William	289
KEEGAN, Rev. George S.	191, 192
Keers, Rev. John	211, 212
Kelburn, Rev. Ebenezer	80, 252, 253
—— Rev. Sinclair	80, 252, 253
Kells congregation	177
Kelly, Rev. Samuel	279
Kelso, Rev. Robert	282, 283
Kennedy, Rev. Robert	168
—— Rev. Thomas	169
Kerr, Rev. Matthew	186, 187, 210, 211, 250
—— Rev. Mr. (Fermoy)	208
Kertland, Rev. J. W.	303
Keys, Rev. William	251
Kilkenny congregation	243, 244
Killala congregation	188-91
Killen, Rev. President, D.D.	146
—— Rev. T. Y.	185

INDEX.

	PAGE
Killucan congregation	244, 245
Kilpedder	228, 241
Kilrush congregation	171, 290
Kimmitt, Rev. Edward	206, 224
King, Archbishop	53
—— Rev. Edward	97
—— Rev. Joseph	183, 192
Kingstown congregation	104, 106, 245-47
Kinnear, Rev. John, D.D.	137
Kirkpatrick, Rev. Dr. W. B.	105, 234, 244, 273-77, 284
Knox, Rev. Hugh M.	184
—— Rev. Robert	113-17, 281
—— Rev. William	267
LABAN, Rev. Dr.	291
Landlordism	62-4, 135, 181
Langford, Sir Arthur	34, 35, 48, 49, 97, 293, 294, 316, 317
La Touche, W. R.	243
Leap congregation	95, 104, 331
Leclew, Rev. William	9
Ledlie, Rev. J. C.	124, 125, 327, 328
Leebody, Professor	146
Leitch, Rev. Professor, D.D.	146
Leland, Rev. John, D.D.	326
Leslie, Bishop	5
Limerick congregation	98, 111
Lindsay, Rev. Colin	308
Lismore congregation	106, 208
Lister, Rev. John	97, 299
Liston, Rev. W.	302
Loftus, Archbishop	4
—— Lady	317
Logan, Rev. Thomas	239
Londonderry, Marquis of	68, 81, 318
Longford congregation	107, 111
Lords, House of, petition for withdrawal of the bounty from the Presbyterians	42-5
Love, Rev. George C.	191
—— Rev. James	188
Lowry, Rev. Archibald	179, 190
Loyalty of Irish Presbyterians	28, 51, 52
Lucan congregation	247, 248
Lunn, Rev. James	306

INDEX.

	PAGE
Lyons, Henry	193
Lyttle, Rev. Thomas	278
McBEATH, Rev. W.	255
McCaldin, Rev. A.	334
McCance, Rev. William	303
McCaughey, Rev. George	248, 285
McCelland, Rev. R.	204
McClinchie, Rev. A.	178
McCorkell, Rev. Joseph	169
McCorkle, Rev. Mr.	291
McCollum, Rev. Charles	69, 267
McCubbin, Rev. John	169
McCullagh, Rev. J. C.	301
McCully, Rev. W. J.	306
McCune, Rev. S.	282
McDowell, Rev. Benjamin, D.D.	69, 96, 268-72
McEwen, Rev. R.	203
—— Rev. W. D. H.	257
McGachin, Rev. J.	222, 331
—— Rev. S.	328
—— Rev. W.	328
McHinch, Rev. William	309
Mackay, Rev. John	287
McKee, Rev. David	185, 277
—— Rev. H. S.	244, 245
MacKeown, Rev. John	209, 303
McKinstry, Rev. Joseph	198
Macknight, Dr.	136
Maclaine, Rev. Archibald, D.D.	319
McLean, Captain	105
McLeod, Rev. Dr.	107
McManus, Rev. Henry	249
MacMaster, Professor	147
—— Rev. Robert	255
MacMillan, Rev. John	309
McMurtry, Rev. D. H.	224
McNeill, Archibald, Malcolm, and Sir John	310
Maconaghie, Rev. James	178
McTaggart, Rev. David	232
Magee, College controversy	139-48
—— Mrs.	139, 141-45, 250
—— Rev. Hamilton, D.D.	186, 190, 229

	PAGE
Magill, Rev. George	210
—— Rev. William, D.D.	214
Mairs, Rev. John	169
Makemie, Rev. Francis	40
Mallow congregation	209
Manor Street College	100
Maquay, Rev. Thomas	252
Marriage Act (1782)	75
—— —— (1844)	130
—— Question (1842-44)	128-30
Marriages by Presbyterian ministers	15 n., 48, 62, 65, 128-30
Marsden, Rev. Gamaliel	9
—— Rev. Josiah	9
Marsh, Primate	21
Marshall, Rev. Alexander	189, 195
—— Rev. James	98, 302
Martin, Rev. Joseph	169
—— Rev. Professor	146
Martineau, Rev. Dr. James	327, 328
Mary's Abbey congregation (*see also* Rutland Square)	106, 111, 117, 118, 124, 126, 263-77
Mass Lane congregation	215-17
Massereene, Lord	322
Mather, Rev. Nathaniel	325
—— Rev. Samuel	9, 324, 325
Mathews, Mr. George	123, 125, 226
Matthews, Rev. Samuel	285
Mawhinney, Rev. James	166
Mears, Rev. John	187, 288, 319
—— Rev. Robert	306
Meath, Countess of	313
—— Earl of	229
Meek, Rev. J. B.	224
Megaw, Rev. James	186
Methodist Church	161, 162
Middleton	204
Millar, Rev. Andrew	295
Milligan, Rev. A.	223
Milling, Rev. John	265
Missionary meeting of Synod of Ulster in Dublin (1853)	107-10
—— effort	27, 95-111
Mitchell, Rev. David	243
—— Rev. James	175, 245

INDEX.

	PAGE
Mogee, Rev. Alexander	223
Montgomery, Rev. W. S.	223
Moody, Rev. John, D.D.	77, 319, 320, 323
Moore, Rev. H. H.	178
—— Rev. Hugh	70, 256, 258
—— Rev. John C.	172
—— Rev. William	174, 175, 229, 233
Moravian settlement	169
Morgan, Rev. Dr. James	102, 140, 231, 249
Morrison, Rev. S. G.	218, 219, 260
Morrow, Rev. J. L.	233
Morton, Rev. J. H.	244
Mountcashel, Lord and Lady	102, 103
Mountmellick congregation	248, 249
Moyvore congregation	173
Muckle, Rev. Roger	230
Mullingar congregation	102, 173, 174
Munster Presbytery	212, 213
Murphy, Rev. Dr. A. C.	277
—— Rev. J. H.	214
—— Rev. Matthew	174
—— Rev. Professor, D.D.	146
NAAS congregation	249, 250
Nairne, Rev. Charles	219
Navan	178
Neely, Rev. G. W.	232
Neilson, Dr. (Killala)	190
—— Rev. William, D.D.	308
Nelson, Rev. Isaac, M.P.	137
Nenagh and Cloughjordan	250, 251
Nesbit, Rev. Hugh	183, 192
Nevin, Rev. Mr.	58
Newport congregation	191, 192
New Row church, Dublin	9
Nichol, Rev. Robert	256
Norbury, Rev. Robert	9
North, Brownlow	150
Northey, Rev. Joseph	184, 196
O'CONNELL, Daniel	134, 135, 323
Orangeism	150
Organ in Dundalk	310

	PAGE
Ormond Quay congregation (*see also* Usher's Quay)	138, 142, 251-60
Ormonde, Duke of	10
Orr, Rev. James	288
Orrery, Earl of	10
Osborne, Rev. Alexander	253
—— Rev. James D.	277
—— Rev. Joseph	169
Owen, Rev. John, D.D.	294, 313
PACIFIC Act	55-8
Parsonstown (*see* Birr)	
Patten, Rev. William	252
Patterson, Rev. James	227, 228
Patteson, Messrs.	310
—— Rev. Thomas J.	174
Paul, Rev. C. E.	226
Peebles, Dr.	137
Petticrew, Rev. Professor, D.D.	147
Philadelphia Presbytery	40, 41
Philips, Rev. J. G.	229
Pinkerton, Rev. John	291
Plunket, Archbishop	84, 161, 320
—— Rev. Thomas	320
—— Street congregation	99, 251-53
—— William Conyngham	84, 85
Poole, Rev. James	208
Porter, Rev. James (Grey Abbey)	81, 82
—— Rev. James (Kilkenny)	243
Portlaw congregation	293
Powell, Rev. John	227, 232
Prenter, Rev. Samuel	260
Presbyterian Churchman	229, 233, 275
Presbyterian emigration to America	62-64
—— Fellows of Trinity College	3, 9
—— marriages	15
—— soldiers	259
Presbyterians and parliamentary representation	137, 138
—— and the Land Question	136, 137
—— and the rebellion of 1798	79-83
—— and the Union	85, 88, 89
—— and the Volunteers	71-4
Pringle, Rev. James	189
Proctor, Rev. William	312

INDEX. 353

	PAG
Provost of Trinity College a Presbyterian	3
Psalms v. hymns	208
QUEEN Anne and the Presbyterians	26, 30
Queen's Colleges	141-43
Queenstown congregation	211
Queen Street church, Cork	210, 284
Quinn, Rev. Robert	207
RAHUE congregation	97, 98, 104, 332-34
Rainey, Rev. John	176, 245
Rathgar congregation	261-63
Rebellion of 1798, The	77-9, 83
Regium Donum 11, 12, 14, 15, 24, 27, 28, 44, 45, 52, 75, 76, 88, 89, 155	
—— withdrawn (1714)	48
—— renewed	51
Reid, Rev. Alexander	306
—— Rev. William	206
Rentoul, Rev. Alexander	173, 279
—— Rev. Alfred H.	173, 279
Repeal movement	134, 135
Revival, The (1859)	148
Ridall, Sir James	105
Robarts, Lord, and the Dublin Presbyterians	10
Robinson, Rev. James	185
—— Rev. Professor, D.D.	146
Rodgers, Rev. David	179, 189, 190
—— Rev. James (Fethard)	289
—— Rev. Robert	169
Rogers, Rev. Professor, D.D.	136
Roman Catholics	63, 77, 79, 88, 89, 134, 158-60
Ronaldson, George	206
Roscrea	104
Rutherford, Rev. Robert	328
Rutland Square congregation (*see also* Mary's Abbey)	263-77
SANDYMOUNT congregation	278
Schism Act	48
Scott, Rev. Jacob	183, 192
—— Rev. Joseph	334
—— Rev. Richard	171
Seawright, Rev. Abraham	98, 291
Seceders, The	66, 67

23

	PAGE
Secession Presbytery of Dublin	112, 113
—— Synod	67
Shannon, Rev. J.	250
Sherlock, Dean : *Vindication* of the doctrine of the Trinity	19
Simms, Rev. J. M.	224
Simpson, Rev. Patrick	308, 310
—— Rev. Samuel	99, 106, 225, 257-59
—— Rev. William	211
Sinclair, Rev. Alexander	33, 251, 252, 302
—— W. P., M.P.	138
Sligo congregation	192, 193
—— Marquis of	103, 197
Sloane, Rev. Dr.	212, 213
Smith, Rev. J. A.	204, 205
—— Rev. James (Capel Street)	267
—— Rev. James (Westport)	197
—— Rev. J. Strothers	186
—— Rev. S. (Limerick)	291
Smyth, Rev. Mr. (Tipperary)	299
—— Rev. Professor, D.D., M.P.	137, 198
—— Rev. William	168
Smythe, Rev. Robert H.	280
Southern Association	28
—— Presbytery	61
Squire, Rev. M.	290
Stafford Street congregation	266
Steen, Rev. James	196, 282
Stephen's Green Church	313, 323, 328
Stephens, James	152, 153
Stevenson, Rev. Dr. W. Fleming	261-63
—— Rev. James	312
Steward, Rev. Dr.	322
Stewart, Mr. Alexander	68, 318
—— Rev. Dr.	101, 230
Stirling, Earl of	252
Strand Street congregation	98, 111, 124
Stratford congregation	106, 334-36
Stuart, Rev. David	99, 216-18
—— Rev. William	187
Subscription controversy	18-23, 54-61, 265, 266
—— of the confession of faith	6, 7, 18, 22, 266
Summerhill congregation	48, 97, 124
Sustentation Fund	293-98

INDEX. 355

	PAGE
Swift, Dean, and the Presbyterians	29-31, 48, 49
Syms, Rev. D.	230
TAIT, Rev. Dr.	219
Taylor, Daniel	138
—— Rev. Philip	77, 326, 327
Temperance	159, 160
Templemore	104
Tenant-right movement	136, 137
Test Act	24-31
Theatre and the Presbyterians, The	11
Thomas, Caleb	20
Three F's	137, 157
Thurles	104
Tipperary congregation	97, 102, 108-10, 299-302
Todd, Mr. William	127, 147
Toleration Act of 1719	53
Topping, Rev. Dr.	173
Tralee congregation	211
Travers, the first regular Provost of T. C. D.	3, 4
Trinity church, Cork	212-14
Trotter, Rev. David	97, 295
Tullamore congregation	279, 280
Tully congregation	174-76
Turlough congregation	193-96
Tyrconnel and Rev. A. Osborne	254
ULSTER Plantation	4
Uniformity, Act of	3, 8, 9, 128
Union Chapel congregation	113, 127, 215-19
—— of the Synods	113
—— The legislative	84-90
Unitarian churches	313-28
Unitarianism (*see* Arianism)	
United Presbyterian Church	311-13
Upton, Colonel Clotworthy	50
Urwick, Rev. Dr.	162, 225
Usher's Quay congregation (*see also* Ormond Quay)	106, 111, 253-60
Ussher, Archbishop	4, 161
VANCE, Rev. Patrick	77, 295
—— Rev. Thomas	69, 255
Veal, Rev. Edward	9

Volunteers, The...	71-4
WALKER, Professor	146
—— Rev. Samuel	165
Walkington, Bishop, and the Presbyterians...	15
Wallace, Rev. Mr. (Limerick)	291
—— Rev. James	189
—— Rev. Professor	172, 213, 214
—— Rev. Robert	222
Wark, Rev. David	198
Warren, Rev. Thomas	170, 171
Waterford congregation	98, 111, 293, 302-4
Watson, Rev. John	185
—— Rev. Mr. (Moyvore)	173
—— Rev. Robert	166
Watters, Rev. F. O. M.	193
Watts, Rev. Professor, D.D.	146, 233
Weld, Rev. Dr. Isaac	326
—— Rev. Nathaniel	56, 325
Wesley	161
Westport congregation	102, 103, 196-98
Wexford congregation...	113, 114, 281, 282
Wharton, Earl of	29, 30
Whately, Archbishop	133
Whigham, Rev. Dr.	167, 168, 170
White, Rev. J. (Bandon)	204
—— Rev. Patrick	178
—— Rev. T. R.	222
—— Rev. W. F.	198, 247, 289
—— Rev. William	69, 267
Whitefield, George	99
Wicklow congregation	282-85
Widows' Fund	68, 69
Wilkin, Rev. James	183
William III. and the Presbyterians	14, 215
Williams, Rev. Dr.	19, 28, 313, 314
Wilson, Rev. David, D.D. (Limerick)	170, 291-93
—— Rev. James (Clonmel)	288, 289
—— Rev. James (Corboy)	169
—— Rev. James (Magherafelt)	108, 299-301
—— Rev. John (Carlingford)	305, 308
—— Rev. John (Killala)	190
—— Rev. Josias (Drogheda)	237

	PAGE
Wilson, Rev. Samuel (Hollymount)	188
—— Rev. Silas E.	187, 224
—— Rev. S. Law	214
—— Rev. William (Gloucester Street)	232
—— Rev. William (Killala)	189
—— Rev. William (Usher's Quay)	69, 256
Winter, Rev. Dr. Samuel	9, 324, 325
Witherow, Rev. Professor, D.D.	18, 146, 192, 253
Wood, Rev. A.	295
—— Street congregation	9, 313-20
Worrall, Rev. James	287
YOUNG Ireland movement	135

Printed by Hazell, Watson, & Viney, Ld., London and Aylesbury.

www.ingramcontent.com/pod-product-compliance
Lightning Source LLC
Chambersburg PA
CBHW030403230426
43664CB00007BB/731